BIBLIOTECA ITALIANA

Cinque Canti

Five Cantos

Cinque Canti

Five Cantos

Ludovico Ariosto

TRANSLATED BY

ALEXANDER SHEERS and DAVID QUINT

WITH AN INTRODUCTION BY

DAVID QUINT

UNIVERSITY
OF CALIFORNIA
PRESS

BERKELEY
LOS ANGELES
LONDON

University of California Press
Berkeley and Los Angeles, California

University of California Press, Ltd.
London, England

The Italian text of the *Cinque Canti* is reprinted from Ludovico
Ariosto, *Opere minori*, edited by Cesare Segre (Milan and Naples:
Riccardo Ricciardi Editore, 1954), by permission.

Library of Congress Cataloging-in-Publication Data

Ariosto, Lodovico, 1474–1533.
   [Cinque canti = Five cantos / Ludovico Ariosto; translated by
Alexander Sheers and David Quint; with an introduction by
David Quint.
         p.   cm.—(Biblioteca italiana)
   Translation based on the Italian text prepared by Cesare Segre
for his edition of Ariosto's Opere minori, 1954.
Sequel to: Orlando furioso.
   Includes bibliographical references.
   ISBN 0-520-20007-1 (alk. paper). —
   ISBN 0-520-20009-8 (pbk.: alk. paper)
   1. Charlemagne, Emperor, 742–814—Romances.   2. Gane-
lon (Legendary character)—Romances.   3. Roland (Legendary
character)—Romances.   I. Sheers, Alexander.   II. Quint,
David, 1950–   .   III. Title.   IV. Title: Five cantos.
V. Series.
PQ4567.A4E5   1996
851'.3—dc20   94-45611
                                                         CIP

Printed in the United States of America
9 8 7 6 5 4 3 2 1

IN MEMORY OF SAM SHEERS

Contents

Preface

OUR TRANSLATION OF the *Cinque Canti* is based on the text of the poem prepared by Cesare Segre for his edition of Ariosto's *Opere minori* (Milan and Naples: Riccardo Ricciardi, 1954), 581–754; the Italian text is reprinted with the gracious permission of the publisher and of Professor Segre. We have aimed at a translation that would be literal and still preserve some of the narrative energy of the original. With the exception of Charles ("Carlo") and Ganelon ("Gano")—and the historical names of Desiderius and Constantine—we have kept the names of Ariosto's characters in their Italian versions. This solution has had the unintended, but to us pleasing, linguistic effect of separating the emperor and his evil courtier from the chivalric heroes of the poem: much as the poem itself separates them off. We have, however, changed place-names, whenever they are recognizable, from Italian to their original or anglicized forms: "Montalbano" becomes "Montauban"; "Reno" becomes "Rhine." These include the unlocatable "Clairmont" ("Chiaramonte"), which should probably be distinguished from modern Clermont, and "Anglant" ("Anglante"), which may be a variant of Angiers. We have tried to keep annotation to the minimum: enough, we hope, to explain the poem's more obscure historical and mythological references without slowing down and distracting the reader from its story. Where pertinent, the reader is referred to more extended discussion in the Introduction.

We would like to thank Albert Ascoli, Daniel Javitch, and Lawrence Manley for their careful reading of the translation and Introduction and for their many helpful suggestions. We are similarly grateful to Alberto Casadei and Sergio Zatti for their detailed criticism, constructive even when in disagreement, of the Introduction. We have consulted, for comparison and reference, the translation of Leslie Z. Morgan. We owe a special debt of gratitude to Louise George Clubb for her support of this project through its many years to completion.

Introduction

David Quint

INCOMPLETE IF NOT, I shall argue, unfinished, the *Cinque Canti* rank among the most striking achievements of Renaissance literature, and they deserve to be better known. Their story begins when mysterious supernatural forces declare war on the Holy Roman Empire of Charles (Charlemagne) and Orlando (Roland), tells how the Empire subsequently breaks apart in civil faction, and ends with the rout of the Emperor's army at Prague and the sight of Charles himself carried by the press of his panicked troops. It presents with uncompromising imaginative power a vision of human betrayal and savagery, of cosmic disorder and ruin, that knows few rivals outside Shakespearean tragedy.

A tradition of Italian criticism of Ariosto's fragment has complained that it lacks many of the features that have delighted readers of the poet's masterpiece, the *Orlando Furioso*, that sprawling, labyrinthine epic-romance to which the *Cinque Canti* were intended to be a sequel. Gone to a considerable extent are the elaborate crisscrossing of narrative threads, the ironic shifting of tones from high seriousness to comedy, the amused and detached narrator of the *Furioso* exercising a godlike control over his poem. Gone, above all, are the love stories that counterbalanced the battles of the *Furioso*: Ariosto seems to have played down the Arthurian or Celtic strain of his long poem and to have privileged its Carolingian matter, whose subject is primarily martial.[1]

1. It was the achievement of Matteo Maria Boiardo in the *Orlando Innamorato* (1483) to have fused together the Carolingian

These observations are correct enough, and next to the extraordinarily capacious and variegated *Furioso*, a poem of forty-six cantos in its final version of 1532, the new poem may seem lean and monochromatic. But such criticism fails to appreciate what the deliberately scaled down *Cinque Canti* have to offer in their very concentration. In such episodes as the opening Council of the Fairies at the hall of Demogorgon, the imprisonment of Ruggiero and Astolfo in the whale of Alcina, or the final siege and battle before Prague, Ariosto's invention and narrative gifts can only be said to have gained new intensity and refinement. If the comedy of the *Furioso* has largely, though not entirely, disappeared, it was because Ariosto had begun to write a different poem, one which would emphasize the dark underside of the imaginative world he had created in the *Furioso*. His new project was to depict, in fact, the tragic disintegration of that world, its fragmentation both inside the fiction and into the fragment that is the *Cinque Canti*: from the chilling decree of his Demogorgon to wipe out all signs of the former kingdom of Charles, to leave not even a trace by which one could say, "Here once stood Paris" (1.30).

A FINISHED FRAGMENT

The *Cinque Canti* were intended to pick up where the *Furioso* left off, and they were themselves left incomplete. This much seems to be clear after nearly four decades of conten-

---

"matter of France" with the Arthurian "matter of England"—a primarily martial chivalric tradition with another more open to stories of love and magical enchantment. Ariosto was the heir to Boiardo's merging of these traditions of chivalric literature in the *Orlando Furioso*, which is a continuation of the *Innamorato*. In the *Cinque Canti* he turned back to the model of Luigi Pulci's *Morgante* (1483), a more characteristically Carolingian poem in which the figures of Ganelon and Charles play a much greater role than they do in the *Innamorato* and where the focus is primarily on war and political intrigue rather than on love.

tious scholarship.[2] Internal evidence indicates that the poet drafted the *Cinque Canti* sometime around 1519, between the first edition of the *Orlando Furioso*, in 1516, and the second, in 1521. The *Cinque Canti* are often identified as the "little addition" ("un poco di giunta") to the *Furioso* which Ariosto, in a letter of October 15, 1519, tells his friend and fellow humanist, Mario Equicola, that he has started to write but has had to set aside. He seems to have returned to touch up the *Canti* in the mid 1520s, until he set them aside again and worked instead on the additions and revisions that he inserted into the expanded third and final version of the *Furioso* in 1532.[3] Ariosto never published the fragment— though, for that matter, he never published his polished *Satires* either. The *Cinque Canti* were lovingly edited by Ariosto's illegitimate son, Virginio, from a manuscript that was missing one or more pages. They appeared in print twelve years after the poet's death as a kind of appendix to a 1545

2. The most important work on the dating of the *Cinque Canti* has been done by Carlo Dionisotti and Cesare Segre. Dionisotti draws attention to the reference (2.52) to Cardinal Bibbiena's mission to France in 1519, in "Per la data dei *Cinque canti*," *Giornale storico della letteratura italiana* 137 (1960):1–40; and "Appunti sui *Cinque canti* e sugli studi arioteschi," in *Studi e problemi di critica testuale* (Bologna: Commissione per i testi di lingua, 1961), 369–382. Segre had earlier concluded on the basis of stylistic elements that Ariosto must also have worked on the *Cinque Canti* sometime between 1526 and 1528; Segre, "Studi sui *Cinque canti*," *Studi di Filologia Italiana* 12 (1954):23–75, reprinted in *Esperienze ariostesche* (Pisa: Nistri-Lischi, 1966), 121–177. For a further discussion of the dating issue, see the summary by Leslie Z. Morgan in her introduction to her translation, *Five Cantos* (New York and London: Garland, 1992), viii–xii.

3. Alberto Casadei has shown how Ariosto took phrases from the *Cinque Canti* and incorporated them into the revisions of the 1532 *Furioso*, indications, he maintains, of the poet's abandoning the fragment. See "I *Cinque canti* o l'ultima eredità di Boiardo," *Italianistica* 21 (1992):739–748, republished in *Il percorso del "Furioso"* (Bologna: Il Mulino, 1993), 113–127.

edition of the *Orlando Furioso* published by the famous Aldine press in Venice. In 1548 the rival Venetian press of Gabriel Giolito published a more complete text, still indicating a lacuna of "many stanzas" in Canto 5.

The nature of sequels is to open up the endings of the works they follow. In the nineteenth century a manuscript of the *Cinque Canti* was found that included at its beginning a stanza that corresponds to stanza 68 in the last canto of the *Orlando Furioso* (stanza 45 in the forty-canto long editions of 1516 and 1521), describing the discontent and resentment of Ganelon and his relatives at the prospect of—hence *before*—the wedding of Ruggiero and Bradamante that concludes the poem. This has led a number of scholars to conclude that the *Cinque Canti* were intended to be attached to the *Furioso* at that juncture, to form part, that is, of the larger body and structure of the epic. But, as a more recent critic has correctly pointed out, the *Cinque Canti* begin right *after* the marriage of Ruggiero and Bradamante at the end of the *Furioso*; in Canto 1, stanza 59 the court of Charles has returned to Paris from the tents and pavilions that the Emperor had put up to handle the overflow of guests at their wedding in the last canto of the *Furioso* (46.74–75), and in the *Cinque Canti* Ruggiero and Bradamante are referred to as husband and wife (3.40).[4] This marriage, which founds the dynasty

4. Alberto Casadei, "Alcune considerazioni sui *Cinque canti*," *Giornale storico della letteratura italiana* 165 (1988):161–179. From his discovery Casadei does not draw the conclusion that the *Cinque Canti* were a separate poem, a sequel to the *Furioso*, though he acknowledges that the debate on whether the fragment was intended to form part of Ariosto's epic or was meant to stand on its own dates back to the first readers of the *Cinque Canti* in the sixteenth century. For the differing opinions of Giraldi Cinzio and Giovanbattista Pigna, see the introduction by Luigi Firpo to his edition of the *Cinque Canti* (Turin: UTET, 1964), 7–19. My contention that the *Cinque Canti* are, indeed, a new poem is something of a minority opinion in the scholarly community, but it has recent support from the literary detective work of Marina Beer in *Romanzi di Cavalleria* (Rome: Bulzoni, 1987), 143–149.

of Ariosto's patrons, the Este Dukes of Ferrara, had been the goal of the epic, and, together with the total defeat of the saracen host of King Agramante, had brought to the *Furioso* a powerful sense of conclusion, a conclusion as well to the *Orlando Innamorato* of Matteo Maria Boiardo to which Ariosto's epic had itself been a sequel and continuation. The climactic duel that interrupts the wedding feast in the final stanzas of the *Furioso*, where Ruggiero fights and kills the pagan warrior Rodomonte, closely imitates the final duel between Aeneas and Turnus at the end of the *Aeneid* and had given to Ariosto's story of dynastic foundation a suitably Virgilian closure. But, as a sequel in turn to the *Furioso*, the *Cinque Canti* undo its happy ending even as Charles and his subjects are still celebrating it. The intrigues of Ganelon have plunged the Empire into a new cycle of warfare.

> This news, arriving by various reports, made Charles abandon his festivals and made the ladies and knights leave off their games and laughter and change their joyful clothes to somber ones. Memories, stirred up hour by hour, of peoples sacked and slaughtered by the sword, by fire, by oppression and plagues, promised new evils just as bad and worse.
>
> (2.33)

"How fleeting is your every happiness," the narrator remarks of the human condition in the following stanza, as his characters brace themselves with a "here we go again" dread of future suffering.

Nor do the *Cinque Canti* themselves come to any definitive ending. We are left in the kind of suspense that Ariosto exploited in the *Furioso*, where descriptions of duels, sea tempests, and attempted rapes would be interrupted by the narrator while his characters were in utmost peril, to be picked up again in subsequent cantos of the poem.[5] But the

5. For a discussion of Ariosto's technique of suspense, see Daniel Javitch, "*Cantus interruptus* in the *Orlando furioso*," *Modern Language Notes* 95 (1980):66–80.

Cinque Canti break off. We do not know whether Ruggiero and Astolfo will escape from the belly of Alcina's whale or will grow old and die like so many of her earlier victims (4.89), whether Orlando will show up for his parley with Rinaldo after they have suspended the battle between them (5.73), what will become of Charles, who has, in the poem's final scene, only just barely escaped being drowned in the general stampede of his army at Prague.

Ariosto stopped writing the *Cinque Canti*, and critics, observing that he abandoned the project—and that for any number of reasons—have not asked why he stopped writing *here*, with so many unresolved plot threads up in the air. But the last scene of the *Cinque Canti* bears a close relationship to the final scene of the most famous unfinished poem of classical literature, the *Pharsalia*, or *De bello civile*, of Lucan, especially in the version of the epic that Ariosto would have known. Lucan was forced by Nero to take his own life in A.D. 65. His poem on the civil wars that destroyed the Roman republic leaves off at the point where Julius Caesar finds himself in a desperate situation, crowded by his own troops on a narrow pier in the harbor of Alexandria ("Molis in exiguae spatio stipantibus armis"), while suddenly surrounded by enemy Egyptian troops seeking to avenge the death of the royal eunuch, Pothinus. The *Pharsalia* breaks off as the perplexed and disheartened Caesar catches sight of the gallant soldier Scaeva, whose exploits have been recounted earlier in the epic. The abruptness of this ending prompted a fifteenth-century humanist, Johannus Sulpicius Verulanus, to add eleven verses explaining how Caesar had escaped; and these lines, published in 1493 along with Sulpicius's commentary on the *Pharsalia*, were included in most early printed editions of Lucan's poem.[6]

---

6. On Sulpicius—Giovanni Antonio Sulpizio—see the biographical entry by Judith Rice Henderson in *Contemporaries of Erasmus*, ed. Peter G. Bietenholz and Thomas B. Deutscher (Toronto,

Erexit mentem trepidi tam fortis imago
Et facturus erat memorandi nobile leti
Exemplum, sed fata vetant & fida salutis
Ostendit fortuna viam. nam levus amicas
Prospexit puppes, nando quas ausus adire,
Ecquid stamus ait? vel iam per tela, fretumque
Eripiar, juguli vel non erit ulla potestas
Eunucho concessa mei. tunc puppe relicta
Prosilit in pontum. siccos fert leva libellos,
Dextra secat fluctus, tandemque illaesus
    amico
Excipitur plausu clamantis ad aethera turbe.[7]

The sight of that valorous man raised his anxious spirits, and he was about to leave a noble example of a memorable death: but the fates forbid him and trusty Fortune shows him a way of safety, for on the left he catches sight of his own friendly ships: daring to reach these by swimming, he says, "Should we perchance stay here? Now either I will escape through the weapons and the waves, or at least the Eunuch will have no power over my death." Then, having left the stern, he leaps into the sea; his left hand carries and keeps dry his manuscripts, his right cuts through the waves; and at length he is fished out unharmed amid the friendly cheers of his troops who shout up to heaven.

The expanded "ending" of the incomplete *Pharsalia* thus depicted a Caesar, routed and at the seeming end of his resources, who dives into the sea at Alexandria and struggles to safety. The *Cinque Canti* leave off with a much more helpless Charles forced ignominiously off the bridge into the Moldau at Prague by the impact of his fleeing troops.

Buffalo, and London: University of Toronto Press, 1987) 3:300. Sulpicius's commentary was included in the edition of the *De bello civile* printed in Venice by Simon Bevilaqua in 1493.

7. I cite from the first Aldine edition: *Lucanus* (Venice, 1502), n.p.

> If Charles had found himself on any horse other than the one on which he rode that day, he could easily have remained in the water and never returned to fair France again. His good horse was white, except for some spots of black which looked like flies and which he had about his neck and flanks right up to the tail: by this horse Charles was finally brought back to shore.
>
> (5.93)

The reduction of the Emperor here is underscored by the lengthy and apparently irrelevant description of his horse, the agent of his salvation.

Both poems end with their commanders escaping a watery death. The parallel between the two episodes is more striking when one turns to the *De bello alexandrino* (20–21), the ancient text that along with Suetonius (*Julius* 64) was the source for Sulpicius Verulanus's addition. Here the pier-front at Alexandria is similarly described as a bridge ("pontem"); Caesar's troops, routed "with no fixed order or formation and no discipline" ("sine signis certisque ordinibus, sine ratione"), cause those arrayed behind them to panic.

> Some of them got on to the nearest ships, only for them to sink under the weight of so many men. Others were killed by the Alexandrians while they hung back wondering what to do. Others, luckier, reached some ships lying at anchor ready for action and got away safely, while a few, lifting up their shields and making determined efforts, swam out to the nearest vessels.
>
> Caesar so long as he was able by exhortation to keep his men by the bridge and the fortification, was exposed to the same danger; when he saw that they were all giving ground, he withdrew to his own vessel. He was followed by a crowd of men who began forcing their way on board and made it impossible to steer the ship or push it off from land; whereupon, Caesar,

who had guessed this would happen, jumped over-
board and swam out to the ships standing farther
off. . . . As for his own ship, it sank under the pres-
sure of the numbers and was lost, with all the men
on board.[8]

The scenario is closely followed in the rout at Prague in the
Cinque Canti, where the fleeing vanguard throws the rest of
Charles's army into disarray, "mixing up every rank and for-
mation" (5.87), where Charles tries to stem their retreat at
the bridge over the Moldau, and where

One drowns, another crosses swimming, another the
water's current drags in circles; one leaps into a boat,
and leaves his horse, one makes his horse swim behind
the skiff; and where a boat appears, the army crowds
in so thickly that, full to overflowing, the vessel either
cannot leave unless it empties or it sinks to the bottom
along its way.

(5.90)

Caesar escapes from the press of his own troops that even-
tually sink his ship, while Ariosto's Charles is caught within
a similar panicked crowd and, "piled together with many
other men and beasts, is himself thrown over into the river
beneath the bridge" (5.91) only to be carried to the shore by
his noble horse. It is a close call in both cases.

If Charles plays the role of Lucan's Caesar at the end of
the *Cinque Canti*, he has already done so earlier in the poem.
The episode in Canto 2 (101–126) where Charles leads his
soldiers to cut down trees in the demon-infested wood in

8. Caesar, *The Civil War, together with The Alexandrian War, The
African War, and The Spanish War by other Hands*, trans. Jane F.
Mitchell (Harmondsworth, England: Penguin, 1967), 177–178.
For the Latin text and commentary, see *Caesar's War in Alexandria*,
ed. Gavin Townsend (Bristol: Bristol Classical Press, 1988), 19–20,
47–48.

the vicinity of a besieged Prague closely imitates *Pharsalia* 3.399–452, where Caesar cuts down a similar forest near Marseilles to which he is laying a similar siege. The *Pharsalia* is, in fact, variously invoked by the *Cinque Canti*, whose depiction of an internal European revolt against the western Emperor Charles—rather than an attack of the external Islamic enemy that was the subject of the *Furioso*—describes a chronicle of civil war, a Rome divided against itself, for which Lucan's poem, with its darkly pessimistic tone, offered the preeminent classical model. In the earlier passage of Canto 2 that I mentioned above, the reaction of the citizens of Paris to the outbreak of a new round of wars (36–37)—their silence, their comparison in simile to a household in mourning, their prayers to heaven—echo the opening of the second book of the *Pharsalia* (20–36), where Lucan describes the dread of the Roman people before the prospect of new civil strife.[9]

9. Compare *Cinque Canti* 2.36–37 and *Pharsalia* 2.20–36:

> Tum questus tenuere suos, magnusque per omnes
> Erravit sine voce dolor. Sic funere primo
> Attonitae tacuere domus, cum corpora nondum
> Conclamata iacent, nec mater crine soluto
> Exigit ad saevos famularum bracchia planctus;
> Sed cum membra premit fugiente rigentia vita
> Voltusque exanimes oculosque in morte minaces;
> Necdum est ille dolor, nec iam metus: incubat amens
> Miratur malum. Cultus matrona priores
> Deposuit, maestaeque tenent delubra catervae.
> Hae lacrimis sparsere deos, hae pectora duro
> Adflixere solo, lacerasque in limine sacro
> Attonitae fudere comas votisque vocari
> Adsuetas crebris feriunt ululatibus aures.
> Nec cunctae summi templo iacuere Tonantis:
> Divisere deos, et nullis defuit aris
> Invidiam factura parens.

Then men withheld their lamentation, and a great grief passed among all without giving voice. So, at the first mo-

If Ariosto modeled the ending of the *Furioso* on the ending of the *Aeneid*, he similarly recalled the truncated end of the *Pharsalia*, the other great Roman epic, where the *Cinque Canti* break off. But the evocation of the "ending" of the *Pharsalia* at the end of the *Cinque Canti* must make us re-evaluate the shape of Ariosto's poem. We can probably assume that Ariosto did not deliberately set out to write his sequel poem as an incomplete fragment. But he did not simply abandon his project. By closing the *Cinque Canti* on the same note as the best known unfinished poem of antiquity, Ariosto decided *consciously* to leave them similarly "unfinished." That is to say, the *Cinque Canti* are *finished* in their present state. Although some stanzas may be missing—especially from the middle of Canto 5, where the sixteenth-century editions and manuscript indicate that their redactors believed that pages had been lost from an original autograph—Ariosto did not intend to write further. He meant for the poem to end where it does, with its loose ends still loose, with its story unresolved. He was thus returning not only to the model of the *Pharsalia* but also to that of the *Orlando Innamorato*, the poem of his own predecessor

---

ment of death, the stunned household is silent, while the body has not yet been laid out and mourned, and the mother, her hair unbound, has not yet urged her attendants cruelly to beat their breasts; she still embraces the limbs stiffening as life escapes from them, and the lifeless face with its eyes fiercely set in death. Grief has not yet set in, fear is no longer: she mindlessly hangs over the body and wonders at her misfortune. Matrons put off their former attire, and in sad groups attend the temples. Some shed tears on the images of the gods, some dashed their breasts against the hard temple floor, some, stunned, scattered their torn hair on the sacred threshold and struck with repeated wailing ears accustomed to be called by prayers. Nor did they all prostrate themselves in the shrine of supreme thundering Jove; they divided up the gods and at no altar was there lacking a mother to look askance at it.

Boiardo, that breaks off in midstory as the poet contemplates the descent upon Italy of the first in what was to be a long succession of foreign invaders, the French army of Charles VIII in 1494. The *Cinque Canti* thus doubly contest the narrative closure—and the sense of political and historical order—achieved by the *Orlando Furioso*: they both reopen the strife that the *Furioso* had put to rest and deny to their own narrative a satisfying ending. Rather, through their imitation of the abrupt close of the *Pharsalia*, they end as a deliberately and pointedly unfinished work, a fragment; at the same time, they end at a point of maximum disarray in their story, the disorganized rout that carries the Emperor before it. The fragmentary form of the *Cinque Canti* thus reinforces—indeed, becomes part of—their subject matter, the dissolution of Charles's Empire, and with it the entire eighth-century Carolingian fantasy world created by four centuries of chivalric literature. And behind this dark fiction and the suspended ending of the *Cinque Canti* may lie an intimation of historical disorder as profound as the alarm with which Boiardo greeted the French invasion on the last page of his interrupted *Innamorato*.

Once the *Cinque Canti* are acknowledged to be finished, even as they present their own narrative as incomplete, one can speak with some confidence of an overall structure, of motifs and thematic concerns that unify them—as, indeed, several critics have already done, though more cautiously and tentatively.[10] My analysis falls into two parts. I examine the sources and literary traditions of the poem's sense of metaphysical crisis, its quasi-apocalyptic vision of universal destruction: both classical models like the *Pharsalia* and more immediate precedents in the fifteenth-century Italian chi-

---

10. See, among others, Eduardo Saccone, "Appunti per una definizione dei *Cinque canti*," in *Il "soggetto" del* furioso (Naples: Liguori, 1974), 119–160; and Sergio Zatti, "I *Cinque canti*: La crisi dell'autorità," *Studi italiani* 8 (1992): 23–40.

valric poems of Boiardo and Luigi Pulci. As I subsequently look at its portrayal of Charlemagne's court, dominated by the presiding allegorical figures of Envy and Suspicion, I will try to suggest how this larger sense of crisis may grow out of the new social and political realities to which Ariosto had been witness in the early sixteenth century. The tragic sense of the *Cinque Canti*, that is, emerges both from within the literary history that they redeploy and as a response to their poet's own historical moment.

A SENSE OF ENDING:
DEMOGORGON'S COUNCIL

If the *Cinque Canti* refuse to end, they nonetheless speak from their opening of an ending, the fall of an Empire that seems to be the end of order itself.[11] The supernatural agents of this destruction are the Fairies—the "fate"—and their governor, Demogorgon, who meet every five years at their Council in the fastness of the Himalayas. When Morgana— an Italian version of Morgan le Fay—shows up at the Council "mournful, dirty, and neglected, with her hair tousled and undone, in the same dress she had been wearing on the day when Orlando chased and later captured her" (1.10), the fiction refers the reader back to a central episode in the *Orlando Innamorato* (2.8–9; 13). There Morgana had been an allegorical personification of Fortune, and Orlando's feat of capturing her had signified the victory of human *virtù*, fortitude and prudence, over temporal contingency. That such a victory over time is possible was a favorite article of faith of Renaissance humanism, one to which even the realist Machiavelli still wants to cling in the famous twenty-fifth chapter of *The Prince*, where he nonetheless concedes to Fortune something more than half the government of hu-

---

11. For powerful critical remarks on the opening of the *Cinque Canti*, see James Nohrnberg, *The Analogy of the Faerie Queene* (Princeton, N.J.: Princeton University Press, 1976), 737–741.

man affairs. In Boiardo's fiction, however, Orlando forces Morgana to swear by her lord Demogorgon that she will never do him injury or in any way hinder him (*Orlando Innamorato* 2.13.26–29): he obtains indemnity from Fortune, from the unpredictable forces of time and change. But Orlando's luck runs out in the *Cinque Canti* where the Fairy Alcina, who has her own motives, uses her sister Morgana's case to convince Demogorgon and the other Fairies to declare all-out war not only on Orlando but also on Charles and his Empire. The human protagonists of the poem become the victims of an outraged and outrageous Fortune.[12]

Who is Demogorgon? He is a monster born of a misprint in the medieval manuscript tradition of a commentary on the *Thebaid*, an epic poem by the first-century Roman writer Statius: when the necromancer Tiresias finds that the spirits of the underworld are recalcitrant to rise to his invocation, he threatens them with the authority of a mysterious chthonic being before whom all Hades trembles (4.503–517). The fifth-century commentator Placidus Lactantius identified this being as the Platonic demiurge, the creator and framer of the universe. Scribal tradition corrupted *demiurgos* into Demogorgon, probably influenced by an analogous passage in the *Pharsalia*, where the witch Erictho menaces the shades she has summoned with the name of him

---

12. Boiardo's episode is now available to English-language readers in the translation by Charles Stanley Ross of the *Orlando Innamorato* (Berkeley, Los Angeles, and Oxford: University of California Press, 1989). For a more extended discussion of the capture of Morgana and the seminal importance of the episode in the Italian tradition of heroic poetry, see David Quint, "The Figure of Atlante: Ariosto and Boiardo's Poem," *Modern Language Notes* 94 (1979):77–91; "La fortuna di Morgana: dal Boiardo al Marino," in *Tipografie e romanzi in val padana fra quattro e cinquecento*, ed. Riccardo Bruscagli and Amedeo Quondam (Modena: Pannini, 1992), 99–106; *Epic and Empire* (Princeton, N.J.: Princeton University Press, 1993), 248–261, 309–311.

"who can look openly at the Gorgon" (6.746). It was a twelfth-century gloss on this passage of Lucan in turn that identified Demogorgon as the hoary progenitor of the gods, the role that he assumes at the beginning of Boccaccio's vastly influential *Genealogy of the Pagan Gods*.[13] There Boccaccio, citing Statius and Lucan, makes Demogorgon the companion of Eternity and Chaos: these are primordial powers indeed. The Demogorgon of the *Cinque Canti* presides over the ranks of Fairies, whose name suggests the classical fates, the spinners of destiny, and who, because in antiquity they were "once called by the fairer names of nymphs and goddesses" (1.9), also seem to embody natural forces. When this Demogorgon decrees the destruction of the Holy Roman Empire, we may feel the turning of a larger cosmic cycle, of the reversion through time of creation back to chaos, carrying all things human with it—not least the humanist belief that people can dominate and create meaning out of time. And we may also sense Ariosto the poetic creator undoing the fictional world he has made.

If the figure of Demogorgon evokes again, if only tangentially, Lucan and his *Pharsalia*, the larger opening episode of the Council of the Fairies imitates another Roman poem, the *In Rufinum* of Claudian. Claudian wrote about contemporary events at the end of the fourth century A.D., and in this poem, which is a combination of invective and historical narrative, he attacks Rufinus, the counselor of the eastern Emperor Theodosius and of his son, Arcadius: after plotting to control the Empire, Rufinus was murdered at the instigation of Claudian's patron, the Vandal general Stilicho.[14]

13. On the tradition of Demogorgon, see David Quint, "Epic Tradition and *Inferno* IX," *Dante Studies* 92 (1975):201–207; Nohrnberg, *Analogy of the Faerie Queene, loc. cit.*

14. See the excellent edition and commentary by H. L. Levy, *Claudian's In Rufinum* (Cleveland and London: Press of Case Western Reserve University, 1971) for the historical background to the

The *In Rufinum* begins with a council of furies in Hades that would inspire many literary imitators and produce a distinguished series of later underworld assemblies, culminating in the council of Milton's devils in the second book of *Paradise Lost*. Ariosto follows Claudian's poem fairly closely in the *Cinque Canti*. The fact that his opening Council of the Fairies is modeled on the demonic council that opens the *In Rufinum* is, in fact, one more indication that the *Cinque Canti* are a new work, independent of the *Furioso*. His Alcina and Morgana take the place of the sister furies Megaera and Allecto (1.25–117); Alcina chooses as her instrument Ganelon, the imperial counselor and high courtier, as Megaera chooses Rufinus as hers (1.86f.). Ganelon arrests Charles's victorious progress before Prague, while he waits for Hungarian reinforcements to come to the aid of its Bohemian defenders. So Rufinus, according to Claudian, "tricked the emperor and put off the instant day of battle" against the Danubian Getae (Visigoths) of Alaric, whom Stilicho had brought to the point of capitulation; in the meantime Rufinus sought "to ally himself with the Huns" (1.316–322; 2.171–219). Ganelon further seeks to bring the Islamic enemies of Spain and Egypt down upon Christendom as Rufinus, with similar treachery, invites the barbarian invasions down upon the Roman Empire (2.22–53).

Those invasions would, in fact, come. In the defeat and death of Rufinus Claudian's poem sees the defeat of the destructive, irrational forces of the underworld; and these forces are a demonic manifestation of the menacing Gothic

poem. In a noteworthy essay, Gordon Braden has discussed the particular qualities of Claudian's poetry and their importance for later medieval and Renaissance imitators in "Claudian and His Influence: The Realm of Venus," *Arethusa* 12 (1979):203–231. Braden (225–227) points out the similarity between the visionary architecture of Claudian's poetry and the descriptions of the heavenly Jerusalem in Revelation; Ariosto, as I indicate below, appears to exploit this similarity in his description of Demogorgon's palace.

hordes poised on the borders of the late Roman Empire.[15]
No small part of the fascination of Claudian's poetry is its
confusion of metaphysical with political anxiety. The fate of
Rufinus has in fact restored the poet's faith in an orderly,
God-governed universe (1.19–20), a faith, he confesses in
the opening verses of the poem, that had been torn by doubt
and by the possibility that the universe operates by chance,
according to the atomic theory of Epicureanism.

> Saepe mihi dubiam traxit sententia mentem,
> curarent superi terras an nullus inesset
> rector et incerto fluerent mortalia casu.
>
> (1.1–3)

> Often this question has drawn my doubting mind:
> whether the gods concern themselves with terrestrial
> matter or whether there is no governor herein and mortal
> affairs fluctuate according to uncertain chance.

But the course of subsequent history casts a considerable
irony on Claudian's affirmation of belief in a providential
law. The poet died around 404; in 408 Stilicho was himself
murdered, and his antagonist Alaric swept down upon Italy
and sacked Rome. Without quite realizing it, Claudian had
been writing about the fall of the Roman Empire. The sense
in the opening scene of the *In Rufinum* that all hell is break-

---

15. Claudian similarly has frequent recourse to the myth of the
war between the giants and the gods, where the giants stand in for
the barbarian enemies of Roman order. See Alan Cameron, *Clau-
dian: Poetry and Propaganda at the Court of Honorius* (Oxford: Clar-
endon Press, 1970), 468–469. Ariosto is also drawn to this myth in
the *Cinque Canti*, both in his early reference to the giants' uproot-
ing of Lemnos, Delos, and Cyprus to hurl against the Olympians
(1.79), a direct allusion to Claudian's poem on the subject, the un-
finished *Gigantomachia*, and in the description of the battle between
Orlando and Rinaldo in Canto 5, where floating islands and bat-
tling giants are a controlling motif (53, 54, 58), suggesting a kind
of cosmic decreation.

ing loose against the imperial order brings the poem close in feeling to the *Pharsalia*, where Lucan repeatedly intimates that chance, not god, rules the universe—"habet mortalia casus" (2.13); "mortalia nulli / Sunt curata deo" (7.454–455)—in passages that Claudian apparently recalls and responds to here.[16]

Ariosto seems to have noted this connection when he put together the models of Claudian and Lucan in the *Cinque Canti*; he found Claudian's poem from the last years of the Roman Empire appropriate for his depiction of the crisis of another, reborn Roman Empire, just as he utilized Lucan's epic on the close of another period of Rome's history, the death throes of her republic. And the *Cinque Canti*, too, may be read as a troubled and doubtful theodicy. In the fifth canto the narrator asserts that Providence has in the end rescued Charles from the schemes of Ganelon.

> And the cruel traitor's astute deceptions, his art and his treasons, could not do so much that He could not do more: He who, dying for our salvation, wanted to drink gall. Ganelon arranged the threads, but in the end the Power on high wove the cloth to his harm: It made him the prisoner of Marfisa and Bradamante and I have told you in what way.
>
> (5.14)

There is an apparent contest for control over the poem's plot among Ganelon, its apparent prime mover, the Christian God who ultimately disposes it, and the poet himself who tells the story; the same Ariostesque narrator took the credit for rescuing Bradamante and for the capture of Ganelon one canto earlier in his address to the lady readers of his poem at the opening of Canto 4: "I kept Ganelon from rejoicing. . . .

16. See Richard T. Bruère, "Lucan and Claudian: The Invectives," *Classical Philology* 59 (1964):223–256. Cameron (*Claudian*, 328) points out that the primary model for the passage is Juvenal 13.86f.

I made the lord of Anglant come at a gallop from Va-
lence. . . . I have Marfisa deal with Lupo" (4.5). This self-
conscious moment, in which the smiling narrator of the *Fu-
rioso* briefly resurfaces in the sequel poem, makes us wonder
about the authorship of literary and providential plots: about
the possibility that the latter may be wishful projections of
the former. Furthermore, while the capture of Ganelon in
Canto 3 seems to promise the reversal and undoing of the
evil he has instigated, his plots continue nevertheless to
work themselves out in his absence and have apparently tri-
umphed in the ignominious defeat of Charles before Prague.
The poem ends before the promised rescue can come to the
Emperor.

Moreover, Ganelon is himself as much the instrument of
a larger plot as the other characters he treacherously manipu-
lates: behind his malice lies the wrath of the Fairies and
Demogorgon, the supernatural rivals in the poem to a Chris-
tian Providence. This rivalry seems particularly marked in
the description of Demogorgon's marvelous temple in the
Himalayas.

It is a hundred yards high, measuring from the first
cornice down to the ground; another hundred from
there to the top of the golden cupola which encloses
it above. It is ten times as big around, if the judgment
of one who measured it at his leisure does not err; and
a single, gorgeous crystal, clear and pure, encircles ev-
erything within and forms its wall and parapet.

It has a hundred sides and a hundred corners, with
equal distances between them. There are two columns
for every corner, supports for the high facade, and all
of them are of one size. Their bases and capitals are of
that rich metal which we value most highly, and they
shine all around with emeralds and sapphires and dia-
monds and rubies.

(1.2–3)

The temple, as Alexander Sheers has noted, bears a shadowy resemblance to the New Jerusalem that, according to the vision of St. John at the end of the Book of Revelation, will descend from heaven and reconstitute the earth at the end of time.

> The angel that was speaking to me was carrying a gold measuring rod to measure the city and its gates and wall. The plan of the city is perfectly square, its length the same as its breadth. He measured the city with his rod and it was twelve thousand furlongs in length and in breadth, and equal in height. He measured its wall, and this was a hundred and forty-four cubits high—the angel was using the ordinary cubit. The wall was built of diamond, and the city of pure gold, like polished glass. The foundations of the city wall were faced with all kinds of precious stone: the first with diamond, the second lapis lazuli, the third turquoise, the fourth crystal, the fifth agate, the sixth ruby, the seventh gold quartz, the eighth malachite, the ninth topaz, the tenth emerald, the eleventh sapphire and the twelfth amethyst. The twelve gates of the city were twelve pearls, each gate being made of a single pearl, and the main street of the city was pure gold, transparent as glass. I saw that there was no temple in the city since the Lord God almighty and the Lamb were themselves the temple.
>
> (Rev. 21:15–22)

Like the angel who takes St. John in spirit to a great and high mountain (21:10) from which he sees the descending apocalyptic city, Ariosto takes his lordly reader to the Himalayan temple of the master of the Fairies. In its geometrical precision, in the curious aside about "one who measured it," in the jewels and gold that makes up its walls, Demogorgon's temple parodies and suggests an alternative version of the New Jerusalem, the city that needs no temple. The crystal that surrounds the temple may be a marvel like the fourth foundation of the wall of the heavenly city and may parody the divine radiance of the New Jerusalem that shines like crystal—"sicut crystallum" (21:11.)[17] Or, as some commentators on the *Cinque Canti* prefer, it may refer to a crystalline stream flowing around the temple: here, too, it would be reminiscent of the river of the water of life, "splendidum tanquam crystallum" (22:1), that flows through the eschatological Jerusalem of St. John.

The intimations of apocalypse surrounding the Council of the Fairies reinforce the sense that the *Cinque Canti* are about the *end*: of a historical-political order, of a former poetic universe, of human meaning itself. But the Christian apocalypse is also a revelation of an ultimate, divine meaning both inside and outside history. Demogorgon and the Fairies present an alternative vision of doom: the revenge of Fortune-Morgana who personifies pure chance ("casus"), a vendetta which may also suggest the annihilating force of time and nature across a great cycle of creation and destruction. In the long run, Demogorgon's mythic coevals, Eternity and Chaos, may turn out to be identical. In this perspective the narrator's protestation of the final order of Providence shines through the darkness of his poem like the "tiny light from a lantern" that appears in response to the devout prayers of Ruggiero, imprisoned in the total obscurity of Alcina's whale (4.35; compare John 8:12). Contemplating Demogorgon and his powers ranged against human

17. Compare the beryl that forms the walls of the palace of Venus in Poliziano's *Stanze* (1.96), another piece of fantastic architecture in Renaissance Italian poetry that takes its inspiration from Claudian. This passage is itself imitated in the palace in Ariosto's Eden in the *Furioso* 34.53. For the similarity to the New Jerusalem, see the discussion by Braden in "Claudian and His Influence," 203–231; and Albert Russell Ascoli, *Ariosto's Bitter Harmony* (Princeton, N.J.: Princeton University Press, 1987), 268. Ascoli (288) further argues that the temple of Immortality on the *Furioso's* Moon (35.16) also echoes—and suggests an alternative to—the Johannine New Jerusalem.

creations and attainments at the opening of the *Cinque Canti*, one may ask the questions posed at the close of the greatest tragic work of Renaissance literature.

> KENT. Is this the promised end?
> EDGAR. Or image of that horror?

A SENSE OF ENDING: RONCEVAUX

It will appear that the trumpet is speaking in the valley of Jehoshaphat: "Come all to the eternal judgment, leave the sepulchre and tomb; bring both the righteous and the evildoer."

(23)

So the narrator of Luigi Pulci's *Morgante* (1483)—the other major chivalric poem, alongside the *Orlando Innamorato*, of Ariosto's preceding literary generation—breaks off the first installment of the poem, as he envisions a second part that would eventually retell Ganelon's betrayal of Orlando and the deaths of Orlando and Oliviero (Oliver) in the defeat at Roncevaux.[18] Although nowhere mentioned in the *Orlando Innamorato* and *Orlando Furioso*, the tradition of chivalric literature about Charlemagne and his peers does contain its own quasi-apocalyptic, tragic ending, a story that is most familiar to modern readers in the eleventh-century *Chanson de Roland* (a poem unknown in the Renaissance and only recovered in the nineteenth century). Versions of the Roncevaux story, in fact, constituted the origin of the tradition whose subsequent elaboration treated earlier events in the career of the Emperor and his knights and put off Orlando's

18. Pulci refers more immediately here to the invasion of Charles's kingdom by Antea, the revengeful Babylonian Princess; but he returns to this apocalyptic imagery in the aftermath of Roncevaux itself, where the battlefield, covered with the maimed bodies of the dead, is twice compared to the valley of Jehoshaphat (27.198; 210).

last stand in the Pyrenees into a distant future, to the point of its virtual disappearance in the poems of Boiardo and Ariosto.[19] But the *Cinque Canti* return to this dark ending of the Carolingian saga and to the model of the *Morgante*, both in the centrality they accord to the treachery of Ganelon and in their own sense of ending and defeat.

Readers of the *Morgante* are familiar with Pulci's slang-filled poetic language and abrupt, sometimes crude shifts into low comedy, which make his poem properly burlesque and distinct from the gentler and superbly controlled irony of the *Furioso*. At the moment of Orlando's pious death at Roncevaux, as hymning angelic voices are heard welcoming the knight's soul on high, the poet cannot resist mentioning a sound of thunder "which was the very gate of heaven slamming shut" (27.158) behind it. But the same scene also rises to a tragic dignity and power. As Orlando recognizes his approaching death, he comments:

19. Roncevaux *is* invoked in the *Orlando Furioso* in the climactic duel of three against three on the island of Lipadusa in Cantos 41–42. Oliviero is a protagonist here, as he is in the rout of Charles's forces before Prague in the last of the *Cinque Canti*; see note 31 below. See Angelo Monteverdi, "Lipadusa e Roncisvalle," *Lettere italiane* 13 (1961):401–409; David Quint, "The Death of Brandimarte and the Ending of the *Orlando furioso*," *Annali d'Italianistica* 12 (1994):75–85.

The death at the hands of Ganelon, not of Orlando, but of the *Furioso's* other hero, Ruggiero, *is* foretold both by Boiardo at the opening of the third book of the *Innamorato* (3.1.3) and by Ariosto, whose hermit knows—but does he ever tell Ruggiero?—that the hero is destined to be treacherously slain four years (37.61 in the 1516 edition; seven years [41.61] in the edition of 1532) to the day from the moment of his baptism and conversion to Christianity. Riccardo Bruscagli suggests that the *Cinque Canti* may represent Ariosto's return to this story of Ruggiero's betrayal and death that parallels the Roncevaux tragedy; see "'Ventura' e 'inchiesta' fra Boiardo e Ariosto," in Bruscagli, *Stagioni di civiltà estense* (Pisa: Nistri-Lischi, 1983), 98–102. This is a persuasive suggestion, but the *Cinque Canti* do not make any mention of the hermit's prophecy, nor do the requisite four years seem to have gone by.

> I grieve that Charles in his old age will perhaps see an
> end put to the fair kingdom of France and of all cour-
> tesy, for he has been a truly worthy emperor; but
> whatever rises must at last decline; all mortal things go
> toward one goal; while one ascends, another falls;
> perhaps the same may happen to Christianity (*cristia-
> nitade*).
>
> (*Morgante* 27.31)

These words contain an element of conventional *contemptus
mundi*. But Orlando's vision comprises the end of Christen-
dom as a political entity—and even, perhaps, of the Chris-
tian faith itself and of its otherworldly anchor against the
finitude of all earthly things. The tragic logic of Pulci's
Orlando is echoed by Ariosto's Alcina in the *Cinque Canti*,
as she enlists Envy in her assault on Charles's Empire.

> God has ordained a certain limit for mortal achieve-
> ment, up to which it is allowed to rise, but passing
> beyond which it would be almost divine, something
> which nature or heaven cannot endure; but He wishes
> instead that, having reached that limit, it may then de-
> cline. Charles has reached that point, if you observe
> him well.
>
> (1.48)

Human greatness, Alcina argues, momentarily creates the il-
lusion of something more than human, participating in the
eternal order of "nature or heaven"—and much of the meta-
physical ambiguity of Ariosto's fragment hangs on that "or."
The illusion, quickly enough dispelled as this greatness falls
inevitably into decline, can once again be labeled as "hu-
manism": even the most optimistic Renaissance hymns to
human dignity must eventually acknowledge the power of
time and death. The tragic principle that the Orlando of the
Morgante intuits as he contemplates the battlefield at Ronce-
vaux becomes the starting point for the action of the *Cinque
Canti*, leading up to their own version of imperial defeat.

24

The focus just before the end of the poem on the defeat and capture of Oliviero (5.78–87), the last champion and bulwark of Charles's routed forces at Prague, is a premonition of Oliviero's death at Roncevaux and draws the parallel more closely between the climax of the *Cinque Canti* and the final, Armageddon-like disaster that the Carolingian cycle has held waiting all along for the Emperor and his paladins.

COURTIER AND PRINCE

The *Cinque Canti* carry manifold intimations that the end is at hand. Their fantasy universe falls apart at the behest of mysterious outside powers—Demogorgon and the *fate*—but, as the poem progresses, these appear more and more as demonizations of forces *inside* its social world, forces that were, moreover, all too actual and part of Ariosto's own society. When one asks just what is it that is coming to an end in the *Cinque Canti*, the answer might be summed up as "chivalry" itself or, more properly, a feudal order of society that constituted chivalry as a system of values. The *Cinque Canti* depict feudalism falling victim to a new social arrangement in which the princely court becomes an increasingly important site of power: it is the site as well of the poem's personified figures of Envy and Suspicion. As its characters act less like traditional chivalric heroes and more like recognizable sixteenth-century social actors, the poem seems to be about contemporary realities that it views with pessimism *and* about the effects of the intrusion of these realities upon its fictions. No sooner had Ariosto completed the ultimate masterpiece of chivalric literature in the *Furioso* than he contemplated that literature's demise.[20] His broken-off se-

20. The *Furioso*, it must quickly be said, already discloses, not least in the central madness of Orlando, a world of chivalry in considerable crisis, and the poet's frequent comparison of the action of the poem to contemporary historical events repeatedly suggests the

quel suggests the inability of chivalric fictions to perpetuate themselves in a modern age that had now definitively outgrown them—an age, for better or worse, without chivalry.

Ariosto published the *Orlando Furioso* in 1516. Meanwhile, Machiavelli was writing *The Prince*, perhaps completing it by 1513; Castiglione would substantially complete the *Book of the Courtier* by 1518, though he would continue to revise and polish his masterpiece for another ten years. These other great classics of the decade gave emblematic treatment to the larger political and social formations emerging on the Italian and European scene. The despotic Prince and his creature, the courtier, were the dominant figures of early modern state-building, whether in small Italian principalities like Ariosto's own Ferrara, ruled by the Este dukes, or in the great nation-states taking shape in Spain, France, and England. The newly powerful institution of the court was the means by which the Prince centralized and consolidated his power, the place where he could transform his martial nobility into dependent princely servants and peaceable bureaucrats.[21] The *Cinque Canti* comment on this new reality

---

evasive nature of its fiction. See the outstanding critical exploration of these issues by Ascoli in *Ariosto's Bitter Harmony*. The *Cinque Canti* seem to break out of the ironic containment that is the supreme artistic achievement of the *Furioso*.

21. The classic accounts of this political and social transformation of the European aristocracy are, for the case of France, Norbert Elias, *The Court Society*, trans. Edmund Jephcott (New York: Pantheon, 1978) and, for the case of England, Lawrence Stone, *The Crisis of the Aristocracy 1558–1641* (1965; abr. ed. Oxford: Oxford University Press, 1967).

For an acute contemporary document that proposes the transformation into courtiers not of feudal aristocrats but of patrician republicans in a sixteenth-century Florence falling under the hegemony of the Medici, see Lodovico Alamanni's letter to Lorenzo de' Medici, Duke of Urbino, written in 1516, the year of the publication of the *Orlando Furioso*; the letter is translated by Anthony Molho in his *Social and Economic Foundations of the Italian Renaissance* (New York and London: Wiley, 1969), 214–220.

in the importance they give to Charles and to Ganelon, whom they depict as Charles's chief courtier. The Emperor had played a lesser role, Ganelon an almost nonexistent one, in the *Furioso*, but they have become the central protagonists of the sequel. The odd man out in the new political arrangement was the old-style aristocrat, clinging to his traditional identity as feudal warrior and independent lord over his domains: it was this independence, with its potential for open rebellion, that the modern state sought to suppress. In the *Cinque Canti* the feudal nobility corresponds to the class of knighthood, itself; by the end of the poem, the machinations of Ganelon have set Charles *against* his greatest paladins, the heroic champions of the *Furioso*. In the process a society that had been held together, in the poem's nostalgic view, by bonds of trust, honor, and obligation finds itself shattered in a world of power-seeking princes and courtiers.

Charles, however, begins the action of the poem by favoring Orlando, Rinaldo, and the other knights who have fought and won the war of the *Furioso*, granting them independent fiefdoms as rewards for their martial service (1.60– 65). He acts, that is, as a traditional feudal monarch and in his relationship to his vassals is likened to a "wise father of a family" (60); the social and political order he presides over is made to seem part of a "natural," patriarchal scheme of things. But he arouses the ire of Ganelon, who has reason to be doubly envious. The *Cinque Canti* have rewritten the ancient rivalry that chivalric tradition ascribed between the clan of Orlando and Rinaldo (Clairmont) and the clan of Ganelon (Mainz) into a competition between a warrior nobility and court nobility. The favor shown to Charles's soldiers appears to bypass the court where Ganelon has tried to rule as a power broker.

> At one time Ganelon was a lord so much in Charles's favor that he had no peer; but later Astolfo, Rinaldo of Montauban, Orlando, and the rest who showed their valor against Marsilio and against the African King worked to deprive him of his high standing.

> Whence the wretched Ganelon, who was all swollen
> up with smoke and wind, lived discontent.
>
> Proud, angry, and malicious, Ganelon hated to the
> death all the great lords surrounding Charles; he could
> not bear to see anyone installed at court except
> through his own patronage and contrivance. He knew
> so well how to feign goodness, with a humble voice
> and a counterfeit smile, and to use every sort of hy-
> pocrisy, that anyone who did not know his ways
> would have lit candles at his feet.
>
> (1.35–36)

This is a satiric portrait of the career courtier. Ganelon has
sought power in peacetime by controlling who is in and
who is out at court, by turning the court itself into his own
system of clientelism. To further his ends he had taken over
that dissimulation which Castiglione's interlocutors in the
Courtier had variously recommended and condemned and
turned it into a high, hypocritical art. Now snubbed by
Charles, Ganelon is consumed by envy even before the per-
sonified Envy, acting at Alcina's behest, pours her venom in
his heart. The dream that Envy shows him (1.53–55) of the
triumph of Orlando and the other paladins and of his own
disgrace merely conforms to Ganelon's actual situation, sup-
planted at court by the heroes of the recent war. Yet the very
fact that this competition takes place at court already sug-
gests the advent of a new political order in which Ganelon
will be at a real advantage, able, through courtly dissem-
bling, to outmaneuver his enemies and regain the all-
important favor of Charles.

Envy was perceived as a particular vice of the Renaissance
court, where subordinates competed with one another for
the Prince's favor; Ariosto's allegorical figure, in fact, re-
serves a special minister to goad courtiers on (1.51).[22] The

22. Castiglione's book attempts, in its picture of the fraternal
"concord of will or cordial love" (1.4) at the court of Urbino, to

second of Matteo Bandello's *Novelle*, which were begun early in the sixteenth century, collected, and published in 1554, depicts envy as the endemic and incurable condition of court society, where the Prince's favor constantly changes, creating new dissensions among his underlings. In the story a high Persian nobleman explains to his King that

> it is very true that in matters of the court one can find some basis for the reason of these changes, and this is the stinging and poisonous goad of pestilential envy, which perpetually weighs the favors of the Prince in a scale, and in one moment lifts him who was low and lowers him who found himself on high, in such a way that there is in courts no plague more harmful and more injurious than the disease of envy. All other vices can be cured very easily and with little effort in those who possess them, and they can almost be pacified, so that they will not do you offense; but with what means, with what art, with what medicine, will you quiet down envy?. . . . And who does not know that if one, who has been stirred by this pestilential disease sees me in court, o most hallowed King, more favored by you than he is, and my services more welcome to you, or that I know better than he how to wield arms, or in any other way be more worthy than he, and he envies me because of such things, who does not know, I say, that he cannot ever be cured, if he does not see

counter a current view that in contemporary "courts nothing prevails save envy, malevolence, corrupt manners" (2.2). Nonetheless, the conversations of the *Book of the Courtier* repeatedly advise the model courtier to observe "a certain decorous mean, which indeed is a very great strong shield against envy, which we ought to avoid as much as possible" (2.41; cf. 2.7, 2.19, 2.22). See *The Book of the Courtier*, trans. Charles S. Singleton (Garden City, N.Y.: Doubleday, 1959), 92, 139. The popular sonneteer and courtier Serafino d'Aquila (d. 1500) had written an invective against the "Envious court" (*Invida corte*) that was a "school of treachery and falsehood" (*Le rime di Serafino de' Ciminelli dall'Aquila*, ed. Mario Meneghini [Bologna: Romagnoli–dall'Acqua, 1894], 127).

me deprived of your grace, driven from court, and cast in extreme ruin? If I were to give to him the greatest gifts all day long, if I were to do him constant honor, if I were to praise him as much as I know how and to do him every service, it would all be thrown away. He will never cease to work against me until he sees me led to the deepest misery, for all other remedies fall short and are worthless. This is the poisonous disease that infects all courts, and injures all virtuous deeds, and seeks to offend all noble spirits. . . . There is not, in sum, any vice in the world that more destroys courts, dissolves the knot of holy companionships, nor that more ruins princes, than this poison of envy, for whoever gives ear to an envious person, whoever listens to his malicious fantasies, cannot possibly do good.[23]

Bandello's character might offer a moralized summary of the action of the *Cinque Canti*, where Charles's eventual willingness to listen to the lies of the invidious Ganelon leads him to disaster. But he also locates the sources of Ganelon's envy in the court system itself, where princely favor could seem to be distributed on a purely random basis, and lay the Prince open to the charge of ingratitude. Bandello's nobleman speaks of one who, like Ganelon, was "the first man at court" and "in the next moment finds himself to be the last" and of another, "diligently anxious and assiduous to serve, experienced in all the doings of the court, and who would care much more about the affairs of the Prince than about his own, but who does all in vain, because he is never rec-

23. *Tutte le opere di Matteo Bandello*, ed. Francesco Flora (Verona: Mondadori, 1966), 1:41–42. It should be pointed out that this whole speech is a piece of courtly hypocrisy; by blaming the vicissitudes that he has suffered at the hands of the King on envy, the nobleman allows an unjust and suspicious monarch to save face. Nonetheless, the nobleman is able to hint that it is the monarch's own capriciousness that causes envy among his courtiers.

ompensed, and sees himself grow old serving without ever obtaining reward."[24] It is just because the courtier is placed in a position of total dependence on the sovereign that the latter's unpredictable shifts of favor arouse such jealousy—and furthermore, the Prince's capriciousness devalues court service itself. Compared to feats of open valor on the battlefield, it looks more and more like the slavish flattery and empty dissimulation of which Ganelon is, in fact, a past master.

Ariosto himself knew only too well the condition of the unrewarded courtier. His first satire, written around 1517—roughly contemporaneous with the *Cinque Canti*—complains of the ingratitude of Cardinal Ippolito d'Este, the patron to whom the *Orlando Furioso* was dedicated: for all his wretched service, he asserts, he has still not received enough to feed himself from the cardinal, who scorns Ariosto's masterpiece and "does not want that the praise I have composed of him be taken for a work meriting compensation" (97–98). Ariosto had seemingly anticipated Ippolito's tightfisted reception of the *Furioso* when he closed the 1516 edition of the poem with the emblem of honeybees being smoked out of their nest and with the motto "Pro bono malum," evil returned for good. In the *Cinque Canti* this emblem turns up, with similar charges of ingratitude against Charles, on the armor of the rebel Rinaldo (5.46), who has mutinied against the Emperor through the machinations of Ganelon. But if Ariosto identifies himself with the heroic Rinaldo, whom the chivalric tradition repeatedly depicts as unjustly

24. *Ibid.*, 39–40. "You will similarly see in the courts of kings and princes one in such favor of his lord that it really seems that his master does not know how to do or say anything without him, and nonetheless when he will endeavor with all his energy and effort to maintain or increase the grace of his lord, the mind of the lord has suddenly changed and turned to another; and he who was before the first man at court in the next moment finds himself to be the last" (39).

31

distrusted and insufficiently honored and rewarded by Charles, his own disappointed experience at the court seems to lie as well behind the resentment and envy of Ganelon, the spinner of plots who seems at times to be the poet's own dark alter ego.[25]

As the Prince of this treacherous courtier, Charles is the most complex character of the *Cinque Canti*. In the *Morgante* and other works of the Carolingian cycle, Charles is the innocent dupe of Ganelon, and here Ariosto even offers a supernatural explanation for the Emperor's credulity in the magic herb that Alcina has given Ganelon (3.21–22), an herb to which the narrator irreverently attributes the success not only of Mohammed but also of Moses. Charles's own guilelessness is later said to cause his downfall: "suspecting no treason in anyone else (since there wasn't any in him)" (4.90). The Emperor is thus placed in opposition to Suspicion itself, the ex-tyrant turned into allegorical personification, who embodies a vice particular to princes—including

25. Ariosto was particularly upset with the Este when he and his family were denied the inheritance of his deceased cousin, Rinaldo di Francesco Ariosti, whose property reverted to Duke Alfonso as a vacant fief. In the *Cinque Canti* he refers at 1.65 to the special beneficence of Charles, who gave his vassals investitures that were "true and free" and unalienable from their heirs—presumably in pointed contrast to the behavior of his own patrons. Ariosto discusses the case in the very same letter to Mario Equicola of October 15, 1519, in which he mentions the "little addition" he is making to the *Furioso*: "It is true that I am making some little addition to my *Orlando Furioso*; that is, I have begun it; but latterly on one side the Duke, on the other the Cardinal [Ippolito d'Este] (the one having taken from me a possession that for more than thirty years belonged to our House, the other another possession worth nearly ten thousand ducats, *de facto* and without even summoning me to show my reasons), have given me other things to think of than fables. Still, notwithstanding this, I am going on, often doing some little thing." The entire letter is cited in Edmund G. Gardner, *The King of Court Poets: A Study of the Work, Life, and Times of Lodovico Ariosto* (1906; rpt. New York: Greenwood Press, 1968), 145–146.

the "many such in Italy in our day" whom the poet prudently declines to name or discuss both at the opening (5) and end (135) of Canto 2. For if Envy is the condition attending modern courtiers, Suspicion is the identifying trait of the new autocratic despot: intent on retaining all power to himself, the Prince mistrusts any potential rival. If Charles is distinguished from such tyrannical princes, so is he distinguished from the deceitful Ganelon, even as the two work together in the Emperor's court: just as the narrator avoids the censure of contemporary princes, his story seems reluctant to criticize the ruler. For most of Canto 2 Charles appears to be the good Prince to whom the canto at its beginning contrasts bad tyrants (1–6), the Prince once again described as father to his people and compared as well to the "true shepherd who lays down his own life for his weak flock" (2). He wisely organizes the defense of his Empire, and by the canto's end he seems on the verge of putting an end to the war raised by his enemies, having defeated Desiderius in Lombardy, forced the surrender of Tassillone in Bavaria, and brought a besieged Prague near to capitulation. But at this point Ganelon arrives on the scene and Charles takes him into his counsel; the narrator cannot withhold comment: "Charles acted like a fool in this regard, as do almost all lords; they neglect the good man and exalt the worst" (134).

It is, however, precisely as a suspicious tyrant that Ganelon represents Charles when he has conveyed to Rinaldo a letter he has forged in the Emperor's hand: Charles, it is made to appear, regrets having given Rinaldo the task of defeating the rebellious Unuldo.

> For once he has conquered Unuldo and taken Gascony from him (and Charles believes Rinaldo will inevitably do so) he will want to be Unuldo's heir, because he longs to expand the state of Montauban; and the suspicion which Charles has about Rinaldo's corrupt loyalty is not just an idle dream: the gist is that

> Charles seems to have decided to remove Rinaldo
> thence, either by force or by love.
>
> (3.30)

The Emperor, Ganelon pretends, suspects the loyalty and is afraid of the power of one of his chief vassals and wants to deprive him of his military forces. Charles, that is, is said to be acting like a modern prince in attempting to consolidate his central authority at the expense of his nobility. And he is said to do so, moreover, as a defense of the court, the site and instrument of his power: "Charles will do more than give you a scare, for Ganelon continually prods him to make the court safe from you altogether—for, so he says, you turn the court upside down every time you want to" (3.33). The apparent victory of the court faction of Ganelon is described as a vindication of the court itself against an unruly martial nobility, knights who have become too errant.[26] The brilliance of Ganelon's plot lies not only in its playing to the secret fears that Rinaldo, as a member of that nobility, may have of being displaced in a new court society allied to a newly autocratic Prince, a society in which his military exploits will be of less importance than the whim of princely favor—especially when the court is dominated by his enemies. By stirring Rinaldo into revolt Ganelon also brings about in reality what had at first been only a fiction: Charles sends Orlando out to quell Rinaldo's rebellion and sanctions Ganelon's actions against Rinaldo's noble kin, Bradamante, Ruggiero, and Marfisa (3.61–64). And Ariosto insinuates that Ganelon's originally false scenario may contain a grain of truth: it suggests why Charles may choose—magic herb or no—to heed the counsel of Ganelon, why like King Lear

26. Charles complains against the commotion that Rinaldo's presence creates at his court in the *Morgante*; see 11.11f. Ariosto, I argue, takes a conventional plot from the chivalric tradition and gives it a fresh social application.

and "almost all lords," he neglects the good and exalts the bad. Lords may prefer bad courtiers to good nobles just because they are courtiers, who (they presume) are their own pacified creatures, rather than independent and armed, if faithful, feudatories. The ascendancy of the courtier Ganelon, even as he seeks to destroy his sovereign from within the latter's center of power, is not possible without Charles's collusion, for courtier and Prince belong to the same modern political configuration.

But if Charles already participates in this new system of strong princes and court servants, he does so without quite realizing it; and he still shares a more traditional view of the feudal polity, bound together by ties of mutual obligation and loyalty. Hence his dismayed reaction to the disloyalty of Rinaldo, described in a series of stanzas (55–58) that take up the numerical midpoint of Canto 3 and thus fall exactly in the center of the *Cinque Canti* themselves. He is like a father who sees his son "raise a knife against him" (55); the image of oedipal struggle undoes the earlier invocations of Charles as a wise father and suggests the extent to which the poem recounts the destruction of a traditional society of feudal chivalry. But there is also something naive and nostalgic in Charles's very dismay, as if one could still believe in the political world as one happy family. It is a remarkable paradox of a poem which laments the disappearance of chivalry that Charles's ruin at Prague is due in no small part to his clinging to outmoded chivalric usages: instead of prosecuting his siege of the beleaguered city he agrees to the offer, presented by the Bohemian King Cardorano but invented by Ganelon himself, to decide the war by a limited trial by combat (3.6–20). The Emperor is urged to seek the "glory" (7–8) of a personal victory, and he is also persuaded to do so as a "good shepherd who lays down his life for his flock" (11) in terms that, with typical Ariostesque irony, recall the narrator's own earlier praise of the good Prince as a Christlike "true shepherd." As it intimates that behind a paternalistic rhetoric of self-sacrifice the chivalric code may all along have concealed an incompatible drive to self-aggrandizement, the poem also suggests that Charles may not be a modern enough Prince, not able to grasp coldly and clearly the facts of power. The narrator finally comes out and openly condemns the Emperor at the beginning of Canto 5 for having allowed the "glorious spectacle" (5.3) of defeating Cardorano to blind him to the precariousness of his military situation and to stop him from calling a strategic retreat from Prague while he still had time to do so.

The tragedy of Charles is that he straddles two different political orders; his lingering attachment to atavistic ideas of chivalric honor and fair play is part and parcel of a guileless-ness that now appears to be a liability in a new, more dangerous world. The *Cinque Canti* lament the passing of those ideas, even as they suggest both their element of self-delusion and the drawbacks of continuing to adhere to them in the face of changing political realities. Sergio Zatti has suggested that in the figure of Charles Ariosto has depicted the dilemma of his contemporary Italian princes, who were too slow to learn the lessons that Machiavelli would draw from the foreign invasions that had wracked the peninsula since 1494—when Boiardo left off the *Innamorato*—since, Ariosto's narrator says as he recalls the good old days of fifteenth-century Ferrara, "the unremitting afflictions began from which every heart in Italy is sick" (2.120).[27]

A DIVIDED EUROPE

Other European princes had already mastered those lessons. There is a telling detail at the end of Canto 4, where we learn that among the troops massed against Charles at Prague is a polyglot army sent by the Byzantine Emperor Constan-

27. See Zatti, "I *Cinque canti*," 34–36.

tine: "Constantine the Greek sent these last, with a brother of his as their captain, because he bore vicious envy and deadly hatred against Charles, the son of Pepin, for having become the Latin Emperor and for usurping the imperial eagle from him" (4.95). The Envy that had seemed to be the peculiarly courtly vice of Ganelon has now spilled out into the larger political world, where the greatest princes are envious of one another. Or, rather, the courtier's envy may be the symptom and extension of the princely power upon which, in a new, modern configuration the court depends: the power of a lord suspicious of rivals among his noble vassals, envious to the point of seeking the overthrow of a rival prince. Prince and courtier, Suspicion and Envy become alike, all part and parcel of an emergent ethos in which the competition for power becomes an end in itself.

We might not wish to grant this passage such importance, did it not appear to allude to a contemporary event to which the *Cinque Canti* have already more directly referred: the struggle in 1519 between François I of France and Charles V of Spain to be elected Holy Roman Emperor. In what is a key passage for the dating of the poem, Ariosto alludes at 2.52 to the mission of his friend Bernardo Bibbiena, the Cardinal of Santa Maria in Portico, who had gone to France to pledge papal support for François, and in the following stanza he lends his own poetic support—and that of his Este patrons—to François by recalling the title, "Most Christian," that had belonged to the French monarchy from the time of Charlemagne. The German electors nonetheless chose the "Catholic" King Charles, initiating the Hapsburg domination of European politics in the sixteenth century, a domination that would eventually be spread to Italy, especially after the defeat and capture of François by Spanish forces at Pavia in 1525. The Este gravitated toward Spain, and in the 1532 revised version of the *Furioso* their poet inserted a passage (15.21–35) celebrating Charles as the "most wise and just emperor that has been or will be since Augustus" (15.24).[28]

The rivalry between France and Spain, in which Italian states like Ferrara became pawns, had aroused Ariosto's indignation in the *Furioso*: "if you want to be called most Christian and you others want to be called Catholics" he had queried, "why do you kill and plunder the goods of Christian men?" (17.83). This appalling picture of Christian Europe divided against itself is actualized in the *Cinque Canti* as the war against Charles, already an internecine European conflict, eventually becomes a fight between two would-be Holy Roman Emperors. And the poem may hint, in addition, at a new, very contemporary cause of dissension in the Christian body-politic. Charles's eighth-century Bohemian adversaries are still pagan.

> Prague . . . was at that time unfriendly to our faith (although I am not certain that the whole country is friendly to it even in our time).
>
> (2.95)

Ariosto refers to the openly schismatic Hussite national Church that held sway in Bohemia in the early sixteenth century. In its rejection of the authority of Rome to decide the interpretation of scripture, the Bohemian Church anticipated Luther. And Luther and his challenge to the papacy and Catholic unity were just being felt in Italy in the years

28. The turn of the Este toward Charles V, reflected in the numerous new encomiastic passages inserted into the 1532 *Furioso*, may help to explain why Ariosto abandoned the *Cinque Canti*. A new imperial hegemony, which may have inspired quite genuine hopes for the restoration of both political order in Italy and religious unity in Europe, could have made the sense of crisis of the *Cinque Canti* already appear superseded and out of date. On the evolution of political allusions in the *Furioso*, see Alberto Casadei, *La strategia delle varianti: le correzioni storiche del terzo "Furioso"* (Lucca: Maria Pacini Fazzi, 1988).

during which Ariosto was composing the *Cinque Canti*. One
year after the 1516 publication of the *Furioso* Luther had
nailed his ninety-five theses on the church door in Witten-
berg; by 1520 a papal bull was issued condemning his writ-
ings, followed swiftly by a bull of excommunication early in
1521. From the very beginning his Italian opponents ac-
cused Luther of trying to foment schism as if, a polemicist of
1518 put it, he "were about to migrate to Bohemia." [29] It is
tempting to read the *Cinque Canti* as a first literary response
to the crisis wrought by the Reformation. The enemies of
Charles include not only Bohemia but also Saxony, the
cradle of Luther's movement. The penitent Astolfo insists,
perhaps in reaction to new Protestant doctrine, upon the
importance of works as well as faith as he catechizes Ruggi-
ero inside Alcina's whale (4.82). When Ariosto later added
his praise of Charles V in the 1532 *Furioso*, he asserted that
God Himself willed that the world should see "only one
sheepfold, only one shepherd" (15.26), under the rule of the
Emperor: the citation of John 10:16 contains the quasi-
messianic hope that Hapsburg power can restore the reli-
gious unity of Europe. But the *Cinque Canti*, with their saga
of warring Christians, would first depict this unity in pieces.

FIGHTING DIRTY

As they comment on an actual political world, the *Cinque
Canti* depict the pervasive breakup of chivalric society. Re-
bellion from the bottom is matched by tyranny from the top.
The larger struggle between Rinaldo and Charles is repeated
farther down the feudal ladder in the foiled attempts by the

29. Silvester Prierias, *Replica ad F. Martinum Luther Ordinis Ere-
mitarum* (1518), cited in Friedrich Lauchert, *Die italienischen literar-
ischen Gegner Luthers* (Freiburg im Breisgau: Herder, 1912), 19. See
also Lauchert's extract, 183, from the *Oratio ad Principes et Populos
Germaniae* (1520) of Thomas Radinus, who accuses Luther of being
a Hussite.

Lombard Penticone (2.66f.) and by the English Paladin As-
tolfo (4.54f.) to force themselves on the wives of their liege-
men, without, as Astolfo ruefully confesses, "regard for my
honor, or for the fact that I was lord there while he was a
vassal (for in using force against someone weaker, the more
powerful a man is, the greater is his fault)" (4.57).

The severing of links of feudal obligation and the frag-
mentation of a larger Christian polity are enacted symboli-
cally on the battlefield in Canto 5. The companies of soldiers
in Rinaldo's and Orlando's armies "had promised to stand
by one another united and in close formation, to be ready
to help each other," but after the impact of battle "no two
were found" together (5.57). "It was enough, it was too
much, for each man to look out for himself," the narrator
comments (5.56), and this same situation prevails during the
rout at Prague in the penultimate stanza of the poem.

> Charles falls into the water below the bridge, and
> there is no one who stops to give him help, for each
> man has so much to do to take care of himself that
> there is little concern for others there: there courtesy,
> charity, love, respect, gratitude for favors received in
> the past, or anything else one can say, is put aside, and
> each one thinks only about himself.
>
> (5.92)

This final vista spells out the moral that the *Cinque Canti*
have been driving at all along. Charles is abandoned as the
routed French army becomes a mass of individuals, each
placing his own survival above all claims of human commu-
nity. This is Renaissance individualism with a vengeance,
and the scene seems to be an emblem of a new era of self-
interest in which the old values of feudalism and chivalry
cannot survive.

In a world where every man is out for himself there can
be no personal loyalty or honor, and the treachery that is
initially the distinguishing trait of Ganelon soon expands

through the poem. The most frequently repeated—and
here, too, morally emblematic—action of the *Cinque Canti*
is the sudden capture of a character, taken unawares and
when least suspecting evil from his or her captors: the cap-
ture of Ganelon in his bed by Gloricia, which goes against
her normal nature as the most hospitable of Fairies (1.84);
Alcina's seizing the terrified Suspicion in his sleep (2.22); the
taking of the Lombard Prince Penticone in the trap laid for
him by Bianca (2.84); Rinaldo's arrest of Namo (3.51) who
has come to him as Charles's envoy; Ganelon's capture
of Bradamante, who rushes into the arms of the shape-
changing Vertumnus—the demonic embodiment of many-
faced treason (3.74); Walter's surprise attack on Astolfo,
leaving him barely the chance to say, "God help me"
(4.73). Both Ruggiero and Rinaldo lead their forces toward
presumed allies, only to discover too late that Ricardo
(4.20) and Orlando (5.39) have been sent out against them.
Canto 3 offers the spectacle of ambush and counterambush:
Ganelon captures Bradamante, is attacked from hiding and
captured in turn by Orlando (85f.), and plots his escape by
means of an ambush by his kinsman Lupo (100f.), a plot that
fails when the concealed Lupo and his men are themselves
ambushed by Marfisa (111f.). Even the stalwartly honorable
Orlando first unhappily accedes to the plan to capture Pen-
ticone (2.85), then resorts himself to the subterfuges of dis-
guise (3.82) and ambush (84) in order to rescue Brada-
mante—directly against the bidding of Charles.

The use of fraud and deception in the poem's warfare, as
well as its ferocity—witness Rinaldo's scorched-earth policy
(3.52) and Orlando's summary execution of captured rebels
(5.38)—may reflect the new military realities that Italy had
come to experience in recent decades.[30] But the "realism"

30. See the fine essay by Stefano La Monica, "Realtà storica e
immaginario bellico ariostesco," *Rassegna della letteratura italiana* 89
(1985), 326–358. La Monica notes several parallels between the

that invades the battlefields of the *Cinque Canti* means the death of chivalry, as a look at one final symbolically charged motif of the fighting will suggest. In Canto 2 the valiant Lombard knight Ottone is captured when his excellent horse—described in detail in stanza 60 as a "Corsican and his grey neck was dappled with red spots, on both sides, from the knee to the shoulder"—is killed by Baldovino (63). It is not clear that Baldovino intended to strike the horse, which was at that moment turning around. His act is as ambiguous as Baldovino is himself: the son of Ganelon and the half-brother of Orlando. For no true knight would ever intentionally wound an adversary's horse, and Baldovino, in spite of his father, is later described as a "courteous knight and paladin" (3.46). But in the battle before Prague in Canto 5, the squire Baraffa quite deliberately attacks the horse that Oliviero's men were bringing to their fallen leader: "he cut off the back legs of the other's horse so that it looked like a giraffe: for it stood tall in front and short behind" (82). Such

---

Cinque Canti and the precepts of Machiavelli's *Arte della guerra*: the condemnation of mercenary soldiers and the depiction of Charles's army as a citizen militia (2.42–44); the depiction of Charles as a reader and imitator of the deeds of ancient military commanders (2.50); the importance of speed in war and of carrying battle into the enemy's country (2.50–51); the hard training and exercise of Charles's knights (4.91); the necessity of prudence in the commander, in which Charles conspicuously fails (5.1–3). Contrary to La Monica's contention, it appears unlikely that Ariosto actually knew Machiavelli's work, probably written around 1520 and published in 1521, during the composition of the *Cinque Canti*; these views on military art were commonplaces of the period. For a discussion of the new brutality that the French armies brought to warfare in Ariosto's Italy, see Michael Murrin, *History and Warfare in Renaissance Epic* (Chicago and London: University of Chicago Press, 1994), 199–204; and for an analysis of the depiction of warfare in the *Orlando Furioso* that insists on its historical *unreality*, see Leonzio Pampaloni, "La guerra nel *Furioso*," *Belfagor* 26 (1971): 627–652.

mistreatment of horses was not new to Ariosto's fiction: in the *Orlando Furioso* (29.68f.) the insane Orlando captures and rides to death the horse of Angelica, doing to the beast what he would like to have done to the lady and in the process offering a dark vision of chivalry gone mad.[31] For chivalry, as the etymology of the word indicates, is the code of the knight on horseback. But in the *Cinque Canti* the assault on the horse is not part of chivalry's mad subconscious. By the end of the poem it has become the willful ploy of a modern warfare, increasingly dominated by the foot soldier, in which the knight and his code of chivalric behavior appear to be things of the past.

But perhaps chivalry may survive after all. The last stanza of the poem—and I want to insist again that this is Ariosto's consciously chosen last stanza—depicts Charles escaping from the waves of the Moldau and the seemingly apocalyptic defeat at Prague. And it is his horse who saves the Emperor when all his men have deserted him, a horse whose lengthy description, "white, except for some spots of black which looked like flies and which he had about his neck and flanks right up to the tail" (93), may now be seen both to recall

31. On this episode of the *Furioso* and its relationship to the revolution in sixteenth century modes of warfare, where the foot soldier had acquired a newly central role, see Beer, *Romanzi di cavalleria*, 109–138. In a second emblematic episode, added to the 1532 version of the poem, Cimosco, the tyrannical inventor of the gun, fires his weapon against Orlando, missing the knight but killing his horse (9.76); here, too, new military technology spells the end of chivalry. For the code of warfare that forbids a knight to attack his adversary's steed, see the *Furioso* 30.50: "it was shame and an infraction and eternal blame for whoever would wound a horse." In the *Furioso*'s climactic duel of three knights against three on the island of Lipadusa, the pagan Sobrino wounds the horse of Oliviero from behind—a blow, the narrator comments, "culpable in its manner" (41.86); this moment of unchivalric sneakiness in battle may be recalled when Oliviero's enemies once again disable his horse at Prague.

Ottone's noble steed and to foreground a last chivalric vestige in the poem.[32] The reader, in fact, knows that Marfisa and Bradamante are at hand and expects—given the narrative conventions of romance that have persisted up to the last-minute arrival of the cavalry in Western movies—that they will renounce their plans to revenge themselves on Charles and intervene to save him instead. So all may not be lost. But the *Cinque Canti* do not end with a final restitution of order, setting everything right once more, but rather they break off at a moment of deepest crisis which intimates that nothing can be the same again. The wan hope of the poem that some remnants of chivalry may still be salvaged out of a general moral and political wreckage rests on the lone figures of man and horse that struggle to the shore.

32. One may remember the care Charles is said to have taken to procure the best horses for his knights at 2.48 and 4.90.

Further Reading

EDITIONS OF THE *CINQUE CANTI*

ARIOSTO, LUDOVICO. *Opere minori.* Edited by Cesare Segre. Milan and Naples: Riccardo Ricciardi, 1954.

——. *Cinque canti di un nuovo libro di M. Ludovico Ariosto.* Edited by Luigi Firpo. Turin: UTET, 1964.

——. *Cinque canti.* Edited by Lanfranco Caretti. Turin: Giulio Einaudi, 1977.

CRITICISM

ASCOLI, ALBERT RUSSELL. *Ariosto's Bitter Harmony: Crisis and Evasion in the Italian Renaissance.* Princeton, N.J.: Princeton University Press, 1987.

BACCHELLI, RICCARDO. *La congiura di Don Giulio d'Este.* Milan: Mondadori, 1958.

BEER, MARINA. *Romanzi di cavalleria: Il "Furioso" e il romanzo italiano del primo Cinquecento.* Rome: Bulzoni, 1987.

BOIARDO, MATTEO MARIA. *Orlando Innamorato.* Translated by Charles Stanley Ross. Berkeley, Los Angeles, and Oxford: University of California Press, 1989.

BRADEN, GORDON. "Claudian and His Influence: The Realm of Venus." *Arethusa* 12 (1979):203–231.

BRUSCAGLI, RICCARDO. *Stagioni di civiltà estense.* Pisa: Nistri-Lischi, 1983.

CASADEI, ALBERTO. "Alcune considerazioni sui *Cinque canti.*" *Giornale storico della letteratura italiana* 165 (1988):161–179.

——. "I *Cinque canti* o l'ultima eredità di Boiardo." *Italianistica* 21 (1992):739–748.

——. *Il percorso del "Furioso."* Bologna: Il Mulino, 1993.

——. *La strategia delle varianti: Le correzioni storiche del terzo "Furioso."* Lucca: Maria Pacini Fazzi, 1988.

CATALANO, MICHELE. *Vita di Ludovico Ariosto.* Geneva: Olschki, 1930.

DIONISOTTI, CARLO. "Appunti sui *Cinque canti* e sugli studi ariosteschi." In *Studi e problemi di critica testuale*, 369–382. Bologna: Commissione per i testi di lingua, 1961.

———. "Per la data dei *Cinque canti*." *Giornale storico della letteratura italiana* 137 (1960):1–40.

FONTANA, PIO. *I "Cinque canti" e la storia della poetica del "Furioso."* Milan: Vita e Pensiero, 1962.

GARDNER, EDMUND G. *The King of Court Poets: A Study of the Work, Life, and Times of Lodovico Ariosto.* 1906; rpt. New York: Greenwood Press, 1968.

GOFFIS, CESARE FEDERICO. "I *Cinque Canti* di un nuovo libro di M. Ludovico Ariosto." *Rassegna della letteratura italiana* 79 (1975):146–168.

LA MONICA, STEFANO. "Realtà storica e immaginario bellico ariostesco." *Rassegna della letteratura italiana* 89 (1985):326–358.

MORGAN, LESLIE Z. *Five Cantos.* New York and London: Garland Publishing, Inc., 1992.

NOHRNBERG, JAMES. *The Analogy of the Faerie Queene.* Princeton, N.J.: Princeton University Press, 1976.

PAMPALONI, LEONZIO. "La guerra nel *Furioso*." *Belfagor* 26 (1971): 627–652.

QUINT, DAVID. "The Death of Brandimarte and the Ending of the *Orlando furioso*." *Annali d'Italianistica* 12 (1994):75–85.

———. "The Figure of Atlante: Ariosto and Boiardo's Poem." *Modern Language Notes* 94 (1979):77–91.

ROSSI, LEA. "Sui *Cinque Canti* di Lodovico Ariosto." *Bolletino storico reggiano* 7 (1974):91–150.

SACCONE, EDUARDO. *Il "soggetto" del* furioso. Naples: Liguori, 1974.

SEGRE, CESARE. *Esperienze ariostesche.* Pisa: Nistri-Lischi, 1966.

ZATTI, SERGIO. "I *Cinque Canti*: La crisi dell'autorità." *Studi italiani* 8 (1992):23–40.

Principal Characters
of the *Cinque Canti*

CHARLES (CHARLEMAGNE): Holy Roman Emperor,
son of Pepin

House of Clairmont (Chiaramonte)

ORLANDO (LORD OF ANGLANT, COUNT OF BRAVA,
ROMAN SENATOR): son of Milone, nephew of
Charlemagne

RINALDO (LORD OF MONTAUBAN): son of Amone,
cousin of Orlando

GUIDON SELVAGGIO: Rinaldo's bastard brother

RICCIARDETTO: Rinaldo's brother

ALARDO: Rinaldo's brother

GUICCIARDO: Rinaldo's brother

BRADAMANTE: woman knight, Rinaldo's sister

RUGGIERO: husband of Bradamante

MARFISA: woman knight, Ruggiero's sister

MALAGIGI: cousin of Orlando and Rinaldo, a
necromancer

ASTOLFO: cousin of Orlando, Rinaldo, and Malagigi,
son of King Ottone of England

TERIGI: Orlando's squire

SINIBALDO: Bradamante's squire

House of Mainz (Maganza)

GANELON: Count of Ponthieu (Pontieri)

BALDOVINO: son of Ganelon, half-brother of Orlando

LUPO: son of Bertolagi

BERTOLAGI AND PINABELLO: killed in the *Orlando Furioso* by members of the House of Clairmont

Allies of Charlemagne

DUKE NAMO: of Bavaria

UGGIERO: the Dane

OLIVIERO: Orlando's brother-in-law

RICARDO: a Norman, commander of Charles's fleet

ARCHBISHOP TURPIN

SANSONETTO: ruler of Jerusalem

Enemies of Charlemagne

MARSILIO: King of Spain

DESIDERIUS: King of the Lombards

PENTICONE: son of Desiderius

OTTONE: a Lombard nobleman

BIANCA: wife of Ottone

TASSILLONE: King of the Bohemians, son-in-law of Desiderius

GORDAMO: ex-King of Saxony

UNULDO: of Aquitaine

CARDORANO: King of Prague

CONSTANTINE THE GREEK: Eastern Emperor

CALIPH OF EGYPT

Fairies

DEMOGORGON: Lord of the Fairies

MORGANA: Fairy of Fortune, conquered by Orlando

ALCINA: her sister, ex-lover of Ruggiero and Astolfo

LOGISTILLA: half-sister of Morgana and Alcina

GLORICIA: a hospitable Fairy

MEDEA

Demons

ENVY

SUSPICION

VERTUMNUS: a shape-changing demon

The Plot So Far

•

THE INTRICATE PLOT of the *Orlando Furioso* revolves around
the war that Charles, the Holy Roman Emperor, wages
against the invading Islamic forces of Agramante, King of
North Africa, and Marsilio, King of Spain. The conflict
ends with the total defeat and death of Agramante; Marsilio
returns to Spain to brace for Charles's retaliation. Early on
in the poem Ruggiero, one of Agramante's pagan champi-
ons, is captivated and loved in turn by the Fairy Alcina on
her island realm in the East Indies; both he and Astolfo, one
of Alcina's former lovers, eventually escape from her impris-
oning charms. Subsequently Ruggiero learns that he and
Marfisa, an indomitable woman warrior, are twin brother
and sister and that they were born of Christian parentage;
both convert to Christianity and in the final canto of the
epic Ruggiero marries his true love, Bradamante, another
woman warrior and the sister of Rinaldo of Montauban,
one of Charles's leading knights. In what seem to be minor
developments in the *Furioso*, Bradamante and Ruggiero
are respectively involved in killing Pinabello and Bertolagi,
members of the House of Mainz and hereditary enemies
of the House of Clairmont, to which Orlando, Rinaldo,
and Bradamante belong. Meanwhile, Astolfo voyages with
St. John the Evangelist to the moon, where he recovers the
lost wits of Orlando, returning him to the Christian fight-
ing forces and ensuring the victory over Agramante; at the
same time, Astolfo has his own sanity fully restored to him,
though it is predicted that his sanity will not last.

Orlando's own madness was triggered when he saw as the proof of his beloved Angelica's betrayal a bracelet he had once given her. This bracelet had belonged to Morgana, the Fairy of Fortune whom Orlando had chased down and captured in the *Orlando Innamorato*. Orlando made Morgana swear by Demogorgon, Lord of the Fairies, never to do him harm or hindrance. This is where matters stand when the Fairies come to their Council, held every five years, in the *Cinque Canti*.

TEXT AND TRANSLATION

Cinque Canti

Five Cantos

Canto Primo

a.   Oₗₜᵣₑ ᴄʜᴇ ɢɪà Rinaldo e Orlando ucciso
molti in più volte avean de' lor malvagi,
ben che l'ingiurie fur con saggio aviso
dal re acchetate, e li comun disagi,
e che in quei giorni avea lor tolto il riso
l'ucciso Pinabello e Bertolagi;
nova invidia e nov'odio anco successe,
che Franza e Carlo in gran periglio messe.

b.   Ma prima che di questo altro vi dica,
siate, signor, contento ch'io vi mene
(che ben vi menerò senza fatica)
là dove il Gange ha le dorate arene;
e veder faccia una montagna aprica
che quasi il ciel sopra le spalle tiene,
col gran tempio nel quale ogni quint'anno
l'immortal Fate a far consiglio vanno.

1.   Sorge tra il duro Scita e l'Indo molle
un monte che col ciel quasi confina,
e tanto sopra gli altri il giogo estolle,
ch'alla sua nulla altezza s'avicina:
quivi, sul più solingo e fiero colle,
cinto d'orrende balze e di ruina,
siede un tempio, il più bello e meglio adorno
che vegga il Sol, fra quanto gira intorno.

Canto 1

a.   R<small>INALDO AND</small> O<small>RLANDO</small> had already, on various occasions, slaughtered many of the wicked clan of Mainz, and the recent killings of Pinabello and Bertolagi had again swept the smiles from their faces. Their injuries, however, and the general unrest were hushed up following the wise advice of the King. Now new envy and new hatred arose to put France and Charles in great peril.[1]

b.   But before I tell you about this other matter, my lord, allow me to take you (for I'll certainly take you there without any trouble) to the golden sands of the Ganges, where you will see a sunny mountain which almost bears the heavens on its shoulders and the great temple to which the immortal Fairies go, every fifth year, to hold their counsel.[2]

1.   There rises between the hardened Scythian and the soft-living Indian a mountain which almost borders on the sky, and it lifts its peak so far above the rest that no other even approaches its height. Here, on the wildest and loneliest rise, girded by awesome cliffs and precipices, sits a temple—the fairest and most beautifully decorated of all that the Sun looks upon as it turns about the earth.

2.   Cento braccia è d'altezza, da la prima
      cornice misurando insin in terra;
      altre cento di là verso la cima
      de la cupula d'or ch'in alto il serra:
      di giro è dieci tanto, se l'estima
      di chi a grand'agio il misurò, non erra:
      e un bel cristallo intiero, chiaro e puro,
      tutto lo cinge, e gli fa sponda e muro.

3.   Ha cento facce, ha cento canti, e quelli
      hanno tra l'uno e l'altro uguale ampiezza;
      due colonne ogni spigolo, puntelli
      de l'alta fronte, e tutte una grossezza;
      di cui sono le basi e i capitelli
      di quel ricco metal che più s'apprezza;
      et esse di smeraldo e di zafiro,
      di diamante e rubin splendono in giro.

4.   Gli altri ornamenti, chi m'ascolta o legge
      può imaginar senza ch'io 'l canti o scriva.
      Quivi Demogorgon, che frena e regge
      le Fate, e dà lor forza e le ne priva,
      per osservata usanza e antica legge,
      sempre ch'al lustro ogni quint'anno arriva,
      tutte chiama a consiglio, e da l'estreme
      parti del mondo le raguna insieme.

5.   Quivi s'intende, si ragiona e tratta
      di ciò che ben o mal sia loro occorso:
      a cui sia danno od altra ingiuria fatta,
      non vien consiglio manco né soccorso:
      se contesa è tra lor, tosto s'adatta,
      e tornar fassi adietro ogni trascorso;
      sì che si trovan sempre tutte unite
      contra ogn'altro di fuor, con ch'abbian lite.

2.　It is a hundred yards high, measuring from the first cornice down to the ground; another hundred from there to the top of the golden cupola which encloses it above. It is ten times as big around, if the judgment of one who measured it at his leisure does not err; and a single, gorgeous crystal, clear and pure, encircles everything within and forms its wall and parapet.

3.　It has a hundred sides and a hundred corners, with equal distances between them. There are two columns for every corner, supports for the high facade, and all of them are of one size. Their bases and capitals are of that rich metal which we value most highly, and they shine all around with emeralds and sapphires and diamonds and rubies.

4.　The other decorations can be imagined by anyone listening or reading without my having to sing or write about them. There Demogorgon, who bridles and rules the Fairies, who gives them power and takes it away, follows observed ritual and ancient law, and calls all to counsel whenever the Lustral cycle reaches its fifth year.[3] He assembles them together from the farthest reaches of the world.

5.　Here they consider, argue, and debate whatever good or ill may have befallen them. There is no shortage of comfort or advice for those to whom some harm or other injury has been done. If there is dissent among them, it is soon resolved, and amends are made for any trespass. Thus they always find themselves united against any outsider with whom they have a quarrel.

6.   Venuto l'anno e 'l giorno che raccorre
    si denno insieme al quinquennal consiglio,
    chi da l'Ibero e chi da l'Indo corre,
    chi da l'Ircano e chi dal Mar Vermiglio;
    senza frenar cavallo e senza porre
    giovenchi al giogo, e senza oprar naviglio,
    dispregiando venian per l'aria oscura
    ogni uso umano, ogni opra di natura.

7.   Portate alcune in gran navi di vetro,
    dai fier demoni cento volte e cento
    con mantici soffiar si facean dietro,
    che mai non fu per l'aria il maggior vento.
    Altre, come al contrasto di san Pietro
    tentò in suo danno il Mago, onde fu spento,
    veniano in collo alli angeli infernali:
    alcune, come Dedalo, avean l'ali.

8.   Chi d'oro, e chi d'argento, e chi si fece
    di varie gemme una lettica adorna;
    portàvane alcuna otto, alcuna diece
    de lo stuol che sparir suol quando aggiorna,
    ch'erano tutti più neri che pece,
    con piedi strani, e lunghe code, e corna;
    pegasi, griffi et altri uccei bizarri
    molte traean sopra volanti carri.

9.   Queste, ch'or Fate, e da li antichi fòro
    già dette Ninfe e Dee con più bel nome,
    di precïose gemme e di molto oro
    ornate per le vesti e per le chiome,
    s'appresentar all'alto Concistoro,
    con bella compagnia, con ricche some,
    studiando ognuna ch'altra non l'avanzi
    di più ornamenti o d'esser giunta innanzi.

6. When the year and the day have arrived for them
    to gather together at their quinquennial council,
    those from the Hebrus and the Indus come
    running, and those from the Caspian and the Red
    Sea.[4] Without bridling a steed, without yoking
    together oxen, without sailing a ship, they come
    through the misty air, disdaining every human
    means and every work of nature.

7. Some are carried in great ships of glass, drawn by a
    hundred ferocious devils, while another hundred,
    with bellows, create a breeze in back. No stronger
    wind ever moved through the air. Others come
    on the necks of infernal angels—as once the
    Magus, in his contest with St. Peter, tried to do to
    his sorrow and was killed.[5] Some, like Daedalus,
    have their own wings.

8. Some make themselves exotic sedan chairs out of
    gold, others out of silver, still others out of various
    precious stones. One is carried by eight, another
    by ten, of the troop that is wont to disappear at
    dawn, all of whom are blacker than pitch, with
    strange feet, long tails, and horns. Winged horses,
    griffins, and other bizarre birds draw many others
    along in flying chariots.

9. These, which we now call Fairies, the ancients
    once called by the fairer names of nymphs and
    goddesses; adorned with precious gems and with
    plenty of gold in their hair and clothing, they
    present themselves at the high consistory with
    handsome retinues and rich baggage, each striving
    that another should not surpass her by having
    more jewelry or by arriving first.

10.   Sola Morgana, come l'altre volte,
      né ben ornata v'arrivò né in fretta;
      ma quando tutte l'altre eran raccolte,
      e già più d'una cosa aveano detta,
      mesta, con chiome rabuffate e sciolte,
      alfin comparve squalida e negletta,
      nel medesmo vestir ch'ella avea quando
      le diè la caccia, e poi la prese, Orlando.

11.   Con atti mesti il gran Collegio inchina,
      e si ripon nel luogo più di sotto;
      e, come fissa in pensier alto, china
      la fronte e gli occhi a terra, e non fa motto.
      Tacendo l'altre di stupor, fu Alcina
      prima a parlar, ma non così di botto;
      ch'una o due volte gli occhi intorno volse,
      e poi la lingua a tai parole sciolse:

12.   —Poi che da forza temeraria astretta,
      non può senza pergiur costei dolerse,
      né dimandar né procacciar vendetta
      de l'onta ria che già più dì sofferse;
      quel ch'ella non può far, far a noi spetta,
      ché le occorrenze prospere e l'avverse
      convien ch'abbiam communi; e si proveggia
      di vendicarla, ancor ch'ella nol chieggia.

13.   Non accade ch'io narri e come e quando
      (perché la cosa a tutto il mondo è piana)
      e quante volte e in quanti modi Orlando,
      con commune onta, offeso abbia Morgana;
      da la prima fïata incominciando
      che 'l drago e i tori uccise alla fontana,
      fin che le tolse poi Gigliante il biondo,
      ch'amava più di ciò ch'ella avea al mondo.

10. Morgana alone arrived there neither well adorned nor in haste, as she had on former occasions; but when all the others were assembled and had already discussed more than one issue, she at last appeared, mournful, dirty, and neglected, with her hair tousled and undone, in the same dress she had been wearing on the day when Orlando chased and later captured her.[6]

11. With a mournful gesture she bows to the great college and seats herself in the lowest place. As though fixed on some deep thought, she bends her forehead and eyes to the ground and says not a word. The others are silent in astonishment. Alcina was the first to speak, though not immediately. Once or twice she cast her eyes about the assembly, and then she loosed her tongue with these words:

12. "Because, bound to her oath by presumptuous human violence, this fay cannot, without foreswearing herself, either lament or ask or pursue revenge for the foul shame which she has already suffered these many days, it is up to us to do that which she cannot do, for it is fitting that we share in common both hardship and prosperity; so let us seek a means to avenge her, even though she herself does not ask it.

13. "I need not tell you how and why and how many times and in how many ways Orlando has offended Morgana, to our common shame, because the matter is well known to all: from the first time, when he slaughtered the dragon and the bulls at the fountain, right up to when he took away Gigliante the Blond, whom she loved more than anything she had in the world.[7]

14. Dico di quel che non sapete forse;
     e s'alcuna lo sa, tutte nol sanno:
     più che l'altre soll'io, perché m'occorse
     gire al suo lago quel medesimo anno:
     alcune sue (ma ben non se n'accorse
     Morgana) raccontato il tutto m'hanno.
     A me ch'a punto il so, sta ben ch'io 'l dica,
     tanto più che le son sorella e amica.

15. A me convien meglio chiarirvi quella
     parte, che dianzi io vi dicea confusa.
     Poi che Orlando ebbe preso mia sorella,
     rubbata, afflitta e in ogni via delusa,
     di tormentarla non cessò, fin ch'ella
     non gli fe' il giuramento il qual non s'usa
     tra noi mai vïolar; né ci soccorre
     il dir che forza altrui cel faccia tòrre.

16. Non è particolare e non è sola
     di lei l'ingiuria, anzi appartien a tutte;
     e quando fosse ancora di lei sola,
     debbiamo unirsi a vendicarla tutte,
     e non lasciarla ingiurïata sola;
     ché siam compagne e siam sorelle tutte;
     e quando anco ella il nieghi con la bocca,
     quel che 'l cor vuol considerar ci tocca.

17. Se toleriam l'ingiuria, oltra che segno
     mostriam di debolezza o di viltade,
     et oltra che si tronca al nostro regno
     il nervo principal, la maiestade,
     facciam ch'osin di nuovo, e che disegno
     di farci peggio in altri animo cade:
     ma chi fa sua vendetta, oltra che offende
     chi offeso l'ha, da molti si difende.—

14. "I speak now of an incident of which perhaps you
have not heard; or if some have heard about it, not
everyone has. I know more about it than anyone
else, for I happened to travel to her lake that same
year, and some of her women told me the whole
story (without Morgana's knowledge). I, who
know the story so well, should be the one to tell
it; and so much the more because I am her sister
and her friend.

15. "I should clear up that part of the story which I
told you before mixed up with everything else.
After Orlando had captured my sister and robbed
and persecuted and humiliated her in every way,
he did not stop tormenting her until she swore to
him the oath which none among us may ever
violate; nor may we plead that duress frees us from
its obligations.[8]

16. "The wrong that has been done is not particular
to her and is not hers alone, but belongs to us all;
and even if it were only hers, we all should still
unite to avenge her and not leave her wronged
alone; for we are all comrades and sisters, and even
if she denies it with her mouth, we ought to
consider what she wishes in her heart.

17. "If we tolerate this injury, aside from the sign we
show of weakness and cowardice, aside from
undercutting that majesty which is our Kingdom's
principal strength, we encourage men to try again,
and plans to do us worse harm may fall into other
minds. Whoever achieves vengeance, beyond
offending the one who has offended her, defends
herself from many others as well."

18.   E seguitò parlando, e disponendo
le Fate a vendicar il commun scorno:
che s'io volessi il tutto ir raccogliendo,
non avrei da far altro tutto un giorno.
Che non facesse questo, non contendo,
per Morgana e per l'altre ch'avea intorno;
ma ben dirò che più il proprio interesse,
che di Morgana o d'altre, la movesse.

19.   Levarsi Alcina non potea dal core
che le fosse Ruggier così fuggito:
né so se da più sdegno o da più amore
le fosse il cor la notte e 'l dì assalito;
e tanto era più grave il suo dolore,
quanto men lo potea dir espedito,
perché del danno che patito avea
era la fata Logistilla rea.

20.   Né potuto ella avria, senza accusarla,
del ricevuto oltraggio far doglianza;
ma perch'ivi di liti non si parla
che sia tra lor, né se n'ha ricordanza,
parlò de l'onta di Morgana, e farla
vendicar procacciò con ogn'instanza;
che senza dir di sé, ben vede ch'ella
fa per sé ancor, se fa per la sorella.

21.   Ella dicea che, come universale
biasmo di lor son di Morgana l'onte,
far se ne debbe ancor vendetta tale
che sol non abbia da patirne il Conte,
ma che n'abbassi ognun che sotto l'ale
de l'aquila alzi la fronte:
propone ella così, così disegna,
perché Ruggier di nuovo in sua man vegna.

18. And Alcina continued speaking, and she
persuaded the Fairies to avenge their common
shame; if I wanted to go on recounting all she
said, I wouldn't be able to do anything else for a
whole day. I don't deny that she did this for
Morgana and for the others there about her, but I
certainly will say that she was moved by her own
self-interest more than by the interests of Morgana
or the others.

19. Alcina could not erase from her heart the fact that
Ruggiero had fled from her the way he did.[9] I
don't know whether her heart tormented her day
and night more with love or with hate. But her
pain was all the heavier because she could not
discuss it openly—because the Fay Logistilla was
responsible for the ills she had suffered.

20. She could not complain about the outrage she had
received without accusing Logistilla; but, because
the Fairies neither discuss nor call to mind in that
place any quarrels they might have among
themselves, Alcina spoke instead of Morgana's
shame and sought with every effort to obtain
revenge for her; and without speaking of herself,
she knows well enough that if she takes her sister's
part, she takes her own as well.

21. She argued that because Morgana's humiliations
were a source of universal reproach, their revenge
should not make Orlando suffer alone but should
crush down everyone else standing beneath the
eagle's imperial wing;[10] she makes her proposals
and schemes in this way so that Ruggiero may
once again fall into her hands.

22. Sapeva ben che fatto era cristiano,
     fatto baron e paladin di Carlo;
     ché se fosse, qual dianzi era, pagano,
     miglior speranza avria di ricovrarlo;
     ma poi che armato era di fede, in vano
     senza l'aiuto altrui potria tentarlo;
     ché se sola da sé vuol farli offesa,
     gli vede appresso troppo gran difesa.

23. Per questo avea fier odio, acerbo isdegno,
     inimicizia dura e rabbia ardente
     contra re Carlo e ogni baron del regno,
     contra i populi tutti di Ponente;
     parendo lei che troppo al suo disegno
     lor bontà fosse avversa e renitente;
     né sperar può che mai Ruggier s'opprima,
     se non distrugge Carlo o insieme o prima.

24. Odia l'imperator, odia il nipote,
     ch'era l'altra colonna a tener ritto,
     sì che tra lor Ruggier cader non puote,
     né da forza d'incanto essere afflitto.
     Parlato ch'ebbe Alcina, né ancor vòte
     restar d'udir l'orecchie altro delitto:
     ché Fallerina pianse il drago morto
     e la distruzïon del suo bell'orto.

25. Poi ch'ebbe acconciamente Fallerina
     detto il suo danno e chiestone vendetta,
     entrò l'aringo e tenel Dragontina,
     fin che tutt'ebbe la sua causa detta;
     e quivi raccontò l'alta rapina
     ch'Astolfo et alcun altro di sua setta
     fatto le avea dentro alle proprie case
     de' suoi prigion, sì ch'un non vi rimase.

22. She knew well that he had been made a Christian and a baron and paladin of Charles.[11] If he were still a pagan, as he had been before, she would have had better hopes of recovering him; now, however, he was armed with faith, and in vain could she tempt him without the help of others. She sees that he is too well defended for her to hope to do him harm all by herself.

23. Because of this she felt savage hatred, bitter disdain, stubborn loathing, and burning rage against King Charles and every baron of the realm and against all the peoples of the West; their goodness seemed to her far too contrary and unyielding to her plans, and she had no hope of ever overcoming Ruggiero without destroying Charles, either with him or beforehand.

24. She detests the Emperor, and she detests his nephew, who was another upright pillar of strength.[12] Between the two of them, Ruggiero could not be brought low or even troubled by the power of enchantment. When Alcina had spoken, the Fairies' ears were not empty for long, for they heard of other crimes. Fallerina lamented her slain dragon and Orlando's destruction of her lovely bower.[13]

25. And after Fallerina had fittingly decried her loss and asked revenge for it, Dragontina entered and held the platform until she had stated her whole case; and she recounted how, in her own house, Astolfo and certain others of his band had robbed her of her prisoners, leaving her nary a one.[14]

26.　　Poi l'Aquilina e poi la Silvanella,
　　　　poi la Montana e poi quella dal Corso;
　　　　la fata Bianca, e la Bruna sorella,
　　　　et una a cui tese le reti Borso;
　　　　poi Griffonetta, e poi questa e poi quella
　　　　(ché far di tutte io non potrei discorso)
　　　　dolendosi venian, chi d'Oliviero,
　　　　chi del figlio d'Amon e chi d'Uggiero;

27.　　chi di Dudone e chi di Brandimarte,
　　　　quand'era vivo, e chi di Carlo istesso.
　　　　Tutti chi in una e chi in un'altra parte
　　　　avean lor fatto danno e oltraggio espresso,
　　　　rotti gli incanti e disprezzata l'arte
　　　　a cui natura e il ciel talora ha cesso:
　　　　a pena d'ogni cento trovavi una
　　　　che non avesse avuto ingiuria alcuna.

28.　　Quelle che da dolersi per se stesse
　　　　non hanno, sì de l'altre il mal lor pesa,
　　　　che non men che sia suo proprio interesse
　　　　si duol ciascuna e se ne chiama offesa:
　　　　non eran per patir che si dicesse
　　　　che l'arte lor non possa far difesa
　　　　contra le forze e gli animi arroganti
　　　　de' paladini e cavallieri erranti.

29.　　Tutte per questo (eccettüando solo
　　　　Morgana, ch'avea fatto il giuramento
　　　　che mai né a viso aperto né con dolo
　　　　procacceria ad Orlando nocumento),
　　　　quante ne son fra l'uno e l'altro polo,
　　　　fra quanto il sol riscalda e affredda il vento,
　　　　tutte approvar quel ch'avea Alcina detto,
　　　　e tutte instar che se gli desse effetto.

26.   Then Aquilina, then Silvanella, then Montana,
        and then the Fairy of the Footrace; the White
        Fairy and the Brown, her sister, and the one for
        whom Borso stretched his snares;[15] then
        Grifonetta, then this one and that one (so many
        that I can't talk about all of them) came
        complaining, some of Oliviero, some of Amone's
        son, and some of Uggiero;

27.   some of Dudone and some of Brandimarte, back
        when he was alive,[16] and some of Charles
        himself—of all who had injured or openly
        insulted them in one place or another, breaking
        their enchantments and scorning their magic arts
        to which nature and the Heavens had at times
        yielded. For every hundred Fairies there was
        scarcely one found who had not had some injury
        done to her.

28.   Those that do not have their own grievances feel
        the weight of the others' wrongs so greatly that
        each laments and declares herself offended no less
        than if her own interest had been at stake; they
        were not about to allow anyone to say their
        cunning could not defend them against the
        strength and arrogant spirits of paladins and errant
        knights.

29.   And so, all of them (excepting only Morgana,
        who had sworn the oath that never, whether
        openly or through subterfuge, would she seek to
        harm Orlando), all those that dwell between one
        pole and the other, all those whom the sun warms
        and the wind cools, unanimously approved what
        Alcina proposed and all insisted it be put into
        effect.

30. Poi che Demogorgon, principe saggio,
     del gran Consiglio udì tutto il lamento,
     disse: —Se dunque è general l'oltraggio,
     alla vendetta general consento;
     che sia Orlando, sia Carlo, sia il lignaggio
     di Francia, sia tutto l'Imperio spento;
     e non rimanga segno né vestigi,
     né pur si sappia dir: "Qui fu Parigi."—

31. Come nei casi perigliosi spesso
     Roma e l'altre republiche fatt'hanno,
     c'hanno il poter di molti a un solo cesso,
     che faccia sì che non patiscan danno;
     così quivi ad Alcina fu commesso
     che pensasse qual forza o qual inganno
     si avesse a usar; ch'ognuna d'esse presta
     avria in aiuto ad ogni sua richiesta.

32. Come chi tardi i suo' denar dispensa,
     né d'ogni compra tosto si compiace;
     cerca tre volte e più tutta la Sensa,
     e va mirando in ogni lato, e tace;
     si ferma alfin dove ritrova immensa
     copia di quel ch'al suo bisogno face,
     e quivi or questa or quella cosa volve,
     cento ne piglia, e ancor non si risolve:

33. questa mette da parte e quella lassa,
     e quella che lasciò di nuovo piglia;
     poi la rifiuta et ad un'altra passa;
     muta e rimuta, e ad una alfin s'appiglia:
     così d'alti pensieri una gran massa
     rivolge Alcina, e lenta si consiglia;
     per cento strade col pensier discorre,
     né sa veder ancor dove si porre.

30. After Demogorgon, that sage prince, had heard all the complaints of the Great Council, he said: "If, then, the offense is general, I consent to a general revenge; let Orlando, let Charles, let the lineage of France, let the entire Empire be wiped out; and let no sign or vestige remain, let no one even know enough to say: 'Here once stood Paris.' "

31. As Rome and other republics would often do in cases of public danger, yielding power to a single dictator who would work to keep them all from harm, so now Alcina was commissioned to consider what force or stratagem was to be used; for she would have each of the others ready to help at her every request.

32. Like one who at the Sensa[17] takes his time in spending his money, and at first is not satisfied with any piece of merchandise but searches three times or more over the entire fair and goes looking on all sides, and is silent; and stops finally where he finds huge supplies of what fills his need and there handles now one object, now another, and takes up a hundred but still does not decide;

33. and puts this aside and leaves that, and takes up again what he put down before; then rejects it and moves on to something new, changes his mind and changes it again, and at last takes hold of something; so Alcina sifts through a great mass of deep schemes and slowly considers; down a hundred paths she runs in her mind, and still cannot see where to come to a halt.

34.   Dopo molto girar, si ferma alfine,
       e le par che l'Invidia esser dea quella
       che l'alto Impero occidental ruine;
       faccia ch'a punto sia come s'appella;
       ma di chi dar più tosto l'intestine
       a roder debba a questa peste fella,
       non sa veder, né che piaccia più al gusto
       creda di lei, che 'l cor di Gano ingiusto.

35.   Stato era grande appresso a Carlo Gano
       un tempo sì, che alcun non gli iva al paro;
       poi con Astolfo quel di Mont'Albano,
       Orlando e gli altri che virtù mostraro
       contra Marsiglio e contra il re africano,
       fér sì che tanta altezza gli levaro;
       onde il meschin, che di fumo e di vento
       tutto era gonfio, vivea mal contento.

36.   Gano superbo, livido e maligno
       tutti i grandi appo Carlo odiava a morte;
       non potea alcun veder, che senza ordigno,
       senza opra sua si fosse acconcio in corte:
       sì ben con umil voce e falso ghigno
       sapea finger bontade, et ogni sorte
       usar d'ippocrisia, che chi i costumi
       suoi non sapea, gli porria a' piedi i lumi.

37.   Poi, quando si trovava appresso a Carlo
       (ché tempo fu ch'era ogni giorno seco),
       rodea nascosamente come tarlo,
       dava mazzate a questo e a quel da cieco:
       sì raro dicea il vero, e sì offuscarlo
       sapea, che da lui vinto era ogni Greco.
       Giudicò Alcina, com'io dissi, degno
       cibo all'Invidia il cor di vizi pregno.

34. After many turns she stops at last and decides that
     Envy should be the one to bring to ruin the lofty
     Empire of the Occident and make it live up to its
     name;[18] and she cannot imagine anyone whose
     innards she ought sooner feed to this fell pest, nor
     does she believe anything would please Envy's
     taste more than the heart of unjust Ganelon.

35. At one time Ganelon was a lord so much in
     Charles's favor that he had no peer; but later
     Astolfo, Rinaldo of Montauban, Orlando, and the
     rest who showed their valor against Marsilio and
     against the African King worked to deprive him of
     his high standing.[19] Whence the wretched
     Ganelon, who was all swollen up with smoke and
     wind, lived discontent.

36. Proud, angry, and malicious, Ganelon hated to the
     death all the great lords surrounding Charles; he
     could not bear to see anyone installed at court
     except through his own patronage and
     contrivance. He knew so well how to feign
     goodness, with a humble voice and a counterfeit
     smile, and to use every sort of hypocrisy, that
     anyone who did not know his ways would have lit
     candles at his feet.

37. Then, when he found himself alone with Charles
     (for there was a time when he was with him every
     day), he would secretly backbite like a worm, and
     rain blows from hiding on this and that person. So
     rarely would he speak the truth, and so well did
     he know how to disguise it, that he outdid any
     Greek. Alcina, as I said, judged this heart
     overflowing with vice to be a worthy dish for
     Envy.[20]

38. Fra i monti inaccessibili d'Imavo,
     che 'l ciel sembran tener sopra le spalle,
     fra le perpetue nevi e 'l ghiaccio ignavo
     discende una profonda e oscura valle;
     donde da un antro orribilmente cavo
     all'Inferno si va per dritto calle:
     e questa è l'una de le sette porte
     che conducono al regno de la Morte.

39. Le vie, l'entrate principal son sette,
     per cui l'anime van dritto all'Inferno;
     altre ne son, ma tòrte, lunghe e strette,
     come quella di Tenaro e d'Averno:
     questa de le più usate una si mette,
     di che la infame Invidia have il governo:
     a questo fondo orribile si cala
     sùbito Alcina, e non vi adopra scala.

40. S'accosta alla spelunca spaventosa,
     e percuote a gran colpo con un'asta
     quella ferrata porta, mezzo rósa
     da' tarli e da la rugine più guasta.
     L'Invidia, che di carne venenosa
     allora si pascea d'una cerasta,
     levò la bocca alla percossa grande
     da le amare e pestifere vivande.

41. E di cento ministri ch'avea intorno,
     mandò senza tardar uno alla porta;
     che, conosciuta Alcina, fa ritorno
     e di lei nuova indietro le rapporta.
     Quella pigra si leva, e contra il giorno
     le vien incontra, e lascia l'aria morta;
     ché 'l nome de le Fate sin al fondo
     si fa temer del tenebroso mondo.

38. Amid the inaccessible Himalayan peaks, which
    seem to hold the sky upon their shoulders, amid
    the perpetual snows and slow-moving ice there
    opens a deep and dark ravine. Thence, through a
    dreadful empty cave, a straight path leads down to
    Hell. This is one of the seven gates which lead to
    the Kingdom of Death.

39. There are seven roads and principal entrances
    through which spirits go directly to Hell; others
    exist, but they are twisted, long, and narrow, like
    those of Tenarus and Avernus:²¹ this one over
    which Envy rules is among the most traveled; to
    its horrible depths Alcina quickly descends,
    without the use of stairs.

40. She approaches the terrifying cave, takes a staff,
    and beats with heavy strokes at the iron-fitted
    door, which is half eaten by worms and wasted
    away for the most part by rust. Envy, who at that
    moment was feeding on the poisonous flesh of a
    horned viper, at those great blows raised her
    mouth from her bitter and pestilential meal.

41. Without delay she sent to the door one of the
    hundred servants she has there about her, who,
    when it recognized Alcina, returned and brought
    back news of her. Lazily, Envy rises up and comes
    toward Alcina and into the light, leaving the dead
    air behind her; for the Fairies' name causes fear
    even in the depths of shadowy Hell.

42. Tosto che vide Alcina così ornata
     d'oro e di seta e di ricami gai
     (ché riccamente era vestir usata,
     né si lasciò non culta veder mai),
     con guardatura oscura e avenenata
     gli lividi occhi alzò, piena di guai;
     e féro il cor dolente manifesto
     i sospiri ch'uscian dal petto mesto.

43. Pallido più che bosso, e magro e afflitto,
     arido e secco ha il dispiacevol viso;
     l'occhio, che mirar mai non può diritto;
     la bocca, dove mai non entra riso,
     se non quando alcun sente esser proscritto,
     del stato espulso, tormentato e ucciso
     (altrimenti non par ch'unqua s'allegri);
     ha lunghi i denti, rugginosi e negri.

44. —O delli imperatori imperatrice,—
     cominciò Alcina—o de li re regina,
     o de' principi invitti domitrice,
     o de' Persi e Macedoni ruina,
     o del romano e greco orgoglio ultrice,
     o gloria a cui null'altra s'avicina,
     né serà mai per appressarsi s'anco
     il fasto levi all'alto Impero franco;

45. una vil gente che fuggì da Troia
     sin all'alte paludi de la Tana,
     dove ai vicini così venne a noia
     che la spinser da sé tosto lontana;
     e quindi ancora in ripa alla Danoia
     cacciata fu da l'aquila romana;
     et indi al Reno, ove in discorso d'anni
     entrò con arte in Francia e con inganni:

42. As soon as she sees Alcina arrayed in gold and silk
     and gay embroidery (for Alcina was accustomed to
     dressing richly and never allowed herself to be
     seen unadorned), Envy, full of woe, raised her
     livid eyes with a dark and venomous look, and the
     sighs that came from her mournful breast made
     clear that her heart was grieving.

43. Paler than boxwood, her unpleasing countenance
     is lean and troubled, withered and dry; her eye
     can never look straight, and laughter never enters
     her mouth except when she hears of someone
     being proscribed, exiled from his country,
     tortured and killed (otherwise it seems that
     nothing can gladden her); her teeth are long,
     rusty, and black.

44. Alcina began: "O Empress of Emperors, O Queen
     of Kings, O mistress of unvanquished Princes, O
     ruin of the Persians and Macedonians, O avenger
     of Greek and Roman pride, O glory which no
     other approaches, and none ever will approach
     you if you also bring down the lofty Empire of the
     Franks,

45. "a vile race that fled from Troy all the way to the
     deep marshes of the Don, where it became such
     an annoyance to its neighbors that they soon drove
     it far away; whence the Roman eagle banished it
     again to the banks of the Danube; and from there
     to the Rhine, where in the course of years,
     through cunning and deceit, it entered France.

46.   dove aiutando or questo or quel vicino
incontra agli altri, e poi, con altro aiuto,
questi ch'ora gli avea dato il domino
scacciando, a parte a parte ha il tutto avuto,
finché il nome regal levò Pipino
al suo signor, poco all'incontro astuto.
Or Carlo suo figliuol l'Imperio regge,
e dà all'Europa e a tutto il mondo legge.

47.   Puoi tu patir che la già tante volte
di terra in terra discacciata gente,
a cui le sedie or questi or quelli han tolte,
né lasciato in riposo lungamente;
puoi tu patir ch'or signoreggi molte
provincie, e freni omai tutto 'l Ponente,
e che da l'Indo all'onde maure estreme
la terra e il mar al suo gran nome treme?

48.   Alle mortal grandezze un certo fine
ha Dio prescritto, a cui si può salire;
che, passandol, serian come divine,
il che natura o il ciel non può patire;
ma vuol che giunto a quel, poi si decline.
A quello è giunto Carlo, se tu mire.
Or questa ogni tua gloria antiqua passa,
se tanta altezza per tua man s'abbassa.—

49.   E seguitò mostrando altra cagione
ch'avea di farlo, e mostrò insieme il modo;
però ch'avria un gran mezo, Ganelone,
d'ogni inganno capace e d'ogni frodo:
poi le soggiunse che d'obligazione,
facendol, le porrebbe al cor un nodo
in suoi servigi sì tenace e forte,
che non lo potria sciòrre altro che morte.

46. "There, first helping this, then that, neighbor
against the others, and then, with the help of a
third, driving out those who had empowered it,
piece by piece this Frankish race acquired the
whole realm, until Pepin took the title of King
from his liege lord, who was not very shrewd in
opposing him.[22] Now Pepin's son Charles rules the
Empire and lays down the law to Europe and the
whole world.

47. "Can you stand it that this race already driven so
many times from one realm to the next, whose
lands one people after another have taken away
and never left in peace very long? Can you stand it
that this race should now govern so many pro-
vinces and may henceforth bridle all the West and
that from the Indus to the farthest Moorish wave
the earth and sea should tremble at its great name?

48. "God has ordained a certain limit for mortal
achievement, up to which it is allowed to rise, but
passing beyond which it would be almost divine,
something which nature or heaven cannot endure;
but He wishes instead that, having reached that limit,
it may then decline. Charles has reached that point, if
you observe him well. Now, if you bring down his
greatness, you will surpass all your former glory."

49. And Alcina went on, giving other reasons for
Envy to accept this challenge, and she showed her
the means as well; for Envy would have a powerful
tool in Ganelon, a man capable of any treachery
and any deception; then she added that by doing
the deed, Envy would place a bond of obligation
in Alcina's heart, a bond for future service so
lasting and strong that nothing but death would
be able to loose it.

50. Al detto de la fata, brevemente
     diè l'Invidia risposta, che farebbe.
     Gli suoi ministri ha separatamente,
     che ciascun sa per sé quel che far debbe:
     tutti hanno impresa di tentar la gente;
     ognun guadagnar anime vorrebbe:
     stimula altri i signori, altri i plebei;
     chi fa gli vecchi e chi i fanciulli rei.

51. E chi gli cortigiani e chi gli amanti,
     e chi gli monachetti e i loro abbati:
     quei che le donne tentano son tanti,
     che seriano a fatica noverati.
     Ella venir se li fe' tutti innanti,
     e poi che ad un ad un gli ebbe mirati,
     stimò sé sola a sì importante effetto
     sufficïente, e ciascun altro inetto.

52. E de' suoi brutti serpi venenosi
     fatto una scelta, in Francia corre in fretta,
     e giunger mira in tempo ch'ai focosi
     destrieri il fren la bionda Aurora metta,
     allor ch'i sogni men son fabulosi,
     e nascer veritade se n'aspetta:
     con nuovo abito quivi e nuove larve
     al conte di Maganza in sogno apparve.

53. Le fantastiche forme seco tolto
     l'Invidia avendo, apparve in sogno a Gano;
     e gli fece veder tutto raccolto
     in larga piazza il gran popul cristiano,
     che gli occhi lieti avea fissi nel volto
     d'Orlando e del signor di Mont'Albano,
     ch'in veste trionfal, cinti d'alloro,
     sopra un carro venian di gemme e d'oro.

50. To the Fairy's speech, Envy briefly replied that she would do it. She has individual ministers, each of whom knows by himself what he has to do. They all have the job of tempting people, and each one tries to win souls; some goad lords, others common folk; one corrupts the old, another children.

51. There is one for courtiers and another for lovers, another for the little monks and their abbots. There are so many to tempt the ladies that they would be tiresome to count. Envy had them all come before her and, after she had inspected them one by one, decided she alone was sufficiently qualified for such an important mission, and everyone else unsuited.

52. Taking a selection from among her foul, poisonous snakes, she hurried on her way to France and looks to arrive by the time that blond Aurora puts the bridle to her fiery steeds, at the hour when dreams are less fabulous and truth is expected to appear in them;[23] taking a new disguise there and accompanied by strange phantasms, she appeared in a dream to the Count of Mainz.

53. Having brought with her some of the fantastic shapes of sleep, Envy appeared to the dreaming Ganelon and made him see the great Christian populace gathered all together in a large square. Their joyful eyes were fixed on the face of Orlando and on the lord of Montauban, who arrived in triumphal attire, crowned with laurel, on a chariot of gems and gold.

54. Tutta la nobiltà di Chiaramonte
    sopra bianchi destrier lor venìa intorno:
    ognun di lauro coronar la fronte,
    ognun vedea di spoglie ostili adorno;
    e la turba con voci a lodar pronte
    gli parea udir, che benediva il giorno
    che, per far Carlo a null'altro secondo,
    la valorosa stirpe venne al mondo.

55. Poi di veder il populo gli è aviso,
    che si rivolga a lui con grand'oltraggio,
    e dir si senta molta ingiuria in viso,
    e codardo nomar, senza coraggio;
    e con batter di man, sibilo e riso,
    s'oda beffar con tutto il suo lignaggio;
    né quei di Chiaramonte aver più loda,
    che gli suoi biasmo, par che vegga et oda.

56. In questa visïon l'Invidia il core
    con man gli tocca più fredda che neve;
    e tanto spira in lui del suo furore,
    che 'l petto più capir non può, né deve.
    Al cor pon delle serpi la piggiore,
    un'altra onde l'udita si riceve,
    la terza agli occhi; onde di ciò che pensa,
    di ciò che vede et ode ha doglia immensa.

57. De l'aureo albergo essendo il Sol già uscito,
    lasciò la visïone e il sonno Gano,
    tutto pien di dolor dove sentito
    toccar s'avea con la gelata mano.
    Ciò che vide dormendo gli è scolpito
    già ne la mente, e non l'estima vano;
    non false illusïon, ma cose vere
    gli par che gli abbia Dio fatto vedere.

54. All the nobility of Clairmont were riding beside them on white steeds, and Ganelon saw each one crown his head with laurels, each one decorated with enemy spoils; and he seemed to hear the crowd praise them with eager voices, blessing the day that that brave lineage had come into the world to make Charles second to none.

55. Then he seems to see the people turn toward him and do him great outrage; he hears them insult him to his face and call him a coward, lacking courage; and with blows from their hands, whistling, and laughter he hears himself and all his lineage mocked; and he seems to see and hear that the clan of Clairmont is praised just as much as his own clan is blamed.

56. During this vision Envy touches his heart with hands colder than snow and breathes so much of her fury into him that his breast cannot and ought not hold any more. She puts the worst of her serpents in his heart, another where his hearing lodges, the third in his eyes; as a result, he suffers terrible agony in what he thinks and in what he sees and hears.[24]

57. The Sun had already left its golden inn when Ganelon departed sleep and this vision, full of pain where he had felt himself touched by Envy's icy hand. What he saw while he was sleeping is now engraved in his mind, and he does not consider it an empty dream; it seems to him that God has made him see not false imaginings but true events.

58. Da quell'ora il meschin mai più riposo
     non ritrovò, non ritrovò più pace:
     da l'occulto venen il cor gli è roso,
     che notte e giorno sospirar lo face:
     gli par che liberale e grazïoso
     sia a tutti gli altri, et a nessun tenace,
     se non a' Maganzesi, il re di Francia;
     fuor che la lor premiata abbia ogni lancia.

59. Già fuor di tende, fuor de padiglioni
     in Parigi tornata era la corte,
     avendo Carlo i principi e baroni
     e tutti i forestier di miglior sorte
     fatto, con gran proferte e ricchi doni,
     contenti accompagnar fuor de le porte;
     e tra' più arditi cavallier del mondo
     stava a goder il suo stato giocondo.

60. E come saggio padre di famiglia
     la sera dopo le fatiche a mensa
     tra gli operari con ridenti ciglia
     le giuste parti a questo e a quel dispensa;
     così, poi che di Libia e di Castiglia
     spentasi intorno avea la face accensa,
     rendea a signori e cavallieri merto
     di quanto in armi avean per lui sofferto.

61. A chi collane d'oro, a chi vasella
     dava d'argento, a chi gemme di pregio;
     cittadi aveano alcuni, altri castella:
     ordine alcun non fu, non fu collegio,
     borgo, villa né tempio né capella,
     che non sentisse il beneficio regio:
     e per dieci anni fe' tutte le genti
     ch'avean patito dai tributi esenti.

58. From that moment on the wretch never again
found any rest, never again found peace; his heart
is eaten away by the hidden poison which makes
him sigh night and day; it seems to him that the
King is liberal and gracious to everyone else and,
aside from the reward given to every lancer, stingy
with no one but the House of Mainz.

59. The court had just returned from its tents and
pavilions to Paris, after Charles had seen to it that
the princes and barons and all the foreign guests of
nobler condition were contented with generous
presents and rich gifts and accompanied outside
the city's gates.[25] Now, in the company of the
boldest knights in the world, he was enjoying his
merry state.

60. And as the wise father of a family, at the evening
supper after the chores, with laughing eyes pays
out among his workers the shares proper to this
one and that, so, now that he had extinguished
everywhere the torch lit by Libya and Castile, he
gave the lords and knights rewards commensurate
with what they had undergone for him in arms.

61. To some he gave necklaces of gold, to others a
vase of silver, to others precious gems; some
received a town, others a castle; there was no
religious order, there was no college, no hamlet,
village, temple, or chapel that did not feel the
royal favor; and he made all the regions that had
suffered during the war exempt from taxes for ten
years.

62. A Rinaldo il governo di Guascogna
diede, e pension di molti mila franchi;
tre castella a Olivier donò in Borgogna,
che del suo antiquo stato erano a' fianchi;
donò ad Astolfo in Picardia Bologna;
non vi dirò ch'al suo nipote manchi:
diede al nipote principe d'Anglante
Fiandra in governo, e donò Bruggia e Guante;

63. e promesse lo scettro e la corona,
poi che n'avesse il re Marsiglio spinto,
del regno di Navara e di Aragona,
la qual impresa allor era in procinto.
Ebbe la figlia d'Amon di Dordona
da quello del fratel dono distinto:
le diè Carlo in dominio quel che darle
in governo solea: Marsiglia et Arle.

64. In somma, ogni guerrier d'alta virtute,
chi città, chi castella ebbe, e chi ville.
A Marfisa e a Ruggier fur provedute
larghe provisïoni a mille a mille.
Se da lo imperator le grazie avute
tutte ho a notar, farò troppe postille:
nessun, vi dico, o in commune o in privato,
partì da lui che non fosse premiato.

65. Né feudi nominando né livelli,
fur senza obligo alcun liberi i doni;
acciò il non sciorre i canoni di quelli
o non ne tòrre a' tempi investigioni,
potesse gli lor figli o gli fratelli,
gli eredi far cader di sue ragioni:
liberi furo e veri doni, e degni
d'un re che degno era d'imperio e regni.

62. To Rinaldo he gave the government of Gascony,
with a pension of many thousands of francs; he
gave to Oliviero three castles, which were on the
borders of his ancient seat in Burgundy; he gave
Boulogne in Picardy to Astolfo; I will not tell you
that his nephew Orlando went without; he gave
his nephew, the Prince d'Anglant, Flanders to
govern and Bruges and Ghent;

63. and promised him the crown and scepter of the
Kingdoms of Navarre and Aragon after he had
driven King Marsilio out of them, an enterprise
which he was just about to begin. The daughter of
Amone of Dordogne[26] had a gift separate from
her brother's; Charles gave her dominion over
what he was accustomed to give her to govern:
Marseilles and Arles.

64. In sum, every knight of great valor received either
a city, a castle, or a country estate. For Marfisa and
Ruggiero ample provision was made, in the
thousands. If I had to keep accounts of all the
favors obtained from the Emperor, I would have
too many entries to make; no one, I assure you,
either in public or in private, left his presence
without reward.

65. The gifts were all free, without obligation or any
talk of fiefs or leases; accordingly, the failure to
pay annual rents or perform rituals of investiture at
the appointed time could not make the sons or
brothers of the new owners fall from their rights as
heirs. The gifts were free and true, and worthy of
a king who was worthy of an empire and
kingdoms.[27]

66. Or, sopra gli altri, quei di Chiaramonte
    nei real doni avean tanto vantaggio,
    che sospirar facean dì e notte il conte
    Gan di Maganza, e tutto il suo lignaggio:
    come gli onori d'un fossero l'onte
    de l'altra parte, lor pungea il coraggio;
    e questa invidia all'odio, e l'odio all'ira,
    e l'ira alfine al tradimento il tira.

67. E perché, d'astio e di veneno pregno,
    potea nasconder mal il suo dispetto,
    e non potea non dimostrar lo sdegno
    che contra il re per questo avea concetto;
    e non men per fornir alcun disegno
    ch'in parte ordito, in parte avea nel petto,
    finse aver voto, e ne sparse la voce,
    d'ire al Sepolcro e al monte della Croce:

68. et era il suo pensiero ire in Levante
    a ritrovar il calife d'Egitto,
    col re de la Soria poco distante;
    e più sicuro a bocca che per scritto
    trattar con essi, che le terre sante
    dove Dio visse in carne e fu traffitto,
    o per fraude o per forza da le mani
    fosser tolte e dal scettro de' Cristiani.

69. Indi andar in Arabia avea disposto,
    e far scender quei populi all'acquisto
    d'Africa, mentre Carlo era discosto,
    e di gente il paese mal provisto.
    Già inanzi la partita avea composto
    che Desiderio al vicario di Cristo,
    Tassillo a Francia, e a Scozia e ad Inghelterra
    avesse il re di Dazia a romper guerra;

66. Now, above and beyond the others, those of Clairmont received so many more of the royal gifts that they made Count Ganelon of Mainz and all of his kindred sigh night and day; as if the honors given to one clan were the shame of the other, it stung their spirit, and this envy drew Ganelon to hatred, from hatred to rage and from rage, at last, to treason.

67. And because he was full of loathing and venom, he could barely conceal his resentment and could not disguise the disdain he had conceived for the King on this account. In part to hide his true feelings, and no less in order to accomplish a plot that he had partly arranged, partly kept in his heart, he pretended and spread word that he had made a vow to go to the Holy Sepulcher, to the mountain of the Cross;

68. and his real intention was to go to the Levant to find the Caliph of Egypt and the neighboring King of Syria and to discuss with them, more safely in person than by letter, how the Holy Land, where God lived in the flesh and was pierced by nails, might be taken from Christian rule either by fraud or force of arms.

69. From there he had arranged to go to Arabia to incite its peoples to descend upon and conquer Africa while Charles was away and the country poorly garrisoned with men. He had already conceived a strategy whereby Desiderius, King of Lombardy, was to declare war on the Vicar of Christ; Tassillone, King of the Bohemians, on France; and the King of Denmark on Scotland and England;

70.   e che Marsilio armasse in Catalogna,
       e scendesse in Provenza e in Acquamorta,
       e con un altro esercito in Guascogna
       corresse a Mont'Alban fin su la porta;
       egli Maganza, Basilea, Cologna,
       Costanza et Aquisgrana, che più importa,
       promettea far ribelle a Carlo, e in meno
       d'un mese tòrli ogni città del Reno.

71.   Or fattasi fornir una galea
       di vettovaglia, d'armi e di compagni,
       poi che licenza dal re tolto avea
       uscì del porto e dei sicuri stagni.
       Restar a dietro, anzi fuggir parea
       il lito, et occultar tutti i vivagni:
       indi l'Alpe a sinistra apparea lunge,
       ch'Italia in van da' Barbari disgiunge;

72.   indi i monti Ligustici, e riviera
       che con aranzi e sempre verdi mirti
       quasi avendo perpetua primavera,
       sparge per l'aria i bene olenti spirti.
       Volendo il legno in porto ir una sera
       (in qual a punto io non saprei ben dirti),
       ebbe un vento da terra in modo all'orza
       ch'in mezo il mar lo fe' tornar per forza.

73.   Il vento tra maestro e tramontana,
       con timor grande e con maggior periglio,
       tra l'orïente e mezodì allontana
       sei dì senza allentarsi unqua il naviglio.
       Fermòssi al fine ad una spiaggia strana,
       tratto da forza più che da consiglio,
       dove un miglio discosto da l'arena
       d'antique palme era una selva amena:

70. Marsilio was to arm in Catalonia and descend on
    Provence and Aigues-Mortes, and with another
    army race into Gascony right up to the gates of
    Montauban. He himself promised to induce
    Mainz, Basel, Cologne, Konstanz, and Aachen,
    which was the most important,[28] to rebel against
    Charles and in less than one month take from the
    Emperor every city on the Rhine.

71. So, having ordered a galley to be furnished with
    provisions, weapons, and men, Ganelon now took
    leave of the King and set out from port and safe
    harbor. The shore seemed to be left behind them,
    indeed to fly away from them, and the whole
    coast to hide from their sight; then, on the left,
    the Alps appeared in the distance, which in vain
    separate Italy from the Barbarians.[29]

72. Then the Ligurian mountains appeared, and the
    Riviera which, with its orange trees and evergreen
    myrtle enjoying an almost perpetual spring,
    spreads sweet-smelling breezes through the air.
    One evening when the ship was making for port
    (just where, precisely, I could not really tell you),
    it met a head wind from the land that forced it to
    return to the high seas.

73. To their great terror and greater peril, the wind,
    between mistral and tramontane, drives the ship
    off course to the southeast for six days without
    ever abating. Drawn by force more than by
    design, the ship came to rest at last upon an
    unknown shore where, a mile distant from the
    beach, there rose a pleasant wood of ancient
    palms.

74.   che per mezo da un'acqua era partita
        di chiaro fiumicel, fresco e giocondo,
        che l'una e l'altra proda avea fiorita
        dei più soavi odor che siano al mondo.
        Era di là dal bosco una salita
        d'un picciol monticel quasi rotondo,
        sì facile a montar, che prima il piede
        d'aver salito, che salir si vede.

75.   D'odoriferi cedri era il bel colle
        con maestrevole ordine distinto;
        la cui bell'ombra al sol sì i raggi tolle,
        ch'al mezodì dal rezzo è il calor vinto.
        Ricco d'intagli, e di soave e molle
        getto di bronzo, e in parti assai dipinto,
        un lungo muro in cima lo circonda,
        d'un alto e signoril palazzo sponda.

76.   Gano, che di natura era bramoso
        di cose nuove, e dal bisogno astretto
        (che già tutto il biscotto aveano roso),
        de' suoi compagni avendo alcuno eletto,
        si mise a caminar pel bosco ombroso,
        tra via prendendo d'ascoltar diletto
        da' rugiadosi rami d'arbuscelli
        il piacevol cantar de' vaghi augelli.

77.   Tosto ch'egli dal mar si pose in via
        e fu scoperto dal luogo eminente,
        diversa e soavissima armonia
        da l'alta casa insino al lito sente:
        non molto va, che bella compagnia
        truova di donne, e dietro alcun sergente
        che palafreni vuoti avean con loro,
        altri di seta altri guarniti d'oro;

74. The wood was divided in the middle by the cool
and playful water of a clear rivulet, which had
strewn either bank with flowers and the sweetest
scents found on earth. Beyond the wood was the
rise of a little hill, almost round, so easy to scale
that you seem to reach the top before you realize
you are climbing.

75. The hill was adorned with an ingenious
arrangement of scented cedar trees. Their lovely
shade blocks so many of the sun's rays that at
noontime the heat is conquered by the breeze. A
long wall circles the top, rich with carvings and
cast of pleasant and soft bronze, with many
paintings here and there. This was the exterior of
a lofty and lordly palace.

76. By nature eager for new things, and driven as well
by need (for they had already eaten all their
hardtack), Ganelon chose a few of his companions
and began to walk through the shaded wood,
enjoying along the way the pleasant song of the
pretty birds on the bushes' dewy branches.

77. As soon as he started on his way from the sea and
could be seen from the high ground, he hears
strange and sweet harmony, reaching from the
lofty house all the way to the shore. He has not
gone far before he finds a lovely band of ladies and
behind them some squires who had riderless
palfreys with them, some caparisoned with silk,
others with gold.

78. che con cortesi e belli inviti fenno
     Gano salir, e chi venìa con lui.
     Con pochi passi fine alla via denno
     le donne e i cavallieri, a dui a dui.
     L'oro di Creso, l'artificio e 'l senno
     d'Alberto, di Bramanti, di Vitrui,
     non potrebbono far, con tutto l'agio
     di ducent'anni, un così bel palagio.

79. E dai demoni tutto in una notte
     lo fece far Gloricia incantatrice,
     ch'avea l'esempio nelle idee incorrotte
     d'un che Vulcano aver fatto si dice;
     del qual restaro poi le mura rotte
     quel dì che Lenno fu da la radice
     svelta, e gettata con Cipro e con Delo
     dai figli de la Terra incontra il cielo.

80. Tenea Gloricia splendida e gran corte,
     non men ricca d'Alcina o di Morgana;
     né men d'esse era dotta in ogni sorte
     d'incantamenti inusitata e strana;
     ma non, com'esse, pertinace e forte
     ne l'altrui ingiurie, anzi cortese e umana,
     né potea al mondo aver maggior diletto
     che onorar questo e quel nel suo bel tetto.

81. Sempre ella tenea gente alla veletta,
     a' porti et all'uscita de le strade,
     che con inviti i pellegrini alletta
     venir a lei da tutte le contrade.
     Con gran splendor il suo palazzo accetta
     poveri e ricchi e d'ogni qualitade;
     e il cor de' vïandanti con tai modi
     nel suo amor lega d'insolubil nodi.

78. With courteous and fair invitations, these made
Ganelon and his companions mount. Two by
two, the ladies and knights reached the end of the
path after just a brief ride. The gold of Croesus,
the art and wisdom of Alberti, Bramante, and
Vitruvius, could not have built such a beautiful
palace even in two hundred years.[30]

79. But the enchantress Gloricia had had it built by
demons in a single night; she found a model for it
among the incorruptible Ideas, in a palace which
Vulcan is said to have made, the walls of which
were ruined the day when Lemnos was torn from
its roots and thrown with Cyprus and Delos
against the heavens by the sons of Earth.[31]

80. Gloricia maintained a great and splendid court, no
less rich than those of Alcina and Morgana, and
she was no less learned than they were in every
variety of rare and unusual enchantment; but she
was not, as they were, strong and persistent in
doing others harm but was instead courteous and
humane and could feel no greater delight in the
world than in honoring this or that guest under
her fair roof.

81. She always kept people standing watch at the ports
and at crossroads to invite travelers from every
country to visit her. Her palace welcomes with
great magnificence the poor and rich and people
of every station, and by these means she binds the
wayfarers' hearts to her love with indissoluble ties.

82. E come avea di accarezar usanza
    e di dar a ciascun debito onore,
    fece accoglienza al conte di Maganza
    Gloricia, quanto far potea maggiore;
    e tanto più, che ben sapea ad instanza
    d'Alcina esser qui giunto il traditore:
    ben sapeva ella, ch'avea Alcina ordito
    che capitasse Gano a questo lito.

83. Ell'era stata in India al gran Consiglio
    dove l'alto esterminio fu concluso
    d'ogni guerriero ubidïente al figlio
    del re Pipino; e nessun era escluso,
    eccetto il Maganzese, il cui consiglio,
    il cui favor stimar atto a quell'uso:
    dunque, a lui le accoglienze e' modi grati
    che quivi gli altri avean, fur radoppiati.

84. Gloricia Gano, com'era commesso
    da chi fatto l'avea cacciar dai venti,
    acciò quindi ad Alcina sia rimesso
    tra' Sciti e l'Indi ai suoi regni opulenti,
    fa la notte pigliar nel sonno oppresso,
    e gli compagni insieme e gli sergenti.
    Così far quivi agli altri non si suole,
    ma dar questo vantaggio a Gano vuole.

85. E benché, più che onor, biasmo si tegna
    pigliar in casa sua ch'in lei si fida,
    et a Gloricia tanto men convegna,
    che fa del suo splendor sparger le grida;
    pur non le par che questo il suo onor spegna:
    ché tòrre al ladro e uccider l'omicida,
    tradir il traditor, ha degni esempi,
    ch'anco si pon lodar, secondo i tempi.

82.   And because it was her custom to lavish welcome
        on everyone and to give them due honor, Gloricia
        made the Count of Mainz welcome as much as
        she could: so much the more because she knew
        very well that the traitor had come at the
        prompting of Alcina. She knew very well that
        Alcina had plotted for Ganelon to arrive on her
        shore.

83.   She had been at the Great Council in India that
        had decided upon the mass extermination of
        every warrior obedient to King Pepin's son; no
        one had been excluded except Ganelon of Mainz,
        whose counsel and favor they deemed suitable for
        this purpose. Accordingly, the greetings and
        gracious manners which others found here were
        redoubled for him.

84.   At Alcina's bidding, Gloricia has Ganelon seized
        that night while he is overcome with sleep,
        together with all of his companions and squires, so
        she can send him east between Scythia and India
        to Alcina and her opulent realm. She does not
        ordinarily treat her guests this way, but she wants
        to grant this special favor to Ganelon.

85.   And although she feels more shame than honor in
        capturing someone who has entrusted himself to
        her in her own house, and although such an
        action is all the less fitting for Gloricia, who prides
        herself on the renowned splendor of her
        hospitality, still she does not feel that it will
        destroy her reputation, because there are worthy
        examples of thieves robbed, murderers killed, and
        traitors betrayed which can even be praised,
        depending on the circumstances.

86.   Quando dormìa la notte più suave,
        Gano e i compagni suoi tutti fur presi,
        e serrati in un ceppo duro e grave,
        l'un presso all'altro, trenta Maganzesi.
        Gloricia in terra disegnò una nave
        capace e grande con tutt'i suo' arnesi,
        e fece gli pregion legare in quella,
        sotto la guardia d'una sua donzella.

87.   Sparge le chiome, e qua e là si volve
        tre volte e più, fin che mirabilmente
        la nave ivi dipinta ne la polve
        da terra si levò tutta ugualmente.
        La vela al vento la donzella solve,
        per incanto allor nata parimente;
        e verso il ciel ne va, come per l'onda
        suol ir nocchier che l'aura abbia seconda.

88.   Gano e i compagni, che per l'aria tratti
        da terra si vedean tanto lontani,
        com'assassini istranamente attratti
        nel lungo ceppo per piedi e per mani,
        tremando di paura, e stupefatti
        di maraviglia de' lor casi strani,
        volavan per Levante in sì gran fretta
        che non gli avrebbe giunti una saetta.

89.   Lasciando Ptolomaide e Berenice
        e tutt'Africa dietro, e poi l'Egitto,
        e la deserta Arabia e la felice,
        sopra il mar Eritreo fecion traghitto.
        Tra Persi e Medi, e là dove si dice
        Batra, passan, tenendo il corso dritto
        tuttavia fra orïente e tramontana,
        e lascian Casia a dietro e Sericana.

86.   So, while he was sleeping the night away in
       sweetest slumber, Ganelon and all his companions
       were seized and bound in solid, heavy stocks,
       thirty men of Mainz one next to the other.
       Gloricia sketched upon the ground a large and
       spacious ship, with all its fittings, and had the
       prisoners bound inside it under the guard of one
       of her damsels.

87.   Gloricia lets down her hair and here and there
       whirls about three times and more, until the ship
       depicted there in the dust wondrously raises itself
       whole out of the earth. Her damsel looses to the
       wind the sails newly brought forth by the same
       enchantment and takes off toward the heavens as
       a helmsman will sail over the waves when he has a
       following wind.

88.   Ganelon and his companions, who saw themselves
       drawn through the air so far from the earth and,
       without explanation, bound hand and foot in the
       long stocks like so many murderers, trembled
       with fear and were stupefied with wonder at their
       extraordinary situation; they were flying through
       the Levant with such speed that an arrow could
       not have overtaken them.

89.   They left behind them Ptolemais and Bengasi and
       all of Africa and then Egypt and both the desert
       and the happy Arabias and made their way over
       the Red Sea. Through the lands of the Persians
       and the Medes and the place which we call
       Bactria they pass, holding a course straight and
       steady between East and West, and leave behind
       Tibet and Northern China.

90.   E sì come veduti eran da molti,
di sé davano a molti maraviglia:
facean tener levati al cielo i volti
con occhi immoti e con arcate ciglia.
Vedendoli passar alcuni stolti
da terra alti lo spazio di due miglia,
e non potendo ben scorgere i visi,
ebbon di lor diversi e strani avisi.

91.   Alcuni imaginar che di Carone,
lo nocchiero infernal, fosse la barca,
che d'anime dannate a perdizione
alla via di Cocito andasse carca.
Altri diceano, d'altra opinïone:
—Questa è la santa nave ch'al ciel varca,
che Pietro tol da Roma, acciò ne l'onde
di stupri e simonie non si profonde.—

92.   Et altra cosa altri dicean dal vero
molto diversa e senza fin remota.
Passava intanto il navilio leggiero
per la contrada a' nostri poco nota,
fra l'India avendo e Tartaria il sentiero,
quella di città piena e questa vuota,
fin che fu sopra la bella marina
ch'ondeggia intorno all'isola d'Alcina.

93.   Ne la città d'Alcina, nel palagio,
dentro alle logge la donzella pose
la nave, e tutti li prigioni adagio,
e l'ambasciata di Gloricia espose.
Nei ceppi, come stavano, a disagio
Alcina in una torre al sole ascose
i Maganzesi, avendo riferite
del dono a chi 'l donò grazie infinite.

90. Many people saw them and were amazed and kept
their faces raised to the sky with eyes fixed and
eyebrows arched. A few fools, seeing them go by
two miles above the ground and not being able to
make out their faces very well, had various strange
opinions about them.

91. Some imagined that the ship belonged to Charon,
the infernal helmsman, and went laden with spirits
damned to perdition on the road to Cocytus.[32]
Others, of another persuasion, would say: "This is
that holy ship that sails to Heaven, which Peter
removes from Rome, so that it does not sink into
the waves of rape and simony."[33]

92. And others said other things very different and
infinitely remote from the truth. Meanwhile, the
light craft was passing through country little
known to us, taking a path between India and
Tartary, the former full of cities, the latter empty,
until it was above the lovely sea that laps about the
island of Alcina.

93. The damsel put the ship and all its prisoners down
softly in the city of Alcina, inside the gallery of
her palace, and revealed her mission from
Gloricia. Leaving the men of Mainz,
uncomfortable as they were, in the stocks, Alcina
hid them from the sun in a dungeon tower and
sent back unbounded thanks to the giver for
her gift.

94. La sera fuor di carcere poi Gano
     fe' a sé condurre, e a ragionar il messe
     de lo stato di Francia e del romano,
     di quel che Orlando e che Ruggier facesse.
     Ebbe l'astuto Conte chiaro e piano
     quanto la donna Carlo in odio avesse,
     Ruggiero, Orlando e gli altri; e tosto prese
     l'util partito, et a salvarsi attese.

95. —S'aver, donna, volete ognun nimico,—
     disse—che de la corte sia di Carlo,
     me in odio avrete ancora, ché 'l mio antico
     seggio è tra' Franchi, e non potrei negarlo;
     ma se più tosto odiate chi gli è amico
     e di sua volontà vuol seguitarlo,
     me non avrete in odio, ch'io non l'amo,
     ma il danno e biasmo suo più di voi bramo.

96. E s'ebbe alcun mai da bramar vendetta
     di tiranno che gli abbia fatt'oltraggio,
     bramar di Carlo e di tutta sua setta
     vendetta inanzi a tutti i sudditi aggio;
     come di re da cui sempre negletta
     la gloria fu di tutto il mio lignaggio,
     e che, per sempre al cor tenermi un telo,
     con favor alza i miei nimici al cielo.

97. Il mio figliastro Orlando, che mia morte
     procurò sempre e ad altro non aspira,
     contra me mille volte ha fatto forte;
     per lui m'ha mille volte avuto in ira:
     Rinaldo, Astolfo et ogni suo consorte
     di giorno in giorno a maggior grado tira;
     tal che sicuro, per lor gran possanza,
     non che in corte non son, ma né in Maganza.

94.   That evening she had Ganelon brought to her
       from prison and started him discussing the state of
       France and Rome and what Orlando and
       Ruggiero were doing. The astute Count realized
       clearly and plainly how much the lady hated
       Charles, Ruggiero, Orlando, and the others, and
       he quickly took the expedient course and sought
       to save himself.

95.   "Lady," he said, "if you wish to be the enemy of
       everyone in Charles's court, you will hate me as
       well, for my ancient seat is among the Franks and
       I could not deny it; but if you hate instead
       Charles's friends, those who want to follow him of
       their own free will, you will not hate me: for I do
       not love him, but instead hunger more than you
       for his destruction and dishonor.

96.   "And if ever anyone longed for revenge against a
       tyrant for the injury he had done him, I have
       more reason than all other subjects to long for
       revenge against him and all his clan, as against a
       king who has always disregarded the prestige of
       my whole family and, in order ever to hold a
       dagger to my heart, raises my enemies to the
       heavens with his favor.

97.   "Thousands of times he has strengthened the hand
       of my stepson Orlando, who has always sought
       my death and aims at nothing else; and thousands
       of times Orlando has inspired Charles's wrath
       against me. Every day he promotes Rinaldo,
       Astolfo, and all their associates to higher rank;
       because of their great power, I am in danger not
       only at court but in Mainz as well.

98.   Or, per maggior mio scorno, un fuggitivo
      del sfortunato figlio di Troiano,
      Ruggier, che m'ha un fratel di vita privo
      et un nipote con la propria mano,
      tiene in più onor che mai non fu Gradivo
      Marte tenuto dal popul romano:
      tal che levato indi mi son, con tutto
      il sangue mio, per non restar distrutto.

99.   Se me e quest'altri ch'avete qui meco,
      che sono il fior di casa da Pontiero,
      uccidete o dannate a carcer cieco,
      di perpetuo timor sciolto è l'Impero;
      ch'ogni nimico suo ch'abbia noi seco
      per noi può entrar in Francia di leggiero;
      ché ci avemo la parte in ogni terra,
      fortezze e porti e luoghi atti a far guerra.—

100. E seguitò il parlar astuto e pieno
      di gran malizia, sempre mai toccando
      quel che vedea di gaudio empirle il seno,
      che le vuol dar Ruggier preso et Orlando.
      Alcina ascolta, e ben nota il veleno
      che l'Invidia in lui sparse ir lavorando:
      commanda allora allora che sia sciolto,
      e sia con tutti i suoi di prigion tolto.

101. Volse che poi le promettesse Gano,
      con giuramenti stretti e d'orror pieni,
      di non cessar, fin che legato in mano
      Ruggier col suo figliastro non le meni:
      ma per poter non darli impresa in vano,
      oltr'oro e gemme e aiuti altri terreni
      promise ella all'incontro di far quanto
      potea sopra natura oprar l'incanto.

98. "Now, to my still greater shame, a deserter from
the unfortunate son of Troiano,[34] Ruggiero, who
with his own hand has deprived my brother and
nephew of life,[35] is held in more honor than ever
was Mars Gradivus by the people of Rome, so that
I have left the court with all my kinsmen in order
not to be destroyed.

99. "If you kill or condemn to dark prison myself and
these others you have here with me, who are the
flower of the house of Ponthieu, the Empire will
be freed from a perpetual dread; for any enemy
that has us on its side can with our help easily
invade France, because we have partisans in every
territory, fortress, harbor, and stronghold good for
making war."

100. Ganelon continued his speech, cunning and full of
the greatest malice, always dwelling on what he
saw filled Alcina's breast with joy, which was his
willingness to deliver Ruggiero and Orlando to
her as prisoners. Alcina listens and notes well how
the poison Envy infused in him is working. She
orders him unbound on the spot and released
from prison with all his men.

101. She wanted Ganelon to promise her, with binding
and dreadful oaths, not to stop until he had
brought Ruggiero and his stepson bound into her
hands; but in order not to send him on a fruitless
enterprise, in addition to helping him with gold
and gems and other worldly goods, she promised
on her part to do as much as she could to work
enchantment over nature.

102. E gli diè ne la gemma d'uno anello
un di quei spirti che chiamiam folletti,
che gli ubedisca, e così possa avello
com'un suo servitor de' più soggetti:
Vertunno è il nome, che in fiera, in ucello,
in uomo, in donna e in tutti gli altri aspetti,
in un sasso, in un'erba, in una fonte
mutar vedrete in un chinar di fronte.

103. Or perché Malagigi non aiuti,
com'altre volte ha fatto, i Paladini,
gli spiriti infernal tutti fe' muti,
gli terrestri, gli aérii e gli marini;
eccetto alcuni pochi c'ha tenuti
per uso suo, non franchi né latini,
ma di lingua dagli altri sì rimota
ch'a nigromante alcun non era nota.

104. Quel ch'alla fata il traditor promise,
promiser gli altri ancor ch'eran con lui.
Fermato il patto, Gano si rimise
nel fantastico legno con gli sui.
Il vento, come Alcina gli commise,
fra i lucidi Indi e gli Cimerii bui
soffiando, ferì in guisa ne l'antenna,
ch'in aria alzò la nave come penna.

105. Né, men che ratto, lo portò quïeto
per la medesma via che venut'era;
sì che, fra spazio di sett'ore, lieto
si ritrovò ne la sua barca vera,
di pan, di vin, di carne e infin d'aceto
fornita e d'insalata per la sera:
fe' dar le vele al vento, e venne a filo
ad imboccar sott'Alessandria il Nilo.

102. And she gave him, inside the stone gem of a ring, one of those spirits which we call goblins, to obey him as the most dutiful of servants. His name is Vertumnus, whom you would see change into a beast, a bird, a man, a woman, and all other shapes, into a rock, a plant, a fountain, all in the twinkling of an eye.[36]

103. And so that Malagigi[37] could not help the paladins the way he had on other occasions, she completely silenced the infernal spirits and the earthly, aerial, and marine ones, too, all except for those few which she kept for her own use, who spoke neither French nor Latin but a tongue so foreign from the rest that no necromancer could understand it.

104. What the traitor promised the Fairy, the others that were with him also promised. With their pact sealed, Ganelon went back into the fantastic ship with his men. The wind, as Alcina ordered it, blew between the sunlit Indians and overcast Cimmerians and struck the mainsail in such a way that the boat rose in the air like a feather.[38]

105. And it carried Ganelon no less quietly than quickly along the same route he had come, so that in the space of seven hours he happily found himself once again aboard his own true ship provisioned with bread, wine, meat, even with vinegar and fresh salad for that evening. He ordered the sheets to be loosed to the winds and sailed a straight course to the entrance of the Nile at Alexandria.

106. E già da l'armiraglio avendo avuto
      salvocondotto, al Cairo andò diritto,
      con duo compagni, in un legno minuto,
      secretamente, e in abito di Egitto.
      Dal calife per Gano conosciuto,
      ché molte volte inanzi s'avean scritto,
      fu di carezze sì pieno e d'onore,
      che ne scoppiò quasi il ventoso core.

107. In questo mezo che l'Invidia ascosa
      il traditor rodea di chi io vi parlo,
      come l'altrui bontà fu da lui rosa,
      ché poco dianzi il simigliavo a un tarlo;
      ira, odio, sdegno, amor facea angosciosa
      Alcina, e un fier disio di strugger Carlo;
      e quanto più credea di farlo in breve,
      tant'ogn'indugio le parea più greve.

108. Il conte di Pontier le avea narrato
      che, prima che di Francia si partisse,
      da lui fu Desiderio confortato,
      per ambasciate e lettere che scrisse,
      che con Tedeschi et Ungheri da un lato,
      che facil fòra che a sue genti unisse,
      saltasse in Francia; e che Marsiglio ispano
      saltar faria da l'altro, e l'Aquitano.

109. E che quel glien'avea dato speranza;
      poi venia lento a metterla in effetto,
      o che tema di Carlo la possanza,
      o sia mal di sua lega il nodo astretto.
      Alcina, che si mor di desïanza
      di por Francia e l'Impero in male assetto,
      adopra ogni saper, ogni suo ingegno,
      per dar colore a così bel disegno.

106.   And, already having a safe-conduct from the
        Emir, he went straight to Cairo with two of his
        companions, secretly and in Egyptian dress,
        traveling in a tiny boat. Once the Caliph knew
        him for Ganelon—for they had written to each
        other many times before—he showered on him
        so many caresses and honors that his inflated heart
        almost burst from it.

107.   In the meantime, while hidden Envy gnawed
        away secretly at the traitor of whom I am telling
        you—just as the happiness of others was gnawed
        away at by him, for just a short time ago I
        compared him to a worm—anger, loathing, spite,
        and love tormented Alcina, together with a fierce
        desire to destroy Charles; and the more she
        believed it could be done quickly, the more any
        delay seemed grievous to her.

108.   The Count of Ponthieu had related to her that
        before he left France he had encouraged
        Desiderius, through ambassadors and letters he
        had written him, to invade France from the east
        together with the Germans and Hungarians with
        whom it would be easy to join forces, and that he
        would make the Spaniard Marsilio invade from
        the west, along with Unuldo of Aquitaine.

109.   Ganelon told Alcina that Desiderius had given
        him hope but had then been slow to put the plan
        into action, either because he feared the power of
        Charles or because the bonds of his alliance were
        poorly tied. Alcina, who is dying from her desire
        to place France and the Empire in a bad way, puts
        all her knowledge and all her ingenuity to work to
        give life to this fine plan.

110. Et è bisogno al fin ch'ella ritruovi,
per far muover di passo il Longobardo,
sproni che siano aguzzi più che chiovi:
tanto le par a questa impresa tardo!
E come fece far disegni nuovi
dianzi l'Invidia a quel cochin pagliardo,
così spera trovar un'altra peste
che 'l pigro re de la sua inerzia deste.

111. Conchiuse che nessuna era meglio atta
a stimularlo e far più risentire,
d'una che nacque quando anco la matta
Crudeltà nacque, e le Rapine e l'Ire.
Che nome avesse e come fosse fatta,
ne l'altro Canto mi riserbo a dire,
dove farò, per quanto è mio potere,
cose sentir maravigliose e vere.

110. And, in the end, she needs to come up with a
spur sharper than nails to make the Lombard take
a step, so slow does he seem to her in this
enterprise! And just as Envy had earlier stirred that
vile wretch Ganelon to new schemes of treachery,
so Alcina now hopes to find another such fiend to
rouse the idle King from his inaction.

111. She decided that none was more suitable to prod
and shake him up than one who was born at the
same time as mad Cruelty was born, together with
Rapine and Wrath. What this fiend was called and
what it looked like I will save for telling in the
next Canto, where, as much as is in my power, I
will have you hear things both marvelous and
true.

Canto Secondo

1. PENSAR COSA MIGLIOR non si può al mondo
    d'un signor giusto e in ogni parte buono,
    che del debito suo non getti il pondo,
    benché talor ne vada curvo e prono;
    che curi et ame i populi, secondo
    che da' lor padri amati i figli sono;
    che l'opre e le fatiche pei figliuoli
    fan quasi sempre, e raro per sé soli:

2. ponga ai perigli et alle cose strette
    il petto inanzi, e faccia agli altri schermo:
    che non sia il mercenario il qual non stette,
    poi che venir vide a sé il lupo, fermo;
    ma sì bene il pastor vero, che mette
    la vita propria pel suo gregge infermo,
    il qual conosce le sue pecorelle
    ad una ad una, e lui conoscono elle.

3. Tal fu in terra Saturno, Ercole e Giove,
    Bacco, Poluce, Osiri e poi Quirino,
    che con giustizia e virtüose prove,
    e con soave e a tutti ugual domino,
    fur degni in Grecia, in India, in Roma, e dove
    corse lor fama, aver onor divino;
    che riputar non si potrian defunti,
    ma a più degno governo in cielo assunti.

Canto 2

1. A BETTER THING cannot be imagined in this world
    than a lord just and good in every way, one who
    does not shirk the burden of his duty even though
    sometimes he may bend and curve his shoulders
    beneath its weight, who cares for his people and
    loves them as fathers love their children, fathers
    who labor and toil almost always for their children
    and rarely for themselves.

2. He should meet dangers and adversity head-on
    and be a shield for others, so that he will not be
    like the hireling who did not stand firm when he
    saw the wolf come at him but, rather, like the true
    shepherd who lays down his own life for his weak
    flock, who knows each one of his sheep
    individually and whose sheep know him.[1]

3. Such on Earth were Saturn, Hercules, Jove,
    Bacchus, Pollux, Osiris, and after them, Quirinus,
    who with justice and valiant deeds, and with a
    rule gentle and equal for all, were honored as gods
    in Greece, in India, in Rome, and everywhere
    their fame has traveled; so that they should not be
    considered dead, but only taken up to a more
    worthy government in the heavens.

4.   Quando il signor è buono, i sudditi anco
fa buoni; ch'ognun imita chi regge:
e s'alcun pur riman col vizio, manco
lo mostra fuor, o in parte lo corregge.
O beati gli regni a chi un uom franco
e sciolto da ogni colpa abbi a dar legge!
Così infelici ancora e miserandi,
ove un ingiusto, ove un crudel commandi;

5.   che sempre accresca e più gravi la soma,
come in Italia molti a' giorni nostri,
de' quali il biasmo in questo e l'altro idioma
faran sentir anco i futuri inchiostri:
che migliori non son che Gaio a Roma,
o Neron fosse, o fosser gli altri mostri:
ma se ne tace, perché è sempre meglio
lasciar i vivi, e dir del tempo veglio.

6.   E dir qual sotto Fallari Agrigento,
qual fu sotto i Dionigi Siracusa,
qual Fere in man del suo tiran cruento;
dai quali e senza colpa e senza accusa
la gente ogni dì quasi a cento a cento
era troncata, o in lungo esiglio esclusa.
Ma né senza martìr sono essi ancora,
ch'al cor lor sta non minor pena ognora.

7.   Sta lor la pena de la qual si tacque
il nome dianzi, e de la qual dicea
che nacque quando la brutt'Ira nacque,
la Crudeltade e la Rapina rea:
e quantunque in un ventre con lor giacque,
di tormentarle mai non rimanea.
Or dirò il nome, ch'io non l'ho ancor detto:
nomata questa pena era il Sospetto.

4.   When the lord is good, he makes his subjects
good as well; for all men imitate the one who
rules; and if anyone still retains his vices, he either
shows them less openly or partly corrects them.
Oh, happy the kingdoms to which a man honest
and free from any fault gives law! How miserable
and wretched, by the same token, those where an
unjust, where a cruel man commands,

5.   for he always increases and adds to his subjects'
burdens: as do many such in Italy in our day
whose censure future writings in this tongue and
in Latin will make known. They are no better
than Caligula or Nero or the other monsters were
in Rome. But let us be silent, for it is always better
to let the living be and to speak of ancient times.

6.   And to speak of what Agrigento was like under
Phalaris, what Syracuse was under Dionysius,
what Pherae was in the hands of its bloody tyrant;[2]
almost every day, without guilt and without
accusation, their citizens were cut down by the
hundreds or banished to long exile. But neither
do the tyrants themselves escape punishment, for a
not lesser torment dwells ever in their hearts.

7.   Theirs is the torment which I did not name
before, and which I said was born when ugly
Wrath was born, with Cruelty and wicked
Rapine; and which, even though it had lain beside
these others in one womb, never stopped afflicting
them. Now I will say the name, which I have not
mentioned earlier; this torment was named
Suspicion.

8. Il Sospetto, piggior di tutti i mali,
    spirto piggior d'ogni maligna peste
    che l'infelici menti de' mortali
    con venenoso stimolo moleste;
    non le povere o l'umili, ma quali
    s'aggiran dentro alle superbe teste
    di questi scelerati, che per opra
    di gran fortuna agli altri stan di sopra.

9. Beato chi lontan da questi affanni
    nuoce a nessun, perché a nessun è odioso!
    Infelici altretanto e più i tiranni,
    a cui né notte mai né dì riposo
    dà questa peste, e lor ricorda i danni,
    e morti date od in palese o ascoso!
    Quinci dimostra che timor sol d'uno
    han tutti gli altri, et essi n'han d'ognuno.

10. Non v'incresca di starmi un poco a udire,
    ché non però dal mio sentier mi scosto;
    anzi farò questo ch'or narro uscire
    dove poi vi parrà che sia a proposto.
    Uno di questi, il qual prima a nudrire
    usò la barba, per tener discosto
    chi gli potea la vita a un colpo tòrre,
    nel suo palazzo edificò una torre,

11. che, d'alte fosse cinta e grosse mura,
    avea un sol ponte che si leva e cala;
    fuor ch'un balcon, non v'era altra apertura,
    ove a pena entra il giorno e l'aria esala:
    quivi dormia la notte, et era cura
    de la moglier di mandar giù la scala:
    di quella entrata è un gran mastin custode,
    ch'altri mai che lor due non vede et ode.

8. Suspicion, the worst of all evils, the worst spirit of
    all the malignant plagues that with their venomous
    sting prey upon the minds of unhappy mortals;
    not upon the minds of the poor and humble but
    upon the minds of these proud and wicked tyrants
    who, by virtue of great fortune, are placed above
    others.

9. Happy the man who, far from these troubles,
    harms no one, for he is hateful to no one! But
    correspondingly wretched and more so are the
    tyrants to whom this plague gives no respite by
    day or night and whom it reminds of their
    misdeeds, and of murders performed openly or in
    secret! Thus is it that while all others must fear but
    one alone, they must fear each and all.

10. Do not mind listening to me a little further, for I
    am not wandering from my path; on the contrary,
    I will make what I am now telling you end up
    where it will seem to be right to the point. One of
    these tyrants—the first to adapt the fashion of
    letting his beard grow long in order to keep away
    anyone who could take his life with a single stroke
    of the razor—built a tower in his palace.

11. Girded by deep moats and a thick wall, the tower
    had a single bridge which could be raised and
    lowered; aside from one balcony, through which
    day might barely enter and air escape, there was
    no other opening. Here he slept at night, and it
    was the duty of his wife to let down the stairs. On
    guard at the entrance was a great hound which
    never saw or heard anyone other than these two.

12.	Non ha ne la moglier però sì grande
	fede il meschin, che prima ch'a lei vada,
	quand'uno e quando un altro suo non mande,
	che cerchi i luoghi onde a temer gli accada.
	Ma ciò poco gli val, ché le nefande
	man de la donna, e la sua propria spada,
	fér d'infinito mal tarda vendetta,
	e all'inferno volò il suo spirto in fretta.

13.	E Radamanto, giudice del loco,
	tutto il cacciò sotto il bollente stagno,
	dove non pianse e non gridò: —I' mi cuoco—,
	come gridava ogn'altro suo compagno;
	e la pena mostrò curar sì poco,
	che disse il giustiziere: —Io te la cagno—;
	e lo mandò ne le più oscure cave,
	dov'è un martìr d'ogni martìr più grave.

14.	Né quivi parve ancor che si dogliesse;
	e domandato, disse la cagione:
	che quando egli vivea, tanto l'oppresse
	e tal gli diè il Sospetto afflizïone
	(che nel capo quel giorno se gli messe,
	che si fece signor contra ragione),
	che sol ora il pensar d'esserne fuore
	sentir non gli lasciava altro dolore.

15.	Si consigliaro i saggi de l'inferno
	come potesse aver degno tormento;
	che saria contra l'instituto eterno
	se peccator là giù stesse contento;
	e di nuovo mandarlo al caldo, al verno
	concluso fu da tutto il parlamento;
	e di nuovo al Sospetto in preda darlo,
	ch'entrasse in lui senza più mai lasciarlo.

12.   Still, the wretch did not have enough faith in his
       wife that before he went to her he did not send
       first one and then another of his men to search the
       places he happened to fear. But it did him little
       good, for at last the wicked hands of his lady and
       his own sword wrought a tardy vengeance for his
       innumerable wrongs, and his spirit flew in haste to
       Hell.

13.   And Rhadamanthus,[3] judge of the place,
       submerged him completely in the boiling pool,
       where, however, he did not wail and cry out,
       "I'm roasting," as all his companions did. He
       showed so little concern for his punishment that
       the judge said, "I'll change it for you," and he sent
       him to the darkest depths, where there is a
       torment that is the worst of all torments.

14.   But even there he did not complain, and when
       asked told the reason: that while he lived
       Suspicion oppressed him and afflicted him so
       much (for it entered his head on the day that he
       unlawfully made himself lord), that now the mere
       thought of being beyond it kept him from feeling
       other pain.

15.   The sages of Hell took counsel among themselves
       about a suitable torment for him, for it would be
       against the eternal statutes were a sinner to be
       happy down below; and it was decided by the
       whole parliament to send him back to Earth, to
       the heat of summer and winter's cold; and to offer
       him up once more as prey for Suspicion, which
       might enter him again and this time stay for good.

16.   Così di novo entrò il Sospetto in questa
       alma, e di sé e di lei fece tutt'uno,
       come in ceppo salvatico s'inesta
       pomo diverso, e 'l nespilo sul pruno;
       o di molti colori un color resta,
       quando un pittor ne piglia di ciascuno
       per imitar la carne, e ne riesce
       un differente a tutti quei che mesce.

17.   Di sospettoso che 'l tiràn fu in prima,
       or divenuto era il Sospetto istesso;
       e, come morte la ragion di prima
       avesse in lui, gli parea averla appresso.
       Ma ritornando al mio parlar di prima,
       ché per questo in oblio non l'avea messo,
       Alcina se ne va dove sul tergo
       d'un alto scoglio ha questo spirto albergo.

18.   Lo scoglio ove 'l Sospetto fa soggiorno
       è dal mar alto da seicento braccia,
       di rovinose balze cinto intorno,
       e da ogni canto di cader minaccia.
       Il più stretto sentier che vada al Forno,
       là dove il Grafagnino il ferro caccia,
       la via Flamminia o l'Appia nomar voglio
       verso quel che dal mar va in cima al scoglio.

19.   Prima che giunghi alla suprema altezza,
       sette ponti ritrovi e sette porte:
       tutte hanno con lor guardie una fortezza;
       la settima de l'altre è la più forte.
       Là dentro, in grande affanno e in gran tristezza,
       ché gli par sempre a' fianchi aver la morte,
       il Sospetto meschin solo s'annida;
       nessun vuol seco e di nessun si fida.

16. So Suspicion entered anew into this soul and of
the two of them made one whole, as on a wild
stock different fruits are grafted and the medlar
tree upon the thorn bush; or as one color comes
of many colors, when a painter takes some of each
in order to simulate flesh and ends up with one
quite different from all those he mixes.

17. From the suspicious man the tyrant had been at
first, he had now become Suspicion itself; and as if
death still retained its old claim on him, it seemed
again to be at his heels. But returning to my
earlier story—for I have not forgotten it with this
other one—Alcina goes off to where this spirit has
its home, at the summit of a lofty promontory.

18. The promontory where Suspicion dwells is six
hundred yards above the sea, encircled by sheer
cliffs, threatening a fall on every side. The
narrowest path that goes to Forno, there where
the Garfagnan seeks for iron, I would call the Via
Flaminia or the Appian Way, beside the one
which went to this ridge's summit from the sea.[4]

19. Before you reach the highest point, you find seven
bridges and seven gates; all have a stockade and
guards, and the seventh is the strongest of all.
There, inside, wretched Suspicion cowers all
alone, in terrible anguish and pain, for he always
seems to have death at his side. He wants nobody
with him, and he trusts in none.

20.   Grida da' merli e tien le guardie deste,
        né mai riposa al sol né al cielo oscuro;
        e ferro sopra ferro e ferro veste:
        quanto più s'arma, è tanto men sicuro.
        Muta et accresce or quelle cose or queste
        alle porte, al serraglio, al fosso, al muro:
        per darne altrui, munizïon gli avanza;
        e non gli par che mai n'abbia a bastanza.

21.   Alcina, che sapea ch'indi il Sospetto
        né a prieghi né a minacce vorria uscire,
        e trarlone era forza al suo dispetto,
        tutto pensò ciò che potea seguire.
        Avea seco arrecato a questo effetto
        l'acqua del fiume che fa l'uom dormire,
        et entrando invisibil ne la rocca,
        con essa ne le tempie un poco il tocca.

22.   Quel cade addormentato; Alcina il prende,
        e scongiurando gli spirti infernali
        fa venir quivi un carro, e su vel stende,
        che tiran duo serpenti c'hanno l'ali;
        poi verso Italia in tanta fretta scende,
        che con la più non van di Giove i strali.
        La medesima notte è in Lombardia,
        in ripa di Ticin dentro a Pavia:

23.   là dove il re de' Longobardi allora
        l'antiquo seggio, Desiderio, avea.
        Nel ciel orïental sorgea l'aurora
        quando perdé il vigor l'acqua letea:
        lasciò il sonno il Sospetto; e quel, che fuora
        e lontan dal castel suo si vedea,
        morto saria, se non fosse già morto;
        ma la fata ebbe presta al suo conforto.

20.   He shouts from the battlements to keep the guards
        alert and never rests, either in daylight or under
        the night sky; he puts on armor over armor and
        then puts on more armor and the more he arms
        himself, the less safe he feels. He changes and
        reinforces first these things, then those, at the
        gates, at the stockade, at the moat, at the wall; he
        has enough extra munitions to give to others, but
        still it seems to him that he never has enough.

21.   Alcina, who knew that Suspicion could never,
        either by prayers or by threats, be induced to leave
        that place willingly and that she would have to
        drag him away against his wishes, had thought of
        everything in advance. For this reason, she
        brought with her water from the river that makes
        men sleep[5] and, entering the castle invisible,
        touched him with a little on his temples.

22.   Suspicion falls asleep; Alcina takes him and,
        conjuring infernal spirits, summons a carriage
        drawn by two winged serpents and puts him in it.
        Then she descends toward Italy with so much
        speed that the shafts of Jove's thunderbolts do not
        go faster. She is in Lombardy the same night,
        inside Pavia on the banks of the Ticino.

23.   In those days Desiderius, the King of Lombardy,
        had his ancient seat there. Dawn was rising in the
        eastern sky when Lethe's water lost its strength;
        Suspicion awoke, and, when he found himself
        outside and so far away from his castle, he would
        have died if he were not already dead; but the
        Fairy was quick to comfort him.

24.   Gli promesse ella indietro rimandarlo
senza alcun danno; e in guisa gli promesse,
che poté in qualche parte assicurarlo,
non sì però ch'in tutto le credesse;
ma prima in Desiderio, che di Carlo
temea le forze, entrasse gli commesse,
e che non se gli levi mai del seno
fin che tutto di sé non l'abbia pieno.

25.   Mentre fu Carlo i giorni inanzi astretto
dal re d'Africa a un tempo e da Marsiglio,
il re de' Longobardi, per negletto
e per perduto avendo posto il giglio,
non curando né papa né interdetto
alla Romagna avea dato di piglio;
po' entrando ne la Marca, con battaglia
e Pesaro avea preso e Sinigaglia.

26.   Indi sentendo ch'era il foco spento,
morto Agramante e il re Marsiglio rotto,
de la temerità sua mal contento
si riputò a mal termine condotto.
Or viene Alcina, e accresceli tormento:
ché fa 'l rio spirto entrar in lui di botto,
che notte e dì l'afflige, crucia et ange,
e più che sopra un sasso in letto il frange.

27.   Gli par veder che lassi il Reno e l'Erra
il popul già troiano e poi sicambro,
et apra l'Alpi e scenda ne la terra
che riga il Po, l'Ada, il Ticino e l'Ambro:
veder s'aspetta in casa sua la guerra,
e sua ruina più chiara che un ambro;
né più certo rimedio al suo mal truova,
che contra Francia ogni vicin commova.

24. She promised to send him back unharmed; and
     she promised to do so in a way which to some
     extent reassured him, though not so much that he
     trusted her completely; but first she ordered him
     to enter Desiderius, who was afraid of Charles's
     powers, and never to leave his breast until he had
     filled it completely.

25. In days just past, while Charles was beset by both
     the King of Africa and Marsilio, the King of the
     Lombards supposed the lily[6] was weakened and
     lost and, caring neither for Pope nor interdict, had
     seized Romagna; then, entering the Marches, he
     had fought and taken both Pesaro and Sinigaglia.[7]

26. Hearing later that the fire of war was put out, that
     Agramante was dead and King Marsilio routed,
     he regretted his boldness and thought himself
     brought to a bad pass. Now Alcina comes, and she
     increases his anguish; for she makes the evil spirit
     Suspicion instantly enter him, and it afflicts him
     day and night, torments him and distresses him
     and racks his limbs on a bed that seems worse than
     a mattress of rocks.

27. He seems to see the race once Trojan, then
     Sicambrian,[8] leave the Rhine and the Loire,
     unlock the passes of the Alps, and descend to the
     lands which the Po, the Adda, the Ticino, and the
     Lambro furrow; he anticipates war in his own
     house, and he sees his impending destruction
     clearer than amber; and he finds no surer remedy
     for his plight than to incite all his neighbors
     against France.

28.   E come quel che gran tesori uniti
      avea d'esazïoni e di rapine,
      et avea i sacri argenti convertiti
      in uso suo da le cose divine;
      con doni e con proferte e gran partiti
      colligò molte nazïon vicine,
      come già il conte di Pontier gli scrisse
      prima che da la corte si partisse.

29.   Tutta avea Gano questa tela ordita,
      che 'l Longobardo dovea tesser poi;
      e quella poi non era oltre seguita,
      e fin qui stava ne' principii suoi.
      Or la mente, d'un stimolo ferita
      piggior di quel che caccia asini e buoi,
      conchiuse e fece nascer com'un fungo
      quel che più giorni avea menato in lungo.

30.   Fe' in pochi dì che Tassillone, ch'era
      suo genero e cugin del duca Namo,
      tutta la stirpe sua fuor di Bavera
      cacciò, senza lasciarverne un sol ramo:
      fe' similmente ribellar la fera
      Sansogna, e ritornar a re Gordamo;
      e trasse, per por Carlo in maggior briga,
      con gli Ungheri Boemi in una liga;

31.   e 'l re di Dazia e il re de le due Marche
      pór tra la Frisa e il termine d'Olanda
      tante fuste, galee, carache e barche,
      per gir ne l'Inghilterra e ne l'Irlanda,
      che per fuggir avean le some carche
      molte terre da mar da quella banda.
      Da un'altra parte si sentiva il vecchio
      nimico in Spagna far grande apparecchio.

28.　He had amassed a great treasure by taxes and by theft and converted the consecrated silver of the Church from divine purposes to his own; with gifts and bribes and generous treaties he gathered together many surrounding nations—just as the Count of Ponthieu had written instructing him to do before he left the court.

29.　Ganelon had plotted all this intrigue which the Lombard was now about to weave, but the plan had not been followed and until now was stalled at its beginning. Now Desiderius, his mind struck by a prod worse than the one that drives asses and oxen, was resolute and made grow like mushrooms what he had temporized over for many days.

30.　In a few days he had Tassillone, who was his son-in-law and the cousin of Duke Namo, drive all of Namo's kindred from Bavaria without leaving a single branch of them behind; he made fierce Saxony rebel also, and return to King Gordamo; and, to put Charles in still bigger trouble, he drew the Bohemians into league with the Hungarians.[9]

31.　He persuaded the King of Denmark and the King of the Two Marches[10] to launch large numbers of light warships, galleys, barks, and carracks between Frisia and Holland, for raids into England and Ireland, causing many seaside peoples to gather their belongings and flee before them. Elsewhere, Charles's old enemy in Spain was heard to be making great preparations.

32. Tutto seguì ciò ch'avea ordito Gano,
     ch'era d'insidie e tradimenti il padre.
     Fu suscitato Unnuldo l'aquitano
     a soldar genti fazïose e ladre:
     mettendo terre a sacco, capitano
     di ventura era detto da le squadre;
     nascosamente da Lupo aiutato,
     di Bertolagi di Baiona nato.

33. Fér queste nove, per diversi avisi
     venute, a Carlo abbandonar le feste,
     e a donne e a cavallieri i giochi e' risi,
     e mutar le leggiadre in scure veste.
     De' saccheggiati populi et uccisi
     per ferro, fiamme, oppressïoni e peste,
     le memorie percosse ad ora ad ora
     prometteano altrotanto e peggio ancora.

34. O vita nostra di travaglio piena,
     come ogni tua allegrezza poco dura!
     Il tuo gioir è come aria serena,
     ch'alla fredda stagion troppo non dura:
     fu chiaro a terza il giorno, e a vespro mena
     sùbita pioggia, et ogni cosa oscura.
     Parea ai Franchi esser fuor d'ogni periglio,
     morto Agramante e rotto il re Marsiglio;

35. et ecco un'altra volta che 'l ciel tuona
     da un'altra parte, e tutto arde de lampi,
     sì che ogni speme i miseri abbandona
     di poter frutto cor de li lor campi.
     E così avvien ch'una novella buona
     mai più di venti o trenta dì non campi,
     perché vien dietro un'altra che l'uccide;
     e piangerà doman l'uom ch'oggi ride.

32.   Everything followed just as Ganelon, who was the
       father of treacheries and betrayals, had plotted it.
       Unuldo of Aquitaine was incited to enlist
       seditious men and thieves; putting lands to sack,
       he was called a soldier of fortune by his troops,
       and he was secretly helped by Lupo, the son of
       Bertolagi of Bayonne.

33.   This news, arriving by various reports, made
       Charles abandon his festivals and made the ladies
       and knights leave off their games and laughter and
       change their joyful clothes to somber ones.
       Memories, stirred up hour by hour, of peoples
       sacked and slaughtered by the sword, by fire, by
       oppression and plagues, promised new evils just as
       bad and worse.

34.   Oh, human life full of travail, how fleeting is your
       every happiness! Your joy is like clear skies in
       winter that do not last for long; the day was clear
       at terce, and at vespers brings sudden rain and
       darkens everything. It seemed to the French that
       they were out of all danger, with Agramante dead
       and King Marsilio put to flight.

35.   And lo, once again, from another quarter, the
       heavens thunder and burn with lightning, and the
       wretched people abandon every hope of being
       able to harvest the fruit of their fields. And so it
       happens that good news never survives more than
       twenty or thirty days, for other tidings come
       afterward to kill it, and the man who laughs today
       will cry tomorrow.

36.   Per le cittadi uomini e donne errando,
        con visi bassi e d'allegrezza spenti,
        andavan taciturni sospirando,
        né si sentiano ancor chiari lamenti:
        qual ne le case attonite avvien, quando
        mariti o figli o più cari parenti
        si veggon travagliar ne l'ore estreme,
        ch'infinito è il timor, poca è la speme.

37.   E quella poca pur spegnere il gelo
        vuol de la tema, e dentro il cor si caccia:
        ma come può d'un piccolin candelo
        fuoco scaldar dov'alta neve agghiaccia?
        Chi leva a Dio, chi leva a' Santi in cielo
        le palme giunte e la smarrita faccia,
        pregandoli che, senza più martìre,
        basti il passato a disfogar lor ire.

38.   Come che il popul timido per tema
        disperi, e perda il cor e venga manco,
        nel magnanimo Carlo non iscema
        l'ardir, ma cresce, e nei paladini anco:
        ché la virtù di grande fa suprema,
        quanto travaglia più, l'animo franco;
        e gloria et immortal fama ne nasce,
        che me' d'ogn'altro cibo il guerrier pasce.

39.   Carlo, a cui ritrovar difficilmente,
        la terra e 'l mar cercando a parte a parte,
        si potria par di santa e buona mente,
        e d'ogni finzïon netta e d'ogn'arte
        (e lasso ancor oltre l'età presente
        volgi l'antique e più famose carte);
        a Dio raccomandò sé, i figli e il stato,
        né più curò ch'esser di fede armato.

36.   Wandering through the cities, their faces
       downcast and emptied of happiness, men and
       women went silent and sighing, although outright
       laments were not yet heard; as happens in stricken
       homes, when husbands, children, or dearest
       relations are suffering in their last hours and fear is
       boundless while hope is small.

37.   And that little hope nonetheless rushes to the
       heart and strives to put out the icy cold of fear;
       but how can the flame of a tiny candle bring
       warmth where deep snow freezes over? One lifts
       to God, another to the Saints in Heaven, his
       joined palms and frightened face beseeching them
       that the past might be enough to appease their
       wrath without further suffering.[11]

38.   Yet, while the timid populace may despair because
       of fear and lose heart and falter, in magnanimous
       Charles courage does not diminish but increases,
       and in his paladins, too; for in a firm soul great
       valor becomes supreme the greater its travails; and
       from its exertions are born glory and immortal
       fame, which nourish the warrior better than any
       other food.

39.   Charles, whose equal for a holy and good mind,
       free of all dissimulation and artifice, it would be
       hard to find searching land and sea everywhere
       (even if, setting aside the present age, you turned
       to ancient and more famous pages), commended
       himself, his children, and his states to God and did
       not worry as long as he was armed with faith.

40. Né men saggio che buono, poi ch'avuto
     ebbe ricorso alla Maggior Possanza,
     che non mancò né mancherà d'aiuto
     ad alcun mai che ponga in lei speranza,
     fece che, senza indugio, proveduto
     fu a tutti i luoghi ov'era più importanza:
     gli capitani suoi per ogni terra
     mandò a far scelta d'uomini da guerra.

41. Non si sentiva allor questo rumore
     de' tamburi, com'oggi, andar in volta,
     invitando la gente di più core,
     o forse (per dir meglio) la più stolta,
     che per tre scudi e per prezzo minore
     vada ne' luoghi ove la vita è tolta:
     stolta più tosto la dirò che ardita,
     ch'a sì vil prezzo venda la sua vita.

42. Alla vita l'onor s'ha da preporre;
     fuor che l'onor non altra cosa alcuna:
     prima che mai lasciarti l'onor tòrre
     déi mille vite perdere, non ch'una.
     Chi va per oro e vil guadagno a porre
     la sua vita in arbitrio di fortuna,
     per minor prezzo crederò che dia,
     se troverà chi compri, anco la mia.

43. O, com'io dissi, non sanno che vaglia
     la vita quei che sì l'estiman poco;
     o c'han disegno, inanzi alla battaglia,
     che 'l piè gli salvi a più sicuro loco.
     La mercenaria mal fida canaglia
     prezzar li antiqui imperatori poco:
     de la lor nazïon più tosto venti
     volean, che cento di diverse genti.

40. No less wise than good, after he had recourse to
the Greater Power which has not failed and will
not fail to help anyone who places his hope in It,
Charles had all the most strategic places provided
for without delay; he sent his captains through
every land to make a levy of warriors.

41. The noise of drums was not heard going about
then as it is today, inviting the most courageous,
or perhaps (to speak more correctly) the most
foolish, who for a price of three crowns or less go
off to places where they can lose their lives: I will
call them foolish sooner than brave, who sell their
lives at so base a price!

42. Honor must be put before life: other than honor
nothing else at all. You should lose your life a
thousand times, not just once, before you ever let
yourself lose your honor. Whoever will put his
own life at the mercy of fortune for gold or base
gain will, I believe, sell mine as well and at a lower
price if he can find a buyer.

43. Either, as I said, they do not know what life is
worth, those who consider it worth so little, or
they are planning, even before the battle, for their
feet to deliver them to safer places. The generals of
former times held the faithless mercenary rabble
of little value; they would sooner have preferred
twenty of their own nation to a hundred
foreigners.

44.   Non era a quelli tempi alcun escluso
che non portasse l'armi e andasse in guerra,
fuor che fanciul da sedici anni in giuso,
o quel che già l'estrema etade afferra:
ma tal milizia solo era per uso
di bisogno e d'onor de la sua terra:
sempre sua vita esercitando sotto
buon capitani, in arme era ognun dotto.

45.   Carlo per tutta Francia e per la Magna,
per ogni terra a' suoi regni soggetta,
fa scriver gente, e poi la piglia e cagna
secondo che gli par atta et inetta;
sì che fa in pochi giorni alla campagna
un esercito uscir di gente eletta,
da far che Marte fin su nel ciel treme,
non che a' nimici l'impeto non sceme.

46.   Gli elmi, gli arnesi, le corazze e scudi,
che poco dianzi fur messi da parte,
e de lor fatte ampie officine ai studi
de l'ingegnose aragne era gran parte,
sì che forse tornar in su gli incudi
temeano, e farsi ordigni a più vil arte;
or imbruniti, fuor d'ogni timore,
godeano esser riposti al primo onore.

47.   Sonan di qua, di là tanti martelli,
che n'assorda di strepito ogni orecchia:
quei batton piastre e le rifanno, e quelli
vanno acconciando l'armatura vecchia;
altri le barde torna alli penelli,
coprirle altri di drappo s'apparecchia:
chi cerca questa cosa, e chi ritrova
quell'altra; altri racconcia, altri rinuova.

44.   In those days no one was excluded from bearing
        arms and going to war, except children of sixteen
        years or less or those already gripped by old age:
        but this militia was only for use at the need or
        honor of the country; everyone was educated in
        arms, drilling their whole lives under good
        captains.

45.   Throughout France and throughout Germany,
        throughout every land subjected to his rule,
        Charles has people enlisted and then chooses and
        removes them according to their ability and
        weakness; so in a few days he sees an army of
        select soldiers emerge for his campaign, a force
        that would make Mars himself tremble up in
        heaven, let alone dishearten an enemy attack.

46.   Helmets, weapons, breastplates, and shields, which
        a little while earlier had been put aside and the
        greater part of which had become the spacious
        workshops of ingenious spiders, had perhaps
        feared being returned to the anvil and made into
        tools for some baser art; now, newly polished, free
        of all fear, they rejoiced to be restored to their
        original honor.

47.   So many hammers sounded here and there that
        every ear was deafened by their noise: these
        pound out armor plate and refashion it, and those
        refurbish old armor; some workmen repaint
        harnesses, others prepare caparisons for the horses;
        one searches out this thing, another finds that;
        some make repairs, others renovations.

48.   Poi che Carlo al tesor ruppe il serraglio,
ebbon da travagliar tutti i mestieri:
ma né maggior né più commun travaglio
era però, che di trovar destrieri:
ché gli disagi e de le spade il taglio
tolto n'avean da le decine i zeri:
quali si fosson (ché i buon eran rari),
come il sangue e la vita erano cari.

49.   Carlo, oltra l'ordinario che solea
aver d'uomini d'armi alle frontiere,
e de la gente che a piè combattea,
che per pace era usato anco tenere,
de l'un canto e de l'altro fatto avea
che pieno era ogni cosa di bandiere:
trenta sei mila armati in su l'arzoni,
e quattro tanto e più furo i pedoni.

50.   E per gli molti esempi che già letto
de' capitani avea del tempo veglio,
com'uom ch'amava sopra ogni diletto
d'udir istorie e farne al viver speglio;
e più perché vedutone l'effetto
per propria esperïenzia, il sapea meglio;
conobbe al tempo la prestezza usata
aver più volte la vittoria data;

51.   e ch'era molto meglio ch'egli andasse
i nimici a trovar ne la lor terra,
e sopra gli lor campi s'alloggiasse,
e desse lor de' frutti de la guerra;
che dentro alle confine gli aspettasse
che l'Alpi e 'l Pireneo fra dui mar serra.
Fatta la mostra, i populi divise
in molte parti, e a' suoi capi i commise.

48. Once Charles has broken open the gates of the
treasury, all the craftsmen have work to do, but
there was still no greater or more general task than
finding horses: hardships and sword wounds had
taken nine out of ten of them: those that were left
(for good ones were rare), cost as dearly as life and
blood.

49. In addition to the normal number of men at arms
that he was used to keeping on the frontiers, and
of the infantry he was accustomed to keeping
even in peacetime, Charles had filled his
territories with banners from one border to the
other: thirty-six thousand men in armor in the
saddle, four times that and more on foot.

50. And from the many examples of captains of
ancient times that he had read, for he loved above
every other pleasure listening to histories and
holding them up as a mirror to life—and because
he knew even better having seen the effect in his
own personal experience—Charles understood
that speed used at the right moment has yielded
victory on many occasions.

51. And he understood that it was much better for
him to go find his enemies in their own territory,
to camp in their fields and give them the fruits of
war, than to wait for them within the confines
that the Alps and the Pyrenees bound between the
two seas. Mustering his troops, he divided them in
many parts and committed them to their captains.

52.   In quel tempo era in Francia il cardinale
        di Santa Maria in Portico venuto,
        per Leon terzo e pel seggio papale
        contra Lombardi a domandarli aiuto;
        ché mal era tra spada e pastorale,
        e con gran disvantaggio combattuto.
        L'imperator, dunque, il primier stendardo
        che fe' espedir, fu contra il Longobardo.

53.   Era Carlo amator sì de la Chiesa,
        sì d'essa protettor e di sue cose,
        che sempre l'augumento e la difesa,
        sempre l'util di quella al suo prepose:
        però, dopo molt'altre, questa impresa
        nome di Cristianissimo gli pose,
        e dal santo Pastor meritamente
        sacrato imperador fu di Ponente.

54.   Mandò il nipote Orlando, e mandò fanti
        seco, a cavallo e una gran schiera d'archi.
        Subito Orlando a pigliar l'Alpi inanti
        fece ir gli suoi più d'armatura scarchi;
        ma trovar ch'i nemici vigilanti
        avean prima di lor pigliato i varchi,
        e fur constretti d'aspettar il Conte
        con tutto l'altro campo a piè del monte.

55.   Orlando quei da l'armi più leggiere,
        quando pedoni e quando gente equestre,
        cominciò a la sua giunta a far vedere
        or su le manche or su le piagge destre;
        e far fuochi avampar tutte le sere,
        di qua e di là, per quelle cime alpestre;
        e di voler passar mostra ogni segno
        fuor ch'ove di passar forse ha disegno.

52.   At that time the Cardinal of Santa Maria in Portico had arrived in France, to request help against the Lombards for Leo III and the Papal See; [12] for there was conflict between the Sword and the Crozier, [13] and it was being fought with greatly uneven odds. Accordingly, the first standard that the Emperor sent out went to fight against the Lombard King.

53.   Charles was such a lover of the Church, so much a protector of it and of its possessions, that he always put its growth, defense, and profit before his own: therefore, after many campaigns, this present one gave him the title of "Most Christian," and he was deservedly consecrated Emperor of the West by the Holy Pastor.

54.   He sent his nephew Orlando and sent with him infantry and a great troop of archers on horseback. Orlando made the more lightly armed troops go on ahead quickly to take the Alps; but they found that their vigilant enemies had seized the passes before them, and they were forced to wait for the Count with all the rest of the army at the foot of the mountains.

55.   .On his arrival, Orlando began to have his lightly armed troops, both infantry and horse, show themselves on the neighboring slopes, now on the left, now on the right, and to have fires burning every evening here and there on the alpine peaks. And he makes all indications of wanting to pass everywhere, except perhaps at the spot where he really intends to pass.

56.   A Mon Ginevra, al Mon Senese avea,
       e a tutti i monti ove la via più s'usa,
       provisto il Longobardo, e vi tenea
       con fanti e cavallieri ogni via chiusa;
       sopra Saluzzo i monti difendea
       un suo figliuolo, et esso quei di Susa.
       Per tutti questi passi, or basso or alto,
       Orlando movea loro ogni dì assalto.

57.   Spesso fa dar all'armi, e mai non lassa
       l'inimico posar né dì né notte:
       né però l'un su quel de l'altro passa,
       e ben si puon segnar pari le botte.
       Ma sarebb'ita in lungo e forse cassa
       d'effetto sua fatica in quelle grotte,
       se non gli avesse la vittoria in mano
       fatta cader un nuovo caso strano.

58.   Nel campo longobardo un giovane era,
       signor di Villafranca a piè de' monti,
       capitan de li armati alla leggiera,
       che n'avea mille ad ogn'impresa pronti,
       di tanto ardir, d'audacia così fiera,
       che sempre inanzi iva alle prime fronti;
       e sue degne opre non pur fra gli amici,
       ma laude anco trovar da gli nimici.

59.   Era il suo nome Otton da Villafranca,
       di lucid'armi e ricche vesti adorno,
       che la fida moglier, nomata Bianca,
       in ricamar avea speso alcun giorno.
       La destra parte era oro, era la manca
       argento, et anco avean dentro e d'intorno,
       quella d'argento e questa in nodi d'oro,
       le note incomincianti i nomi loro.

56. The Lombard had provided for Monginevro, for
Moncenisio, for all the mountains through which
the customary routes pass, and had closed off
every path there with infantry and knights; one of
his sons defended the mountains above Saluzzo,
and he himself defended those of Susa. Orlando
launched attacks against all these passes, whether
high or low, every day.

57. He often made the enemy sound the call to arms
and never let them rest day or night; still, neither
one gained on the other, and the blows could
easily be scored even. Orlando's toil in those
rocky heights would have gone on a long time
and perhaps ineffectually, had not a strange new
development made the victory fall into his hands.

58. In the Lombard camp there was a young man, the
lord of Villafranca, a town at the foot of the
mountains. A captain of the light troops, he led a
thousand men who were ready for any adventure.
He was of such ardor and such fierce daring that
he always went first in the front lines, and his
worthy deeds found praise, not only among his
friends but among his enemies as well.

59. His name was Ottone da Villafranca, and he
dressed in shining armor and rich vestments which
his faithful wife, named Bianca, had spent many
days embroidering. The right side was gold, and
the left silver, and his initials and hers, one in
braids of silver, the other in gold, were entwined
in the lining and all around.

60. Avea un caval sì snello e sì gagliardo,
    che par non avea al mondo, et era còrso,
    sparso di rosse macchie il col leardo,
    l'un fianco e l'altro, e dal ginocchio al dorso.
    Men sicuro di lui parea e più tardo,
    volga alla china o drizzi all'erta il corso,
    quell'animal che da le balze cozza
    coi duri sassi, e lenta la camozza.

61. Su quel destrier Ottone, or alto or basso
    correndo, era per tutto in un momento,
    quando lanciando un dardo e quando un sasso,
    ché la persona sua ne valea cento.
    Or s'opponeva a questo, or a quel passo;
    né sol valea di forza e d'ardimento,
    ma facea con la lingua e con la fronte
    audaci mille cor, mille man pronte.

62. Poi che Fortuna a quella audacia arriso
    ebbe cinque o sei giorni, entrò in gran sdegno;
    ché pur troppa baldanza l'era aviso
    ch'Otton pigliasse nel suo instabil regno,
    ch'avendo di lontano alcuno ucciso,
    d'entrar nel stuol facesse anco disegno;
    e gli ruppe in un tratto, come vetro,
    ogni speranza di tornar a dietro.

63. Baldovin con molt'altri gli la tolse,
    ch'a un stretto passo il colse per sciagura:
    il cavallo al voltar dietro gli colse
    dove i schinchi e le cosce hanno giuntura;
    sì che lo fe' prigion, volse o non volse,
    quantunque il cavallier senza paura
    non si rendette mai, fra la tempesta
    di mille colpi, fin ch'ebbe elmo in testa.

60. He had a horse so nimble and spirited that his
equal was nowhere in the world; he was a
Corsican, and his grey neck was dappled with red
spots, on both sides, from the knee to the
shoulder. The wild boar charging down the cliffs
and butting its head against their hard rocks seems
less sure-footed and more sluggish than this horse,
when he turns his course down the incline, or
directs it up the slope, and the chamois seems
slower.

61. On that horse Ottone was everywhere in an
instant, coursing now high, now low, sometimes
hurling a spear, sometimes a rock, so that his one
person was worth a hundred. Now he defended
this pass, now that one; and not only was he
worth much in strength and courage, but he made
a thousand hearts brave and a thousand hands
ready with his tongue and his demeanor.

62. After Fortune had smiled on his daring for five or
six days, she became very indignant; for it seemed
to her that Ottone took too many liberties in her
unstable realm when, after having killed a few
men from afar, he now planned to enter into the
thick of things; and in one blow, she shattered like
glass every hope he had of returning home.

63. Baldovino, with many others, took that hope
from him when he caught the unlucky Ottone at
a narrow pass; he struck Ottone's horse where the
shins join the thighs while it was turning around,
and he took him prisoner whether he liked it or
not, even though the fearless knight never yielded
amid the storm of a thousand blows, as long as he
had a helmet on his head.

64. Perduto l'elmo, non fe' più contrasto,
    ma disse: —Io mi vi rendo—; e lasciò il brando,
    molto più del destrier che vedea guasto
    che del maggior suo danno sospirando.
    La presa di quest'uomo venne il basto,
    com'io vi dirò appresso, rassettando,
    sul qual fur poi le gravi some poste
    ch'a Desiderio sì rupper le coste.

65. Lasciato a Villafranca avea la fida,
    casta, bella, gentil, diletta moglie,
    quando di quella schiera si fe' guida,
    seguendo più l'altrui che le sue voglie:
    or restando prigion, n'andar le grida
    là dove più poteano arrecar doglie;
    alla moglie n'andar casta e fedele,
    che mandò al cielo i pianti e le querele.

66. Sparso la Fama avea, com'è sua usanza
    di sempre aggrandir cosa che rapporte,
    che Otton preso e ferito era, non sanza
    grandissimo periglio de la morte.
    Perciò il figliuol del re, ch'avea la stanza
    vicino a lei con parte di sua corte,
    andò per visitarla e trar di pianto,
    se valesse il conforto però tanto.

67. Penticon (ché quel nome avea il figliuolo
    del re de' Longobardi) poi che venne
    a veder la beltà che prima, solo
    conoscendo per fama, minor tenne;
    com'augel ch'entra ne le panie a volo,
    né può dal visco poi ritrar le penne,
    si ritrovò nel cieco laccio preso,
    che nel viso di lei stava ognor teso.

64.   Having lost his helmet, he made no more
       resistance but said, "I surrender to you," and let
       go of his sword, sighing much more for his horse,
       which he saw ruined, than for his own greater
       harm. The capture of this man, as I will tell you
       below in due course, was to become the load that
       afterward broke Desiderius's back.

65.   Ottone had left in Villafranca his faithful, chaste,
       beautiful, noble, and beloved wife when,
       following others' wishes more than his own, he
       made himself head of that brigade; now that he
       was a prisoner, news of it went where it could
       bring the most sorrow: it went to his chaste and
       faithful wife, who sent her cries and lamentations
       up to Heaven.

66.   As is always her custom, Fame exaggerated her
       report and spread word that Ottone had been
       taken wounded and not without the greatest
       danger of death. Accordingly, Desiderius's son,
       who had lodgings next to Ottone's wife, went
       with part of his court to visit and comfort her, if
       any comfort were still to be found.

67.   There Penticone (for the son of the Lombard
       King was called by this name) saw her beauty
       which before, knowing it only by report, he had
       thought much less than it was; like a bird that flies
       into a snare and then cannot withdraw its feathers
       from the lime, he found himself taken in the
       hidden trap which was laid in her face.

68. E dove era venuto a dar conforto,
non si partì che più bisogno n'ebbe.
Dal camin dritto immantinente al torto
voltò il disio, che smisurato crebbe:
or, non che preso, ma che fosse morto
Otton suo amico, intendere vorrebbe:
l'uom che pur dianzi con ragione amava,
contra ragione or mortalmente odiava.

69. Né può d'un mutamento così iniquo
render la causa o far scusa migliore,
che attribuirlo all'ordine che, obliquo
da tutti gli umani ordini, usa Amore;
di cui per legge e per costume antiquo
gli effetti son d'ogn'altro esempio fuore.
Non potea Penticon al disio folle
far resistenza; o se potea, non volle.

70. E lasciandosi tutto in preda a quello,
senza altra escusa e senza altro rispetto,
cominciò a frequentar tanto il castello,
ch'a tutto il mondo dar potea sospetto:
indi fatto più audace, col più bello
modo che seppe, a palesarle il petto,
a pregar, a promettere, a venire
a' mezi onde aver speri il suo desire.

71. La bella donna, che non men pudica
era che bella, e non men saggia e accorta,
prima che farsi oltre il dovere amica
di sì importuno amante, esser vuol morta.
Ma quegli, avegna ch'ella sempre dica
di non voler, però non si sconforta;
et è disposto di far altre prove,
quando il pregar e proferir non giove.

68. And where he had come to give comfort, he left in greater need of being comforted himself. His desire, which grew boundless, turned at once from the straight path to the crooked: now he wished to hear not that his friend Ottone had been captured but that he had been killed: the man that just yesterday he had loved with good reason, now against reason he mortally hated.

69. And he could not find a cause or make a better excuse for such a wicked transformation than to attribute it to the law of Love that is contrary to all human laws: Love, whose workings, by edict and by ancient custom, follow no pattern. Penticone could not resist his mad desire; or if he could, he did not want to.

70. And letting himself fall prey to it completely, without further excuse and without further regard, he began to visit the castle often enough to make the whole world suspicious; then, made bolder, he began to make the feelings of his heart known in the fairest way he knew, to beg, to promise, to find some means by which he might hope to obtain his desire.

71. The beautiful lady, who was no less chaste than lovely and no less wise and shrewd, would rather die than be anything more than a proper friend to such an importunate lover. But, even though she constantly refuses him, he does not despair and is determined to try some other means when his prayers and promises do not work.

72.   Ella conosce ben di non potere
      mantener lungamente la contesa;
      e stando quivi, se non vuol cadere,
      non può, se non da morte, esser difesa.
      Ma questa suol, fra l'aspre, orride e fiere
      condizïon, per ultima esser presa:
      quindi, prima fuggir, e perder prima
      ciò ch'altro ha al mondo, che l'onor, fa stima.

73.   Ma dove può ella andar, ch'ogni cittade
      che tra il mar, l'Alpi e l'Appennino siede,
      del padre de l'amante è in podestade,
      né sicuro per lei luogo ci vede?
      Passar l'Alpi non può, ch'ivi le strade
      chiude la gente, chi a caval, chi a piede:
      non ha il destrier che fe' alle Muse il fonte,
      né il carro in che Medea fuggì Creonte.

74.   Di questo fe' tra sé lungo discorso,
      né mai seppe pigliar util consiglio.
      Ad un suo vecchio al fin ebbe ricorso,
      che amava Otton come signore e figlio.
      Costui s'imaginò tosto il soccorso
      di trar l'afflitta donna di periglio,
      e le propose per segreti calli
      salva ridurla alle città dei Galli.

75.   Stato era cacciator tutta sua vita,
      ma molto più quand'eran gli anni in fiore;
      et avea per quei monti ogni via trita,
      di qua errando e di là, dentro e di fuore.
      Pur che non fosse nel partir sentita,
      la condurrebbe salva al suo signore:
      solo si teme che la prima mossa
      occulta a Penticon esser non possa;

72. She knows very well that she cannot keep up the
     fight for long and that in such a situation, if she
     does not wish to fall, she cannot defend herself
     except by death. But death is usually the last
     recourse to be taken, however bitter, terrible, and
     dire one's predicament; and so she resolves to flee
     first and to lose everything else she has in the
     world before she loses her honor.

73. But where can she go, when every city that stands
     between the sea, the Alps, and the Apennines is in
     the power of her lover's father and there is no safe
     place for her in sight? She cannot cross the Alps
     when troops, some on horseback, some on foot,
     block the passes. She has neither the horse that
     made the Muses' fount nor the chariot in which
     Medea fled Creon.[14]

74. Inwardly she talked this problem out at length,
     but could not find a good solution. Finally she
     had recourse to an aged servant of hers, who loved
     Ottone both as a master and as a son. He soon
     contrived a means to help lead the troubled lady
     out of danger and proposed to conduct her safely
     by secret trails to the cities of the Gauls.

75. He had been a hunter all of his life, but much
     more in the flower of his youth; and he had worn
     out every path through those mountains,
     wandering here and there, inside and out.
     Provided that she were not detected leaving, he
     would lead her safely to her lord: his only fear is
     that their first move cannot be hidden from
     Penticone.

76.   che, non che un dì, ma poche ore interpone
        che non sia seco, e v'ha sempre messaggio.
        Mentre va d'una in altra opinïone
        come abbia a proveder il vecchio saggio,
        vede che lei salvar, e con ragione
        Otton può vendicar di tanto oltraggio,
        portar facendo al folle amante pena
        di quel desir ch'a tanto obbrobrio il mena.

77.   Esorta lei ch'anco duo dì costante
        stia, fin che di là torni ove andar vuole;
        e, come saggia, intanto al sciocco amante
        prometta largamente e dia parole.
        Fatto il pensier, si parte in uno instante
        per una via ch'in uso esser non suole,
        con lunghi avolgimenti, ma assai destra
        quanto creder si può d'una via alpestra.

78.   Tosto arrivò dove occupava il monte
        la gente del figliuol del re Pipino,
        e dimandò voler parlar al Conte;
        ma la guardia il condusse a Baldovino,
        che del campo tenea la prima fronte.
        Costui d'Orlando frate era uterino:
        vuo' dir ch'ambi eran nati d'una madre;
        ma l'un Milon, l'altro avea Gano padre.

79.   Il Maganzese, poi che di costui
        attentamente ebbe il parlar inteso,
        di liberar il signor suo, e per lui
        darli il figliuol del re nimico preso;
        non lasciò che parlasse al Conte, in cui
        di virtù vera era un disio sì acceso,
        che di ciò non seria stato contento,
        ch'aver gli parria odor di tradimento.

76.   For not a whole day goes by, but scarcely a few
      hours, when Penticone isn't with her, and he has
      his messengers there constantly. As the shrewd old
      man considers one plan of action after another, he
      sees that he can both save Bianca and rightfully
      avenge the outrage done to Ottone; he will have
      the foolish lover punished for his shameful desire.

77.   He urges Bianca to remain constant for two more
      days, until he can return from a place he wants to
      visit; and that in the meantime she may, as an
      astute woman, make generous promises to the silly
      lover and give him her word. He made up his
      mind and leaves immediately by an unused path
      that has long twists and turns, but as smooth as
      one can expect of a mountain path.

78.   He soon arrived where the troops of King Pepin's
      son occupied the mountain and expressed his
      desire to speak to the Count; but the guard led
      him to Baldovino, who held the vanguard of the
      army. He was the uterine brother of Orlando,
      which is to say that both were born of a single
      mother, but one had Milone as a father, the other
      Ganelon.

79.   The son of Mainz listened carefully to the old
      man's speech, in which he proposed to have his
      lord freed and in return to hand over the captured
      son of the enemy King. But Baldovino did not let
      him speak to the Count; such desire for true
      virtue burned in Orlando that he would not have
      been happy with this plan, which would have
      reeked to him of treason.

80.   E dubitava non facesse Orlando
      quel che Fabrizio e che Camil già féro,
      che l'uno a Pirro, e l'altro già assediando
      Falisci, in mano i traditor lor diero.
      Finse voler la notte occupar (quando
      la strada avea imparata) un poggio altiero
      che si vedea all'incontro oltre la valle,
      e i nimici assalir dietro alle spalle.

81.   Con volontà d'Orlando, in su la sera
      Baldovin se ne va con buona scorta
      de cavallieri armati alla leggiera,
      e un fante ognun di lor dietro si porta.
      La luna in mezo 'l ciel, che ritond'era,
      vien lor mostrando ogni via dritta e torta:
      appresso a terza, si trovar dal loco
      dove s'hanno a condur lontani poco.

82.   Si fermar quivi, e ricrear alquanto
      sé et i cavalli in una occulta piaggia;
      che seco vettovaglia aveano, quanto
      bastar potea per quella via selvaggia.
      Il vecchio corre alla sua donna intanto,
      e le divisa ciò ch'ordinato aggia.
      A Villafranca Penticon rimena
      il suo desio, che 'l giorno spunta a pena.

83.   La donna, che dal dì che le fu tolto
      il suo marito andò sempre negletta;
      questo, che spera di vederlo sciolto
      e far d'ogni sua ingiuria alta vendetta,
      ritrova i panni allegri, e il crine e 'l volto,
      quanto più sa, per più piacer rassetta;
      e fe' quel dì, quel che non fe' più inante,
      grata accoglienza al poco cauto amante.

80.   Baldovino feared that Orlando might do what
       Fabricius and Camillus had done, who returned
       traitors into enemy hands, the first to Pyrrhus, the
       second to the besieged Falisci.[15] That night (when
       he had learned the way), he feigned a desire to
       occupy a high hill which one could see across the
       other side of the valley and to attack the enemy
       from behind.

81.   With Orlando's consent, Baldovino goes off
       toward evening with a good escort of lightly
       armed knights, each of them bringing a foot
       soldier behind him. The full moon came out in
       the middle of the heavens and showed them every
       straight and turning path; nigh terce they find
       themselves not far from their destination.

82.   They pause there and refresh themselves and their
       horses for a time in a secluded vale, for they had
       brought along sufficient provisions to sustain them
       in those inhospitable parts. The old man,
       meanwhile, hurries to his lady and explains to her
       what he has arranged. When the day has barely
       broken, Penticone's desire leads him back to
       Villafranca.

83.   From the day her husband was taken away from
       her, the lady always neglected her appearance; this
       day, on which she hopes to see him freed and to
       work high vengeance for all her injuries, she puts
       on gay attire again and arranges her hair and face
       to be as pleasing as she knows how; and she did
       this day what she had not done before: she
       graciously welcomed the incautious lover.

84.   E con onesta forza, la mattina,
      e dolci preghi, a mangiar seco il tenne.
      Il vecchio intanto a Baldovin camina,
      ch'al venir ratto aver parve le penne:
      piglia tosto ogni uscita, indi declina
      ove il dì si facea lieto e solenne;
      e quivi, senza poter far difese,
      e Penticone e de' suoi molti prese.

85.   Lasciato avea chi sùbito al fratello
      la vera causa del suo andar narrassi;
      ch'avea per prender Penticon, non quello
      monte occupar, volti la sera i passi;
      sì che per l'orme sue verso il castello
      pregava che col resto il seguitassi.
      Benché non piacque al Conte che tacciuto
      questo gli avesse, pur non negò aiuto:

86.   e con tutti gli altri ordini si mosse,
      senza che tromba o che tambur s'udisse;
      e perché inteso il suo partir non fosse,
      lasciò chi 'l fuoco insino al dì nutrisse.
      La presa del figliuol, non che percosse,
      ma al vecchio padre in modo il cor trafisse,
      che si levò de l'Alpi; e mezza rotta
      salvò a Chivasco et a Vercei la frotta.

87.   Né a Vercei né a Chivasco il paladino
      di voler dar l'assalto ebbe disegno;
      anzi i passi volgea dritto al Ticino,
      alla città che capo era del regno.
      Desiderio, per chiuderli il camino,
      lo va a trovar, ma non gli fa ritegno;
      et è sì inferïor nel gran conflitto,
      che ne riman perpetuamente afflitto.

84. And with chaste insistence and sweet beseeching,
she keeps him there to dine with her that
morning. The old servant, meanwhile, goes to
Baldovino, who came up so swiftly with his forces
that he seemed to have wings; he quickly seizes
every escape route, then he descends to the house
where Bianca and Penticone were passing the day
with merriment and ceremony; and there he
captured Penticone and many of his men, who
were unable to muster a defense.

85. Baldovino had left someone behind who would
promptly tell his brother the real reason for his
going, that he had changed his course that evening
to take Penticone and not to occupy that
mountain; and for this reason he requested that
Orlando follow upon his tracks toward the castle
with the rest of the army. Although it did not
please the Count that Baldovino had hidden this
from him, still he did not deny him help.

86. And he advanced with all the rest of the troops,
without a trumpet or drum to be heard; and so that
his departure might not be noticed, he left behind
people who would feed the campfires until day. The
capture of his son not only wounded but, indeed,
pierced the heart of old Desiderius, who retreated
from the Alps and delivered his army half-broken to
Vercelli and Chivasso.

87. The paladin had no intention of making an attack
on either Vercelli or Chivasso; instead, he turned
his course straight to the Ticino, to the city that
was the capital of the kingdom. Desiderius, to
block his way, goes to meet him but is unable to
hold Orlando off; his defeat in this great battle is
so bad that his power is forever crippled as a result.

88.   Quivi cader de' Longobardi tanti,
        e tanta fu quivi la strage loro,
        che 'l loco de la pugna gli abitanti
        Mortara dapoi sempre nominoro.
        Ma prima che seguir questo più inanti,
        ritornar voglio agli altri gigli d'oro,
        che Carlo ai capitani raccommanda
        ch'alle sue giuste imprese altrove manda.

89.   Con dieci mila fanti e settecento
        lance e duo milla arcier andò Rinaldo
        verso Guascogna, per far mal contento
        di sua perfidia l'Aquitan ribaldo.
        Bradamante e Ruggier, che 'l regimento
        avean del lito esposto al fiato caldo,
        ebbon di fanti non so quanti miglia,
        e legni armati a guardia di Marsiglia.

90.   Come chi guardi il mar, così si pone
        chi a cavallo, chi a piè, che guardi il lito.
        Olivier guardò Fiandra, Salamone
        Bretagna, Picardia Sansone ardito:
        dico per terra; ch'altra provisione,
        altro esercito al mar fu statüito.
        Con grossa armata cura ebbe Ricardo
        da la foce del Reno al Mar Picardo.

91.   E dal Picardo al capo di Bretagna
        avendo uomini e legni in abondanza,
        uscì Carlo col resto alla campagna,
        e venne al Reno, e lo passò a Costanza;
        et arrivò sì presto ne la Magna,
        che la fama al venir poco l'avanza;
        passò il Danubio, e si trovò in Bavera,
        che mosso Tassillone anco non s'era.

88.   So many Lombards fell there and such was their
      slaughter that the inhabitants have called the
      battleground Mortara ever since. But before
      following these events any further, I want to
      return to the other lilies of gold, the standards that
      Charles entrusts to the captains he sends elsewhere
      in his righteous enterprise.

89.   Rinaldo went to Gascony with ten thousand foot
      soldiers, seven hundred lances, and two thousand
      archers to make the scoundrel of Aquitaine sorrow
      for his treason. Bradamante and Ruggiero, who
      were assigned the governorship of the shore that is
      exposed to the hot winds of the south, had I don't
      know how many thousands of foot soldiers and
      armed ships to guard Marseilles.

90.   And just as there are those to guard the sea, so
      others are placed, some on horseback, some on
      foot, to guard the Atlantic coast: Oliviero oversaw
      Flanders; Salamone, Brittany; brave Sansone,
      Picardy. I speak of those on land; other provisions,
      other forces, were established for the sea. With a
      large fleet, Ricardo was in charge from the mouth
      of the Rhine to the Sea of Picardy.

91.   And when he had positioned men and ships in
      abundance from Picardy to the cape of Brittany,
      Charles left to campaign with the rest of his army
      and came to the Rhine and crossed it at Konstanz;
      and he arrived so quickly in Germany that news of
      his coming scarcely preceded him. He crossed the
      Danube and found himself in Bavaria, where
      Tassillone still had not stirred.

159

92. Tassillon, de Boemi e de Sassoni
     esercito aspettando e d'Ungheria,
     alle squadre di Francia e legïoni
     tempo di prevenirli dato avia.
     Carlo fermò ad Augusta i confaloni,
     e mandò all'inimico ambasceria
     a saper se volesse esperïenza
     far di sua forza o pur di sua clemenza.

93. Tassillon, impaurito de la presta
     giunta di Carlo, ch'improviso il colse,
     con tutto il stato se gli diè in podesta,
     e Carlo umanamente lo raccolse;
     ma che rendesse alla prima richiesta
     il tolto a Namo et a' consorti, volse;
     e che lor d'ogni danno et interesse
     ch'avean per questo avuto, sodisfesse;

94. e settecento lance per un anno,
     e dieci mila fanti gli pagasse;
     la qual gente volea ch'allora a danno
     di Desiderio in Lombardia calasse.
     Con gli statichi i Franchi se ne vanno;
     e prima che 'l passaggio altri vietasse
     (ché de' Boemi prossimi avean dubio),
     tornar ne l'altra ripa del Danubio.

95. E verso Praga in tanta fretta andaro,
     di nostra fede a quella età nimica
     (ben che né ancora a questa nostra ho chiaro
     che le sia tutta la contrada amica),
     ch'a prima giunta i varchi le occuparo,
     cacciato e rotto con poca fatica
     re Cardoranno, che mezo in fracasso
     quivi era accorso a divietar il passo.

92.   By waiting for the army of the Bohemians,
       Saxons, and Hungarians, Tassillone had given the
       troops and legions of France time to anticipate
       them. Charles halted the standards at Augsburg
       and sent an embassy to the enemy to find out
       whether he wished to make trial of his force—or,
       rather, of his clemency.

93.   Terrified by Charles's sudden arrival, which took
       him by surprise, Tassillone gave himself and his
       entire state into Charles's power, and Charles
       humanely accepted it; but he first ordered that
       Tassillone return upon request everything he had
       taken from Namo and his associates and that he
       repay with interest every injury they had suffered
       as a result of his actions;

94.   and that he pay to Charles the cost of maintaining
       for one year seven hundred lancers and ten
       thousand foot soldiers; he ordered these troops to
       descend now into Lombardy to help with the
       destruction of Desiderius. The French leave with
       their hostages; and before anyone might prevent
       their crossing (for they feared the nearby
       Bohemians), they return to the other bank of the
       Danube.

95.   And they marched with such haste to Prague,
       which was at that time unfriendly to our faith
       (although I am not certain that the whole country
       is friendly to it even in our time), that at their first
       encounter they occupied the passes and with little
       trouble drove back and routed King Cardorano,
       who had rushed there half in disarray to stop their
       passage.

161

96. Gli Franceschi cacciar fin su le porte
di Praga gli Boemi in fuga e in rotta.
Quella città, di fosse e mura forte,
salvò col suo signor la maggior frotta:
le diè Carlo l'assalto; ma la sorte
al suo disegno mal rispose allotta,
ch'a gran colpi di lance il popul fiero
fe' ritornar la gente de lo Impero.

97. Ché, mentre era difeso et assalito
da un lato il muro, il forte Cardorano
(di cui se si volesse un uom più ardito,
si cercheria forse pel mondo in vano)
fuor d'una porta era d'un altro uscito,
et avea fatto un bel menar di mano;
e dentro, con prigioni e preda molta,
sua gente seco salva avea raccolta.

98. E fe' che Carlo andò più ritenuto
et ebbe miglior guardia alle sue genti,
avendo lor d'un sito proveduto
da porvi più sicuri alloggiamenti,
dove il fiume di Molta è ricevuto
da l'acque d'Albi all'Oceàn correnti:
la barbara cittade in loco sede,
che quinci un fiume e quindi l'altro vede.

99. Tra le due ripe, alla città distanti
un tirar d'arco, s'erano alloggiati,
sì che s'avean la città messa inanti,
che gli altri fiumi avea dietro e dai lati.
Carlo, perché dai luoghi circonstanti
non abbian vettovaglia gli assediati,
e perché il campo suo stia più sicuro,
tra un fiume e l'altro in lungo tirò un muro;

96. The French drove back the Bohemians, who fled
in a rout, right up to the gates of Prague. That
city, fortified with moats and walls, saved the
greater part of the army with its lord: Charles
attacked every day, but chance now responded ill
to his plan, for with heavy blows from their lances,
that fierce people made the troops of the Empire
turn back.

97. For while the walls were being attacked and
defended on one side, the powerful Cardorano
(than whom, if one wanted to find a bolder man,
one would perhaps search in vain throughout the
world) went out through the gate on another side
and made a fine sortie, and he brought his men
safely back inside with him with many prisoners
and much plunder.

98. And he made Charles proceed more cautiously
and keep his troops better protected; Charles
provided them with a site where they could build
a safer encampment, at the place where the River
Moldau is received by the Elbe flowing to the
ocean. The barbarian city overlooked one river on
this side and another on that.

99. They were camped between the two banks, a
bowshot distant from the city, so that they had the
city situated before them, which had the two
rivers behind it and on both sides. To keep the
besieged city from receiving supplies from the
surrounding area and to make his own camp safer,
Charles erected a long wall between the one river
and the other;

100.   che era di fuor di travi e di testura
di grossi legni, e dentro pien di terra;
e perché non uscisson de le mura
dal canto ove la doppia acqua gli serra,
su le ripe di fuor ebbe gran cura
di por ne le bastie genti da guerra,
che con velette e scolte a nissun'ora
lassassino uomo entrar o venir fuora.

101.   Quindi una lega appresso, era una antica
selva di tassi e di fronzuti cerri,
che mai sentito colpo d'inimica
secure non avea né d'altri ferri:
quella mai non potesti fare aprica,
né quando n'apri il dì né quando il serri,
né al solstizio, né al tropico, né mai,
Febo, vi penetrar tuoi chiari rai.

102.   Né mai Dïana, né mai Ninfa alcuna,
né Pane mai, né Satir, né Sileno
si venne a ricrear all'ombra bruna
di questo bosco di spavento pieno;
ma scelerati spirti et importuna
religïon quivi dominio avieno,
dove di sangue uman a Dei non noti
si facean empi sacrifici e voti.

103.   Quivi era fama che Medea, fuggendo
dopo tanti inimici al fin Teseo,
che fu, con modo a ricontarlo orrendo,
quasi ucciso per lei dal padre Egeo;
né più per tutto il mondo loco avendo
ove tornar se non odioso e reo,
in quelle allora inabitate parti
venne, e portò le sue malefiche arti.

100. which was made of beams and interwoven with
heavy logs outside and inside was full of earth; and
to keep the enemy from leaving the city walls on
the side where the waters of both rivers enclosed
it, he was very careful to station men–at–arms in
stockades on the far banks, with lookouts and
sentries who never allowed anyone to enter or go
out.

101. A league away from there was an ancient forest of
yew trees and leafy oaks, which had never felt the
blow of an unfriendly axe or of any other blade:
that forest, Phoebus, you could never make sunny,
not as you opened the day or as you closed it, not
at the winter solstice or at the summer one, nor
could your bright rays ever penetrate there.[16]

102. Nor did Diana, or any Nymph, or Pan, or Satyr,
or Silenus ever come to play in the dark shadow of
this fearful wood; but wicked spirits and ill-starred
superstition had dominion there, where impious
rites and sacrifices of human blood were made to
gods unknown.

103. Here fame reported that Medea, after fleeing so
many other enemies, fled from Theseus, who, at
her instigation, had almost been killed, in a way
horrendous to tell, by his father, Aegeus; having
no other place in the whole world to turn to
except hateful and wicked ones, she came to those
still uninhabited parts and brought along her
maleficent arts.[17]

165

104. So ch'alcun scrive che la via non prese,
quando fuggì dal suo figliastro audace,
verso Boemia, ma andò nel paese
che tra i Caspi e l'Oronte e Ircania giace,
e che 'l nome di Media da lei scese:
il che a negar non serò pertinace;
ma dirò ben ch'anco in Boemia venne
o dopo o allora, e signoria vi tenne;

105. e fece in mezo a questa selva oscura,
dove il sito le parve esser più ameno,
la stanza sua di così grosse mura
che non verria per molti secol meno;
e per potervi star meglio sicura,
di spirti intorno ogn'arbor avea pieno,
che rispingean con morti e con percosse
chi d'ir nei suoi segreti ardito fosse.

106. E perché, per virtù d'erbe e d'incanti,
de le Fate una et immortal fatt'era,
tanto aspettò, che trionfar di quanti
nimici avea vid'al fin Morte fiera:
indi a grand'agio ripensando a tanti
a' quai fatt'avea notte inanzi sera,
all'ingiurie sofferte, affanni e lutto,
vid'esser stato Amor cagion di tutto.

107. E fatta omai per lunga età più saggia
(ché van di par l'esperïenze e gli anni),
pensa per lo avvenir come non caggia
più negli error ch'avea passati, e danni;
e vede, quando Amor poter non v'aggia,
ch'in lei né ancor avran poter gli affanni;
e studia e pensa e fa nuovi consigli,
come di quel tiran fugga gli artigli.

104.   I know that some write that she did not take the
       road to Bohemia when she fled her brave stepson
       but went to the country which lies within the
       Caspian and the Orontes and Hyrcania and which
       took from her the name of Media; I will not be
       stubborn about denying this, but I surely will say
       that she also came to Bohemia, either afterward or
       before, and held dominion there;

105.   and in the middle of this dark wood, at what
       seemed to her the most pleasant site, she built her
       dwelling with such a thick wall that it would not
       decay for many centuries; and in order to feel
       even more secure there, she filled every tree
       around with spirits, to repel with death and blows
       whoever was bold enough to enter its secret
       places.

106.   And because, by the power of herbs and
       enchantments, she had been made one of the
       Fairies and immortal, she waited long enough to
       see cruel Death triumph in the end over whatever
       enemies she had; and there, thinking again at her
       leisure about all those to whom she had made death
       come before their time, and about the injuries she
       herself had suffered, her pains and sorrows, she saw
       that Love had been the cause of it all.

107.   And by now grown wiser with age (because
       experience and years go hand in hand), she
       considers how she might not fall again in the
       future into the errors and wrongs which she has
       undergone; and she perceives that if Love were no
       longer to hold power over her, her suffering
       would also cease; and she ponders and studies and
       makes new plans about how she might escape this
       tyrant's clutches.

108.   Ma perché, essendo de la stirpe antica
        che già la irata Vener maledisse,
        vide che non potea viver pudica,
        et era forza che 'l destin seguisse;
        pensò come d'amor ogni fatica,
        ogni amarezza, ogni dolor fuggisse;
        come gaudi e piacer, quanti vi sono,
        prender potesse, e quanto v'è di buono.

109.   Cagion de la sua pena l'era aviso
        che fosse, com'avea visto l'effetto,
        il tener l'occhio tuttavia pur fiso,
        e l'animo ostinato in uno oggetto;
        ma quando avesse l'amor suo diviso
        fra molti e molti, arderia manco il petto:
        se l'un fosse per trarla in pena e in noia,
        cento serian per ritornarla in gioia.

110.   Di quel paese poi fatta regina,
        che venne a lungo andar pieno e frequente,
        perché ammirando ognun l'alta dottrina
        le facea omaggio volontariamente;
        nuova religïone e disciplina
        instituì, da ogn'altra diferente:
        che, senza nominar marito o moglie,
        tutti empìano sossopra le sue voglie.

111.   E de li dieci giorni aveva usanza
        di ragunarsi il populo gli sei,
        femine e maschi, tutti in una stanza,
        confusamente i nobili e i plebei:
        in questa dimandavan perdonanza
        d'ogni gaudio intermesso agli lor Dei,
        ch'era a guisa d'un tempio fabricata
        di vari marmi, e di molt'oro ornata.

108.   But, because she was of the ancient stock that
        angry Venus once cursed,[18] she saw that she could
        not live chaste and was obliged to follow her
        destiny; she thought of how she might flee all of
        Love's troubles, all of its bitterness and sorrow, and
        how she might have whatever delights and
        pleasures it possesses, whatever there is in Love
        that is good.

109.   Having seen its effects, she decided that the cause
        of her distress was fixing her eyes and mind
        obsessively on a single object; but if she were to
        divide her love among many, her breast would
        burn at a lower flame; if one lover were about to
        drag her into misery and pain, there would be a
        hundred others who would restore her to joy.

110.   She was later made Queen of this land, which
        over time became populous and was much
        frequented, for everyone did homage to her
        voluntarily, in admiration of her high learning.
        She instituted a new religion and rule, different
        from any other, in which everyone might satisfy
        their desires without restraint, and without taking
        the name of husband or wife.

111.   And six days out of ten she had the custom of
        bringing all her people together in a mass, males
        and females, nobles and commoners, in one room;
        in this place, which was like a temple made of
        various marbles and decorated with much gold,
        they asked their gods to pardon them for every
        pleasure they had deferred.

112.   Finita l'orazion, facean due stuoli,
         da un lato l'un, da l'altro l'altro sesso;
         indi levati i lumi, a corsi e a voli
         venian al nefandissimo complesso;
         e meschiarsi le madri coi figliuoli,
         con le sorelle i frati accadea spesso:
         e quella usanza, ch'ebbe inizio allora,
         tra gli Boemi par che duri ancora.

113.   Deh! perché quando, o figlia del re Oeta,
         o d'Atene o di Media tu fuggisti,
         deh! perché a far l'Italia nostra lieta
         con sì gioconda usanza non venisti?
         Ogni mente per te seria quïeta,
         senza cordoglio e senza pensier tristi;
         e quella gelosia che sì tormenta
         gli nostri cor, serìa cacciata e spenta.

114.   Oh come, donne, miglior parte avreste
         d'un dolce, almo piacer, che non avete!
         Dove voi digiunate, e senza feste
         fate vigilie in molta fame e sete,
         tal satolle e sì fatte prendereste,
         che grasse vi vedrei più che non sete.
         Ma bene io stolto a porre in voi desire
         da farvi, per gir là, da noi fuggire!

115.   Visse più d'una età leggiadra e bella,
         regina di quei populi, Medea;
         ch'ad ogni suo piacer si rinovella,
         e da sé caccia ogni vecchiezza rea;
         e questo per virtù d'un bagno ch'ella
         per incanto nel bosco fatto avea;
         al qual, perché nissun altro s'accosti,
         avea mille demoni a guardia posti.

112.   Having finished their prayer, they formed two
        groups, one sex on one side, the other on the
        other; then they put out the lights and came
        together racing and flying into the most
        unspeakable embraces, and it often happened that
        mothers mingled with sons and brothers with
        sisters; and it seems that this custom, which had its
        beginning then, still goes on among the
        Bohemians.

113.   Alas! Aetes's daughter, why, when you fled from
        either Athens or from Media, why, oh why, did
        you not come to gladden our Italy with so merry
        a custom? Because of you, every mind would be
        tranquil, free of heartache and mournful thoughts;
        and that jealousy which so torments our hearts
        would be dispelled and extinguished.

114.   Oh ladies, how much better a portion of sweet,
        dear pleasure would you have then! Whereas now
        you fast and without feast days you keep vigils in
        great hunger and thirst, then you would take such
        full meals, so well prepared, that you would see
        yourselves plumper than you are now. But I am
        stupid indeed to instill desires in you that will
        make you flee from us to go there!

115.   Medea lived happy and beautiful as Queen of
        those people for more than an eon; for she
        rejuvenates herself when she wishes and banishes
        from herself every wicked sign of old age; and this
        by virtue of a bath which she had made by
        enchantment in the forest, around which she had
        put a thousand demons as a guard, so that nobody
        else might approach.

116.   Questa fata del populo boemme
    ebbe per tanti secoli governo,
    che 'l tempo si potria segnar con l'emme,
    e quasi credea ognun che fosse eterno:
    ma poi che a partorir in Bettelemme
    Maria venne il figliuol del Re superno;
    quivi regnare non poté, o non volse,
    e di vista degli uomini si tolse.

117.   E ne l'antiqua selva, fra la torma
    de li demoni suoi tornò a celarsi,
    dove ogni ottavo dì sua bella forma
    in bruttissima serpe avea a mutarsi.
    Per questa opinïon, vestigio et orma
    di piede uman nissun potea trovarsi
    inanzi a questo dì di ch'io vi parlo,
    che l'aurea fiamma alzò in Boemia Carlo.

118.   L'imperador commanda che dal piede
    taglin le piante a lor bisogno et uso:
    l'esercito non osa, perché crede,
    da lunga fama e vano error deluso,
    che chi ferro alza incontra il bosco, fiede
    sé stesso e more, e ne l'inferno giuso
    visibilmente in carne e in ossa è tratto,
    o resta cieco o spiritato o attratto.

119.   Carlo, fatta cantar una solenne
    messa da l'arcivescovo Turpino,
    entra nel bosco, et alza una bipenne,
    e ne percuote un olmo più vicino:
    l'arbor, che tanta forza non sostenne,
    ché Carlo un colpo fe' da paladino,
    cadde in duo tronchi, come fu percosso;
    e sette palmi era d'intorno grosso!

116.   This Fairy governed the Bohemian people for so
       many centuries that one could mark the time with
       an "M"[19] and nearly everyone believed her reign
       to be eternal; but when Mary came to Bethlehem
       to give birth to the son of the King on High, she
       could no longer rule there, or she did not want to,
       and she removed herself from the sight of men.

117.   And she returned to hide in the ancient wood,
       among the throng of her demons, where once
       every week she had to change her beautiful shape
       into a very ugly serpent.[20] Because of her reported
       presence, no man set foot in that place until the
       day I am telling you about, when Charles raised
       the Oriflamme in Bohemia.[21]

118.   The Emperor commands his men to cut down the
       trees at their base for their need and use; the army
       does not dare because, deluded by old stories and
       foolish error, it believes that any man who raises
       his blade against that forest will strike himself and
       die and be dragged downward, visibly in his flesh
       and bone, to Hell, or be left blind or possessed by
       demons or paralyzed.

119.   Charles, having had a solemn mass sung by
       Archbishop Turpin, goes into the forest, lifts a
       double-edged axe, and strikes the nearest elm
       with it: the tree, which could not resist so much
       force, because Charles struck a blow worthy of a
       paladin, fell cut in two as it was struck; and it was
       seven palms thick!

120. Chi si ricorda il dì di san Giovanni,
     che sotto Ercole o Borso era sì allegro?
     che poi veduto non abbian molt'anni,
     come né ancora altro piacere integro,
     di poi che cominciar gli assidui affanni
     dei quali è in tutta Italia ogni core egro:
     parlo del dì che si facea contesa
     di saettar dinanzi alla sua chiesa.

121. Quel dì inanzi alla chiesa del Battista
     si ponean tutti i sagittari in schiera;
     né colpo uscia fin ch'al bersaglio vista
     la saetta del principe non era;
     poi con la nobiltà la plebe mista
     l'aria di frecce a gara facea nera:
     così ferito ch'ebbe il bosco Carlo,
     fu presto tutto il campo a seguitarlo.

122. Sotto il continuo suon di mille accette
     trema la terra, e par che 'l ciel ribombi;
     or quella pianta or questa in terra mette
     il capo, e rompe all'altre braccia e lombi.
     Fuggon da' nidi lor guffi e civette,
     che vi son più che tortore o colombi;
     e, con le code fra le gambe, i lupi
     lascian l'antiche insidie e i lochi cupi.

123. Per la molta bontà ch'era in effetto
     e vera in Carlo, non mendace e finta,
     fu sì la forza al diavol maladetto
     da l'aiuto di Dio quivi rispinta,
     ch'a lui non nocque, né, per suo rispetto,
     a chi s'avea per lui la spada cinta:
     sì che mal grado de l'inferno tutto
     alli demoni il nido era distrutto.

120.   Who remembers the feast day of Saint John,
which under Ercole and Borso was so merry?[22]
They have not seen it for many years, or any other
unmitigated pleasure either, since the unremitting
afflictions began from which every heart in Italy is
sick: I speak of the day on which they used to
have an archery contest in front of the church.

121.   On that day, before the Church of the Baptist, all
the archers lined up in a group; and no shot left
before the Prince's own arrow was seen in the
target; then the common people, mixed together
with the nobility, blackened the air with their
arrows in competition: in the same way, once
Charles had struck the forest, the whole camp was
ready to follow his example.

122.   The earth trembles under the continuous sound of
a thousand hatchets, and the heavens seem to
echo; first that tree, then this one, drops headlong
to earth and breaks the arms and limbs of others as
it falls. Hoot owls and screech owls, which are
more numerous there than turtledoves or pigeons,
flee from their nests, and wolves, with their tails
between their legs, abandon their ancient coverts
and dark lairs.

123.   Through Charles's great goodness, which in his
case was real and genuine, not feigned and lying,
the power of the cursed Devil was defeated there
with the help of God: it could injure neither him
nor any of the soldiers who girded sword for his
sake; and in spite of Hell, the demons' nest was
destroyed.

124.   Un fremito, qual suol da l'irate onde
         del tempestoso mar venir a' lidi,
         cotal si udì fra le turbate fronde,
         meschio di pianti e spaventosi gridi;
         indi un vento per l'aria si difonde
         che ben appar che Belzebù lo guidi:
         ma né per questo avvien ch'al saldo e fermo
         valor di Carlo abbia la selva schermo.

125.   Cade l'eccelso pin, cade il funebre
         cipresso, cade il venenoso tasso,
         cade l'olmo atto a riparar che l'ebre
         viti non giaccian sempre a capo basso;
         cadono, e fan cadendo le latebre
         cedere agli occhi et alle gambe il passo:
         piangon sopra le mura i Pagan stolti,
         vedendo alli lor Dei gli seggi tolti.

126.   Alcun dentro ne gode, ché n'aspetta
         di veder sopra a Carlo e tutti i Franchi
         scender dal ciel così dura vendetta
         ch'a sepelirli il populo si stanchi.
         Com'è troncato un arbore, si getta
         nel fiume ch'alla selva bagna i fianchi;
         e quello, ubidïente, ai corni sopra
         lo porta al loco ov'è poi messo in opra.

127.   In questo tempo avea l'iniquo Gano,
         per dar a Carlo in ogni parte briga,
         composto il re d'Arabia e il Sorïano
         col Calife d'Egitto in una liga;
         e dopo il colpo, per celar la mano,
         in guisa d'uom che conscïenza instiga,
         per voto a cui già s'obligasse inanti,
         era andato al Sepolcro, ai Luoghi santi.

124. A roaring was heard throughout the shaking branches, like that which comes from the angry waves of a stormy sea upon the shore, mixed with wails and fearful screams; then a wind, which truly seemed to be sent by Beelzebub, blows through the air: but not even this could defend the wood against Charles's firm and steadfast valor.

125. The lofty pine falls, the mournful cypress falls, the poisonous yew falls, the elm falls, good for supporting drunken vines. They fall and in falling open up hidden recesses to the eyes and pathways for the feet: the foolish Pagans lament upon their city walls, seeing the seats of their gods taken away.

126. Some within the city rejoice at it, because they expect to see so dire a vengeance descend from Heaven upon Charles and the French that the people will grow weary of burying them. As a tree is cut down, it is thrown into the river that bathes the flanks of the forest; and the river obediently carries it on its branching streams to the place where it is put to work.

127. Meanwhile, in order to give Charles trouble in every region, the villainous Ganelon had bound the Kings of Arabia and Syria in a league with the Caliph of Egypt; and, after striking this blow, to hide his hand in it he had gone to the Sepulcher, to the Holy Land, in the manner of a man whose conscience pricks him because of a vow to which he had formerly bound himself.

128.   Quivi da Sansonetto ricevuto,
        che da Carlo in governo avea la terra,
        era stato alcun giorno, e poi venuto
        verso Costantinopoli per terra;
        dove certa notizia avendo avuto
        di Carlo che in Boemia facea guerra,
        s'era voltato, per la dritta via
        di Servia e di Belgrado, in Ungheria.

129.   Ritrovò, essendo già Filippo morto,
        aver il regno un figlio d'Otacchiero,
        che come l'avol dritto, così ei torto
        ebbe l'animo sempre da lo Impero.
        Gano gli venne in tempo a dar conforto,
        ch'era pel re di Francia in gran pensiero,
        del qual nimico discoperto s'era
        per la causa del duca di Baviera:

130.   e molto si dolea di Tassillone
        ch'avesse senza lui fatta la pace,
        di che il Boemme e l'Ungaro e il Sassone
        restava in preda alla francesca face.
        Avea d'aiutar Praga intenzïone,
        ma de lo assunto si vedea incapace:
        impossibil gli par che in così breve
        tempo far possa quel ch'in ciò far deve.

131.   Ma se lo assedio si potea produrre,
        se potea andar in lungo ancora un mese,
        tanta gente era certo di condurre,
        oltre il soccorso che daria il paese,
        che i gigli d'or ne le bandiere azzurre
        quivi restar faria con l'altro arnese:
        ma s'ora andasse, non farebbe effetto
        se non d'attizzar Carlo a più dispetto.

128.   He was received there by Sansonetto, who had
       been assigned the governorship of the land by
       Charles, and spent some days there before he went
       by land to Constantinople. There, having received
       authoritative reports that Charles was waging war
       in Bohemia, he turned back, by the direct route
       through Serbia and Belgrade, toward Hungary.

129.   He found, now that King Philip was dead, a son
       of Ottachiero reigning there who opposed the
       Empire as much as his grandfather had supported
       it. Ganelon came at a good time to give him
       comfort, for he was very worried about the King
       of France, whose enemy he had openly declared
       himself to be in the cause of the Duke of Bavaria;

130.   He complained much of Tassillone, who had
       made a treaty without him by which the
       Bohemian, the Hungarian, and the Saxon now
       became fodder for the French torch. He had
       intended to help Prague but considered himself
       incapable of the undertaking: it seemed to him
       impossible that he would be able to do what the
       situation called for in such a short time.

131.   But if the siege could be prolonged, if it could go
       on still another month, he was sure he could add
       so many men to the forces the city itself would
       provide that they would strew the field with the
       azure flags and the lilies of gold and the other
       baggage of the routed French; but if he went now,
       he would accomplish nothing except arouse
       Charles's greater wrath.

132.   Gano promesse che farebbe ogn'opra
        che Praga ancor un mese si terrebbe;
        e poi che molto han ragionato sopra
        quanto far ciascun d'essi in questo debbe,
        parte Gano da Buda, e tra via adopra
        lo 'ngegno che molt'atto a tradire ebbe:
        va da Strigonia in Austria, indi si tiene
        a destra mano et in Boemia viene.

133.   Il peregrino di Gerusalemme,
        con quanti avea condotti a' suoi servigi,
        umilmente, senza oro e senza gemme
        ma di panni vestiti grossi e bigi,
        nel campo tolto al popolo boemme
        baciò la mano al buon re di Parigi,
        ch'avendolo raccolto ne le braccia,
        di qua e di là gli ribaciò la faccia.

134.   Era inclinato di natura molto
        a Gano Carlo, e ne facea gran stima,
        e poche cose fatte avria, che tolto
        il suo consiglio non avesse prima;
        com'ogni signor quasi in questo è stolto,
        che lascia il buono et il piggior sublima;
        né, se non fuor del stato, o dato in preda
        degli inimici, par che 'l suo error veda.

135.   Per non saper dal finto il vero amico
        scernere, in tal error misero incorre.
        Di questo vi potrei, ch'ora vi dico,
        più d'un esempio inanzi agli occhi porre;
        e senza ritornar al tempo antico,
        n'avrei più d'uno a nostra età da tòrre:
        ma se più verso a questo Canto giungo,
        temo vi offenda il suo troppo esser lungo.

132. Ganelon promised he would do everything he could so that Prague would hold out another month; and after they have discussed at length how much each of them has to do, Ganelon leaves Budapest, and along the way he employs his apt talent for treason to think up a plan: he goes from Esztergom into Austria, then keeps to his right hand and arrives in Bohemia.

133. The pilgrim from Jerusalem, with those servants he had brought with him, humbly, without gold and without gems but clothed in coarse, gray habits, came to the camp Charles had taken from the Bohemian army and kissed the hand of the good King of Paris, who welcomed him into his arms and returned his kiss here and there upon his face.

134. Charles was by nature very well disposed toward Ganelon and esteemed him highly, and there were not many things that he would do without first asking Ganelon's advice; Charles acted like a fool in this regard, as do almost all lords: they neglect the good man and exalt the worst; nor does it appear that they will ever perceive their mistake unless they are banished from their states or given into the hands of their enemies.

135. The wretched King falls into this error by not being able to tell the true friend from the false. I could show you more than one example of what I am describing to you now; and I could take more than one from our own age, without going back to older times: but, I fear, if I add more verses to this Canto, you might be offended by its being too long.

Canto Terzo

1. D' OGNI DESIR CHE tolga nostra mente
    dal dritto corso et a traverso mande,
    non credo che si trovi il più possente
    né il più commun di quel de l'esser grande:
    brama ognun d'esser primo, e molta gente
    aver dietro e da lato, a cui commande;
    né mai gli par che tanto gli altri avanzi,
    che non disegni ancor salir più inanzi.

2. Se questa voglia in buona mente cade
    (ch'in buona mente ha forza anco il desire),
    l'uom studia che virtù gli apra le strade,
    che sia guida e compagna al suo salire:
    ma se cade in ria mente (ché son rade
    che dir buone possiam senza mentire),
    indi aspettar calunnie, insidie e morte,
    et ogni mal si può di piggior sorte.

3. Gano, non gli bastando che maggiore
    non avea alcuno in corte, eccetto Carlo,
    era tanto insolente, che minore
    lui vorria ancora, e avea disio di farlo;
    et or che sopranatural favore
    si sentia da colei che potea darlo,
    oltra il desir avea speme e disegno
    fra pochi giorni d'occupargli il regno.

Canto 3

1. OF ALL THE DESIRES that turn our minds from the right path and send it astray, I do not believe there is any more powerful or more common than the desire for greatness. Every man hungers to be first and to have many others behind and beside him at his command; nor does he ever feel that he is far enough ahead of the rest that he stops scheming to climb still farther beyond them.

2. If this desire occurs in a good mind (for it does have power over good minds as well as bad), a man studies how virtue may open paths for him, how it may be the guide and companion to his ascent; but if it occurs in a wicked mind (for those we can honestly call good are rare), then one can expect calumnies, betrayals, and death and every evil of the worst sort.

3. Not satisfied that he had no one greater than himself at court except Charles, Ganelon was insolent enough to want Charles his inferior, too, and desired to make him so; and now that he enjoyed the supernatural favor of one who had such gifts within her power,[1] he had, in addition to his desire, hopes and plans to occupy the throne in a few days.

4. E pur che fosse il suo desir successo,
    non saria dal fellon, senza rispetto
    che tra gli primi suoi baroni messo
    Carlo l'avea di luogo infimo e abietto,
    stato ferro né tòsco pretermesso,
    né scelerato alcun fatto né detto;
    e mille al giorno, non che un tradimento,
    ordito avria per conseguir suo intento.

5. Carlo tutto il successo de la guerra
    narrò senza sospetto al Maganzese,
    e gli mostrò ch'avria in poter la terra
    prima ch'a mezo ancor fosse quel mese.
    Questo nel petto il traditor non serra,
    ma tosto a Cardoran lo fa palese;
    e per un suo gli manda a dar consiglio
    come possa schifar tanto periglio.

6. Da quella volpe il re boeme instrutto,
    mandò un araldo in campo l'altro giorno,
    che così disse a Carlo, essendo tutto
    corso ad udir il populo d'intorno:
    —Il mio signor, da la tua fama indutto,
    o imperador d'ogni virtute adorno,
    per crudeltà non pensa né avarizia
    ch'abbi raccolto qui tanta milizia;

7. né che tu metta il fin di tua vittoria
    in averli la vita o il stato tolto,
    ma solo in aver vinto; ché tal gloria
    più che sua morte o che 'l suo aver val molto
    acciò che il nome tuo ne la memoria
    del mondo viva e mai non sia sepolto:
    ché contra ogni ragion saresti degno,
    come tu sei, se fessi altro disegno.

4. And, as long as it accomplished his desire, the villain would not forgo sword or poison, or any wicked deed or word; nor was he deterred by the fact that Charles had raised him from a base and abject estate to a position among his foremost barons; to pursue his intent, he would have plotted not just one but a thousand treasons every day.

5. Suspecting nothing, Charles innocently recounted to the Count of Mainz every event in the war and showed him that he could take possession of Prague before less than half that month had passed. The traitor does not lock this in his heart but quickly discloses it to Cardorano, sending a servant with advice on how to escape the imminent peril.

6. Instructed by that fox, the Bohemian King sent a herald to the camp the next day, who, with the whole army gathered about to listen, spoke to Charles thus: "Persuaded by your fame, O Emperor adorned with every virtue, my master does not imagine that you have gathered this great army here through cruelty or avarice;

7. "or that you make the goal of your victory depriving him of his life or state rather than simply conquering him; for the glory of conquest is far more valuable than his death or possessions: through it your name may live in the world's memory and never be interred. If you had other intentions, you would be held praiseworthy, as you are, against all reason.

8. Ma tu non guardi forse che l'effetto
    tutto contrario appar a quel che brami:
    tu brami d'esser glorïoso detto,
    e con l'effetto tuttavia t'infami.
    Che tu sia entrato nel nostro distretto
    con cento mille armati, gloria chiami;
    ma quanto ella sia grande estimar déi,
    che noi siamo a fatica un contra sei.

9. Milziade e Temistocle converse
    a parlar in suo onor tutte le genti,
    perché con pochi armati, questi Xerse,
    quel vinse Dario, in terra e in mar possenti.
    Vincer pochi con molti, mai tenerse
    non sentisti fra l'opere eccellenti.
    S'in te è valor, pon giù il vantaggio, e poi
    vien alla prova, e vincine, se puoi.

10. Da sol a sol la pugna t'offerisce,
    da dieci a dieci, o voi da cento a cento,
    il mio signor; e accresce e minuisce,
    secondo che accettar tu sei contento:
    con patto che se Dio lui favorisce,
    sì che tu resti vinto o preso o spento,
    che tu gli abbi a rifar e danni e spese,
    e tornar col tuo campo in tuo paese;

11. né chi la Francia e chi l'Imperio regge
    fino a cento anni lo guerreggi mai:
    ma se tu vinci lui, torrà ogni legge
    ch'imporre a senno tuo tu gli vorrai.
    Il buon pastor pon l'anima pel gregge:
    essendo tu quel re di che fama hai,
    la tua persona o di pochi altri arrisca,
    acciò così gran popul non perisca.—

8. "But perhaps you do not see how the outcome appears in every way contrary to your desires: you may want to be called glorious, but you are dishonored nevertheless. You call it glory to have invaded our territory with a hundred thousand soldiers, but you should consider just how great a deed this is when we are scarcely one against six.

9. "Miltiades and Themistocles induced all men to speak in their honor because, with a few men, the latter conquered Xerxes, the former Darius, both of whom were powerful on land and sea.[2] You never heard that conquering a few with many was considered among excellent deeds. So, if there is valor in you, put aside advantage and then come to the test, and win it if you can.

10. "My lord offers you combat one against one, ten against ten, or if you wish, a hundred against a hundred; he makes the number larger or smaller according to your pleasure with the agreement that, if God favors him and you should be beaten, taken, or killed, you will restore to him his damages and expenses and return with your army to your country;

11. "and that whoever may rule France and the Empire will never wage war on him for a hundred years. But if you conquer him, he will accept every law your good judgment may impose on him. The good shepherd lays down his life for his flock; if you are the kind of king your fame reports you to be, risk your own person, or that of a few others, so that many need not die."

12. Così disse lo araldo, né risposta
     lo imperador gli diede allora alcuna;
     ma da la moltitudine si scosta
     e i consiglieri suoi seco raguna,
     ché lor sentenzie sopra la proposta
     de l'araldo udir vuol ad una ad una.
     Il primo fu Turpin che consigliasse
     che l'invito del Barbaro accettasse,

13. non già da sol a sol, ma in compagnia
     di quattro o sei de' suoi guerrier più forti;
     dei quali egli esser uno si offeria.
     Così Namo et Uggier par che conforti;
     e che fra dieci dì la pugna sia,
     o quanto può che 'l termine più scorti:
     perché, successo che lor sia ben questo,
     possano volger poi l'animo al resto.

14. Era in quei cavallier tanta arroganza
     pei fortunati antichi lor successi,
     che tutti in quella impresa, con baldanza
     di restar vincitor, si sarian messi.
     Poi disse il suo parer quel di Maganza,
     che la pugna accettar pur si dovessi;
     ma non però venir a farla inante
     che Rinaldo ci fosse o quel d'Anglante;

15. che ci fosse Olivier con ambi i figli,
     Ruggier et alcun altro dei famosi:
     ché quando senza questi ella si pigli,
     fòran di Carlo i casi perigliosi.
     —Tenete voi sì privi di consigli
     gli inimici,—dicea—che fosser osi
     di domandar a par a par battaglia,
     se non han gente ch'al contrasto vaglia?

12. So spoke the herald, and the Emperor gave him
    no response at all at first, but took himself away
    from the crowd and gathered his counselors
    together with him because he wanted to hear their
    opinions of the herald's proposals one by one. The
    first was Archbishop Turpin, who advised him to
    accept the Barbarian's invitation;

13. Not, however, just one against one, but in the
    company of four or six of his strongest fighters; as
    one of these he would offer himself. Namo and
    Uggiero seem to counsel the same thing and that
    the battle should be within ten days, or that the
    date should be brought as near as possible, because
    once this turned out well for them, they could
    then turn their minds to other fronts.

14. These knights were so arrogant because of their
    past success and good fortune that they all would
    have joined in this enterprise, confident of victory.
    Then the Count of Mainz spoke his mind,
    advising that the challenge be accepted, yes, but
    by no means held before Rinaldo or the knight of
    Anglant[3] were there;

15. before Oliviero were there with both of his sons,[4]
    and Ruggiero or another one of those famous
    knights: for if it were undertaken without these
    men, Charles's situation would be perilous. "Do
    you take your enemies to be so short of wisdom,"
    he said, "that they would dare to request a battle
    at equal strength unless they had people worthy of
    the contest?

16. Se non ci intervenisse la corona
     di Francia, non avrei tanti riguardi;
     benché, né senza ancor, di scelta buona
     si de' mancar in tòrre i più gagliardi:
     ma dovendo venirci il re in persona,
     come a bastanza potremo esser tardi
     a darli, con consiglio ben maturo,
     compagnia con la qual sia più sicuro?

17. Io non vi contradico che valenti
     cavallier qui non sian come coloro
     che nominati v'ho per eccellenti;
     ma non sappiàn così le prove loro.
     Questo luogo non è da esperimenti
     di chi sia, al paragon, di rame o d'oro:
     vogliàn di quei che cento volte esperti,
     de la virtute lor n'han fatti certi.—

18. E seguitò mostrando, con ragioni
     di più efficacia ch'io non so ridire,
     che non doveano senza i dui campioni,
     lumi di Francia, a tal pruova venire;
     e la sua vinse l'altre opinïoni,
     che la pugna si avesse a diferire
     fin che venisse a così gran bisogna
     l'uno d'Italia e l'altro di Guascogna.

19. Queste parole et altre dicea Gano
     per carità non già del suo signore;
     ma di vietar che non gli andasse in mano
     quella città studiava il traditore,
     e tanto prolungar, che Cardorano
     l'aiuto avesse che attendea di fuore;
     in somma, il suo parer parve perfetto,
     e fu per lo miglior di tutto eletto.

16. "If the crown of France were not taking part here,
I would not be so concerned; even without his
presence, one should not forgo a good selection of
men from whom to choose the most valiant. But
because the King is going to be there in person,
how can we be too deliberate in providing for
him, after full and mature consideration, the
company in which he will be safest?

17. "I do not deny there may be knights here as
worthy as those I have just called excellent before
you; but we do not know their mettle so well.
This is no place for discovering who, at the
touchstone, may be copper or gold: let us look to
those who, put to the proof a hundred times, have
made us certain of their valor."

18. And he continued, showing with reasons more
compelling than I know how to retell, that they
should not come to this test without those two
champions who were the lights of France; and his
opinion—that the battle would have to be
deferred until, at so critical a need, the one could
come from Italy, the other from Gascony—
vanquished all the others.

19. Ganelon spoke these words and others not, of
course, out of love for his lord; the traitor was
working to prevent the city from falling into
Charles's hands and to delay long enough to
enable Cardorano to have the assistance that he
awaited from outside: in the end, his opinion
seemed perfect and was chosen as the best of all.

20.   Che dieci guerrier fossero, si prese
        conclusïon, pur come Gano volse;
        e da' dieci di maggio al fin del mese
        di giugno un lungo termine si tolse.
        In questo mezo si levar le offese,
        e quello assedio tanto si disciolse,
        che Praga potea aver di molte cose
        che fossino alla vita bisognose.

21.   Nuove intanto venian de l'apparecchio
        che l'Ungaro facea d'armata grossa;
        ma sempre Gano a Carlo era all'orecchio,
        che dicea: —Non temer che faccia mossa.—
        Io lessi già in un libro molto vecchio,
        né l'auttor par che sovvenir mi possa,
        ch'Alcina a Gano un'erba al partir diede,
        che chi ne mangia fa ch'ognun gli crede.

22.   Quella mostrò nel monte Sina Dio
        a Moise suo, sì che con essa poi
        il popul duro fece umile e pio,
        e ubidïente alli precetti suoi.
        Poi la mostrò il demonio a Macon rio,
        a perdizion degli Afri e degli Eoi:
        la tenea in bocca predicando, e valse
        ritrar chi udiva alle sue leggi false.

23.   Gano, avendo già in ordine l'orsoio,
        di sì gran tela apparecchiò la trama;
        e quel demon che d'uno in altro coio
        si sa mutar, a sé da l'anel chiama.
        —Vertunno,—disse—di disir mi moio
        di fornir quel che da me Alcina brama;
        e pensando la via, veggio esser forza
        che d'alcun ch'io dirò tu pigli scorza.—

20. It was decided that there would be ten warriors, just as Ganelon wished, and a long interim was established from the tenth of May to the end of the month of June. In this period hostilities were suspended and the siege was loosened enough to allow Prague again to obtain many of the things that were necessary for its life.

21. Meanwhile, news arrived that the Hungarian was preparing a huge army, but Ganelon was always at Charles's ear, saying, "Don't be afraid; he won't make a move." I read once in a very old book, although I can't seem to remember the author, that Alcina gave Ganelon an herb when he left her which made whoever ate it believed by all.

22. God showed this herb to Moses on Mount Sinai, whereupon, by its power, he made his stubborn people humble and pious and obedient to his commandments. Then the devil showed it to wicked Mohammed, to the perdition of Africans and Orientals; he held it in his mouth while preaching and it worked to draw whoever heard him to his false laws.

23. Having already set the threads in the warp, Ganelon prepared the woof of the plot he was weaving and summoned from his ring that devil who knew how to change himself from one skin to another. "Vertumnus," he said, "I am dying from the desire to give Alcina what she wants from me, and, considering how we best may go about it, I see that you must take the outward appearance of some people I will describe to you."

24.   E le parole seguitò, mostrando
    che tramutar s'avea prima in Terigi:
    Terigi che scudiero era d'Orlando,
    venuto da fanciul ai suo' servigi;
    e dopo in altre facce, e seminando
    dovea gir sempre scandali e litigi.
    Presa che di Terigi ebbe la forma,
    di quanto avesse a far tolse la norma.

25.   Di sua mano le lettere si scrisse
    credenzïal, come dettolli Gano;
    che, con stupor vedendole, poi disse
    Orlando, e Carlo, ch'eran di sua mano.
    Postole il sigil sopra, dipartisse
    Vertunno, e col signor di Mont'Albano,
    ch'era a campo a Morlante, ritrovosse
    prima che giunto al fin quel giorno fosse.

26.   Presso a Morlante avea Rinaldo, e sotto
    il vicin monte, avuto aspra battaglia;
    et in essa lo esercito avea rotto
    de li nimici, e morto e messo a taglia.
    Unuldo ne la terra era ridotto,
    e Rinaldo gli avea fatto serraglia,
    pien di speranza, in uno assalto o dui,
    d'aver in suo poter la terra e lui.

27.   Veduto il viso et il parlar udito,
    che di Terigi avean chiara sembianza,
    Rinaldo fa carezze in infinito
    al messaggier del conte di Maganza:
    che sia d'Orlando, e quello avea sentito
    per fama, gli dimanda con instanza;
    come abbia a piè de l'Alpi, et indi appresso
    Vercelli, in fuga il Longobardo messo.

24. And he followed these words, describing how
Vertumnus first had to transform himself into
Terigi, who was Orlando's squire and who had
come into his service as a little boy. Afterward,
taking other guises, he was to go about sowing
scandals and disputes everywhere he went. When
he had taken Terigi's form, Vertumnus received
instructions for all he had to do.

25. With his own hand he wrote himself credentials,
as Ganelon dictated them to him, which afterward
Orlando and Charles, looking on them in
amazement, said were written in their own hands.
Vertumnus sealed them and departed and, before
he had come to the end of that day, he found
himself with the lord of Montauban, who was
camped at Morlaas.[5]

26. Rinaldo had fought a fierce battle near Morlaas
and under the neighboring mountain where he
had routed the army of his enemies, slaughtering
some, capturing others for ransom. Unuldo had
been forced back to his castle, and Rinaldo had
him cornered and was hopeful of taking him and
the castle in another assault or two.

27. When he saw the face and heard the voice that so
clearly had the semblance of Terigi's, Rinaldo
endlessly greeted the messenger of the Count of
Mainz and pressed him with questions about how
Orlando was and about what he had heard, by
rumor, concerning how Orlando had put the
Lombard to rout at the foot of the Alps and then
near Vercelli.

28.   Come presente alle battaglie stato
       fosse il demonio, gli facea risposta;
       e la lettera intanto, che portato
       di credenza gli avea, gli ebbe in man posta.
       Quel l'apre e legge; e lui per man pigliato,
       da chi lo possa udir seco discosta.
       Vertunno, prima ch'altro incominciasse,
       di petto un'altra lettera si trasse.

29.   Poi disse: —Il cugin vostro mi commise
       ch'io vi facessi legger questa appresso.—
       Rinaldo mira le note precise,
       che gli paion di man di Carlo istesso;
       il qual Orlando di Boemia avise
       d'esser pentito senza fin, che messo
       così potente esercito abbia in mano
       de l'audace signor di Mont'Albano:

30.   però che, vinto Unuldo (come crede
       che vincer debbia) e toltoli Guascogna,
       egli d'Unuldo esser vorrà l'erede,
       ché crescer stato a Mont'Alban agogna;
       e la sospizïon c'ha de la fede
       di Rinaldo corrotta, non si sogna:
       in somma, par che sia disposto Carlo,
       per forza o per amor, quindi levarlo.

31.   Ma che prima tentar vuol per amore:
       finger ch'al maggior uopo lo dimande
       per un dei dieci il cui certo valore
       abbatta a Cardoran l'orgoglio grande;
       e vuol per questo che dia un successore
       all'esercito c'ha da quelle bande;
       e che disegna mai più non gli porre
       governo in man, se gli può questo tòrre.

28. The devil answered him as if he had been present at those battles and in the meantime put in Rinaldo's hands the letter of credentials which he had brought him. Rinaldo opens and reads them and, taking Vertumnus by the hand, leads him aside from anyone who might overhear them. Before he could begin to speak, Vertumnus drew another letter from his breast.

29. Then he said: "Your cousin ordered me to have you read this immediately." Rinaldo looks at the unmistakable script and believes it comes from the hand of Charles himself, informing Orlando from Bohemia that he repents without end having put so powerful an army in the hands of the daring lord of Montauban;

30. For once he has conquered Unuldo and taken Gascony from him (and Charles believes Rinaldo will inevitably do so) he will want to be Unuldo's heir, because he longs to expand the state of Montauban; and the suspicion which Charles has about Rinaldo's corrupt loyalty is not just an idle dream: the gist is that Charles seems to have decided to remove Rinaldo thence, either by force or by love;

31. But first he wants to try out love by pretending that he has a greater need for Rinaldo in Prague, where he wants him to be one of the ten whose trusty valor will beat down the arrogance of Cardorano. By this stratagem, Charles plans to give the army he has in Gascony to a new general—and if he can relieve Rinaldo of this command, he plans never to put another in his hands.

32. Vuol ch'Orlando gli scriva ch'esso ancora
     serà in questa battaglia un degli eletti,
     e gl'insti che, rimossa ogni dimora,
     veduto il successor venire, affretti.
     Rinaldo, mentre legge, s'incolora
     per ira in viso, e par che fuoco getti;
     morde le labbia, or l'uno or l'altro; or geme,
     e più che 'l mar quand'ha tempesta freme.

33. Letta la carta, il spirto gli soggiunge,
     pur da parte d'Orlando: —Abbiate cura,
     che se alla discoperta un dì vi giunge,
     vi farà Carlo peggio che paura;
     però che tuttavia Gano lo punge
     che la corte di voi faccia sicura:
     la qual, sì come dice egli, ogni volta
     che voglia ve ne vien, sossopra è volta.

34. Al cugin vostro acerbamente duole
     che 'l re tenga con voi questa maniera,
     che cerchi, a instanza di chi mal vi vuole,
     far parer vostra fé men che sincera;
     e che più creda alle false parole
     d'un traditor, ch'a tanta prova vera
     che si vede di voi: ma dagli ingrati
     son le più volte questi modi usati.

35. Ché, quando l'avarizia gli ritiene
     di render premio a chi di premio è degno,
     studian far venir causa, e se non viene,
     la fingon, per la quale abbiano sdegno;
     e di esilio, di morte o d'altre pene,
     in luogo di mercé, fanno disegno;
     per far parer ch'un vostro error seguito
     quel ben che far voleano abbia impedito.

32. He wants Orlando to write Rinaldo that he, too,
will be one of those chosen for this battle and to
insist that Rinaldo make haste as soon as he sees
his successor coming. Rinaldo's face colors with
fury as he reads this and he seems to breathe fire;
he bites his lips, first one, then the other; he
groans and he shudders more than the sea in a
tempest.

33. When Rinaldo had finished the letter, the spirit
added, still as if on behalf of Orlando: "Take care,
for if one day he should take you unawares,
Charles will do more than give you a scare, for
Ganelon continually prods him to make the court
safe from you altogether—for, so he says, you turn
the court upside down every time you want to.

34. "It pains your cousin cruelly that the King should
take this attitude toward you and should seek, at
the bidding of one who wishes you ill, to make
your loyalty appear less than pure and that he
should believe more in the false words of a traitor
than in all your real and proven deeds: but these
ways are often used by the ungrateful.

35. "For when avarice restrains them from giving
reward to whomever reward is due, they seek to
come up with a reason; and if no reason appears,
they make one up, because of which they may
then show displeasure. They plan exile, death, or
other punishments in place of meed, to make it
seem that some error you have committed
prevented them from showing you the favor they
wanted to show.

36.   Orlando, perché v'ama, e perché aspetta
        il medesmo di sé fra pochi giorni,
        che 'l re in prigion, Gano instigando, il metta,
        o gli dia bando o gli faccia altri scorni
        (ché, come contra voi, così lo alletta
        contra esso ancor), senza far più soggiorni
        per me vi esorta a prender quel partito
        ch'egli ha di tòr di sé già statüito:

37.   che di quel mal che senza causa teme
        facciate morir Carlo, come merta.
        Prendete accordo con Unuldo, e insieme
        con lui venite a fargli guerra aperta:
        vegga se Gano, e se 'l suo iniquo seme,
        contra il valor e la possanza certa
        di Chiaramonte, e l'una e l'altra lancia
        tanto onorata, può difender Francia.—

38.   E seguitò dicendoli che Orlando
        prima favor occulto gli darebbe;
        poscia in aiuto alla scoperta, quando
        fosse il tempo, in persona li verrebbe.
        Rinaldo avea grand'ira, et attizzando
        il fraudolente spirto, sì l'accrebbe,
        ch'allora allora pensò armar le schiere
        e levar contra Carlo le bandiere;

39.   poi diferì fin che arrivasse il messo
        ch'alla pugna boemica il chiamasse,
        e che sentisse commandarsi appresso
        ch'in guardia altrui l'esercito lasciasse.
        Quel che Gano gli avea quivi commesso,
        Vertunno a fin con diligenzia trasse:
        poi, con lettere nuove e nuovo aspetto,
        venne a Marsiglia e fece un altro effetto.

36. "Because Orlando loves you and because he shortly expects the same for himself—that the King, at Ganelon's instigation, will put him in prison, or send him into exile, or do him other injury (for, just as Ganelon incites Charles against you, he will incite him against Orlando, too)— through me he urges you to take without delay the part he has already decided to take for himself:

37. "to make Charles die, as he deserves to, of that disease which he now fears without reason. Make peace with Unuldo and together with him begin to make open war on Charles: see if Ganelon and his iniquitous seed can defend France against the valor and proven power of Clairmont and against our two lances, which are held in such honor."

38. Vertumnus continued, telling Rinaldo that Orlando would at first give him secret assistance and afterward, when the time was right, would help him openly and in person. Rinaldo was very angry, and the deceiving spirit stirred him up and so intensified his wrath that he decided then and there to arm the troops and raise his ensigns against Charles.

39. Later he decided to wait for the envoy to arrive and summon him to the battle in Bohemia, so he could hear himself ordered firsthand to leave his army to the command of another. Vertumnus diligently drew to a close what Ganelon had commissioned him to accomplish there; then, with new letters and a new disguise, he came to Marseilles and carried out another plan.

40. D'Arriguccio s'avea presa la faccia,
ch'era di Carlo un cavallaro antico:
egli scrive le lettere, egli spaccia
se stesso e chiude egli in la bolgia il plico:
l'insegna al petto e il corno al fianco allaccia,
e fu a Marsiglia in men ch'io non lo dico;
e le dettate lettere da Gano
pose a Ruggiero et alla moglie in mano.

41. Alla sorella di Ruggier, Marfisa,
mostrò che Carlo lo mandasse ancora,
come a tutti tre insieme, e poi divisa-
mente a ciascun da Carlo scritto fòra.
Sotto il nome del re Gano gli avisa
che navighi Ruggier senza dimora
ver' le colonne che Tirinzio fisse,
e sorga sopra la città d'Ulisse;

42. e Marfisa con gli altri da cavallo
si vada con Rinaldo a porre in schiera;
ché vinto Unuldo, come senza fallo
vederlo vinto in pochi giorni spera,
vuol ch'assalti Galizia e Portogallo;
né l'impresa esser può se non leggiera:
ché gli dà aiuto, passo e vettovaglia
Alfonso d'Aragon, re di Biscaglia.

43. Appresso scrive all'animosa figlia
del duca Amon che stia sicuramente:
che né da terra né da mar Marsiglia
ha da temer di peregrina gente.
Se false o vere son non si consiglia,
né si pensa alle lettere altrimente:
Ruggier va in Spagna, Marfisa a Morlante,
resta a guardar Marsiglia Bradamante.

40. He had taken the appearance of Arriguccio,
    who was an old courier of Charles; he writes the
    letters, he despatches himself, as rider, and he
    fastens the flap of his mail sack; he ties the
    standard to his breast and the horn to his side[6] and
    is in Marseilles in less time than it takes to say it;
    there he put the letters Ganelon had dictated into
    the hands of Ruggiero and his wife.

41. He pretended that Charles had sent him as well to
    Marfisa, Ruggiero's sister, that his message was
    intended for all three of them together, and that
    afterward Charles would write something to each
    of them individually. In the name of the King,
    Ganelon informs them that Ruggiero must sail
    immediately toward the pillars that Tirynthian
    Hercules made fast and drop anchor by Lisbon,
    the city of Ulysses;[7]

42. Marfisa must go with the rest of the cavalry to
    join Rinaldo's army, which, once it has defeated
    Unuldo (as Charles expects to see it do without
    fail and in a few days), Charles wants to attack
    Galicia and Portugal. This campaign cannot be
    anything but easy, for Alfonso of Aragon, King of
    Biscayne, is giving them assistance, passage, and
    provisions.

43. Next Charles writes to the valiant daughter of
    Duke Amone[8] that she should rest assured:
    Marseilles has nothing to fear from foreign forces
    either by land or by sea. Ruggiero, Marfisa, and
    Bradamante do not consider whether these letters
    are true or false, nor do they give them another
    thought; Ruggiero heads for Spain, Marfisa for
    Morlaas, Bradamante stays to guard Marseilles.

44.   L'imperadore, intanto, che le frode
       non sa di Gano, e solo in esso ha fede,
       di tutti gli altri amici il parere ode,
       ma solamente a quel di Gano crede;
       né cavallier, se non che Gano lode,
       a far quella battaglia non richiede:
       con lui consiglia chi si debba porre
       nei luoghi onde gli due s'aveano a tòrre.

45.   Quando Gano ha risposto, ogn'altro chiude
       la bocca, né si replica parola.
       In luogo di Rinaldo egli conclude
       che mandi Namo; e l'intenzion è sola
       perché Rinaldo, a cui le voglie crude
       l'ira facea, lo impichi per la gola;
       ché pensarà che sol lo mandi Carlo
       per levarli l'esercito e pigliarlo.

46.   Consiglia che si lassi Baldovino
       a governar in Lombardia le squadre;
       il qual fratel d'Orlando era uterino,
       nato, com'ho già detto, d'una madre;
       cortese cavalliero e paladino,
       e degno a cui non fosse Gano padre,
       per consiglio del qual Carlo lo elesse
       ch'all'imperio fraterno succedesse.

47.   Gli dieci eletti alla battaglia fòro
       Carlo, Orlando, Rinaldo, Uggier, Dudone,
       Aquilante, Grifone, il padre loro,
       e con Turpino il genero d'Amone.
       Fatta la elezïone di costoro,
       si spacciaro in diversa regïone
       prima gli avisi, e poi quei che ordinati
       in luogo fur dei capitan chiamati.

44. Meanwhile, the Emperor, who does not know about Ganelon's treachery and has faith only in him, hears the advice of all his other friends, but believes only Ganelon; he asks no knight to fight in the duel with Cardorano unless Ganelon praises him. With Ganelon he considers whom to put in charge of the two commands that Rinaldo and Orlando have to leave.

45. When Ganelon answers, everyone else keeps his mouth shut and no one adds a word. He concludes that Charles should send Namo to take Rinaldo's place; and his sole intention is to have Rinaldo, made bloodthirsty by his wrath, hang Namo by the neck; for Rinaldo will think Charles has only sent Namo to take away his army and arrest him.

46. Ganelon also counseled that Baldovino should be left to govern the troops in Lombardy. He was the uterine brother of Orlando, as I have said already, both born of one mother: a courteous knight and paladin, worthy of a father other than Ganelon, through whose counsel he was selected by Charles to succeed to his brother's command.

47. The ten chosen for the battle were to be Charles, Orlando, Rinaldo, Uggiero, Dudone, Aquilante and Grifone and their father Oliviero, along with Turpin and the son-in-law of Amone.[9] The selection made, proclamations were dispatched at once to the various regions and promptly followed by the knights who had been ordered to take the places of the captains who were being recalled.

48.   Namo fu il primo, il qual, correndo in posta,
      insieme con l'aviso era venuto.
      Già Rinaldo sua causa avea proposta,
      e dimandato alla sua gente aiuto;
      che tanto in suo favor s'era disposta,
      che, dai maggiori al populo minuto,
      tutti affatto volean prima morire
      che Rinaldo lasciar così tradire.

49.   Tra Rinaldo et Unuldo già fatt'era
      accordo et amicizia, ma coperta.
      Allo arrivar del duca di Baviera
      Rinaldo, che la fraude avea per certa,
      di sdegno arse e di còlera sì fiera,
      che tre volte la man pose a Fusberta,
      con voglia di chiavargliela nel petto;
      pur (non so già perché) gli ebbe rispetto.

50.   Ma spesso nominandol traditore,
      e Carlo ingrato, e minacciandol molto
      che lo faria impiccar in disonore
      di Carlo, lo raccolse con mal volto.
      Namo, a cui poco noto era l'errore
      in che Vertunno avea Rinaldo involto,
      mirando ove da l'impeto era tratto,
      stava maraviglioso e stupefatto:

51.   ma magnanimamente gli rispose
      che, traditor nomandolo, mentia.
      Rinaldo, se non ch'uno s'interpose,
      alzò la mano e percosso lo avria:
      prender lo fece, et in prigion lo pose;
      e tolto ch'ebbe Unuldo in compagnia,
      le ville, le cittadi e le castella
      dal re per forza e per amor rubella.

48.   Namo was the first, and, riding by post-horse, he arrived at the same time as the proclamation. Rinaldo had already pled his case to his men and requested their help; they were so disposed in his favor that, from the highest rank to the lowest, they would all rather die before allowing Rinaldo thus to be betrayed.

49.   Agreement and friendship had already been reached between Rinaldo and Unuldo, but secretly. At the coming of the Duke of Bavaria, Rinaldo, who was certain of the fraudulent plot against him, burned furiously with indignation and with such rage that three times he put his hand to Fusberta[10] with the intention of driving it into Namo's breast; yet (I still do not know why) he had respect for him.

50.   But, often calling him a traitor and Charles an ingrate and strongly threatening that he would have him hanged to Charles's shame, Rinaldo welcomed Namo with evil looks. Namo, who knew nothing of the error in which Vertumnus had entangled Rinaldo, stood amazed and bewildered, wondering where Rinaldo was being carried by the force of his rage.

51.   But he answered him loftily that he lied in calling him a traitor. Rinaldo raised his hand and would have struck him, had not someone intervened: he had Namo arrested and put him in prison and, taking Unuldo for his ally, by force or by love caused towns, cities, and castles to rebel against the King.

52. E dovunque ritrovi resistenza
     o dà il guasto o saccheggia o mette a taglia:
     gli dà tutta Guascogna ubidïenza,
     e poche terre aspettan la battaglia.
     Gan da Pontier, che n'ebbe intelligenza,
     ché del tutto Vertunno lo raguaglia,
     con lieto cor, ma con dolente viso,
     fu il primo che ne diede a Carlo aviso.

53. Gano gli diè l'aviso, e poi che 'l varco,
     come bramato avea, vide patente
     di potersi cacciar a dire incarco
     et ignominia del nimico absente,
     sciolse la crudel lingua, e non fu parco
     a mandar fuor ciò che gli venne in mente:
     dei falli di Rinaldo, poi che nacque,
     che fece o puoté far, nessuno tacque.

54. Come si arruota e non ritruova loco
     né in ciel né in terra un'agitata polve,
     come nel vase acqua che bolle al foco,
     di qua di là, di su di giù si volve:
     così il pensier gira di Carlo, e poco
     in questa parte o in quella si risolve.
     Provisïon già fatta nulla giova;
     tutta lasciar conviensi, e rifar nuova.

55. Se padre, a cui sempre giocondo e bello
     fu di mostrarsi al suo figliuol benigno,
     se lo vedesse incontra alzar coltello,
     fatto senza cagione empio e maligno;
     più maraviglia non avria di quello
     ch'ebbe Carlo, vedendo in corvo il cigno
     Rinaldo esser mutato, e contra Francia
     volta senza cagion la buona lancia.

52.   Wherever he finds resistance he either lays waste,
        sacks, or extorts ransom; all Gascony obeys him,
        and not many cities wait for a battle. Ganelon of
        Ponthieu had intelligence of these events because
        Vertumnus gave him reports of everything; and,
        with a happy heart but a sorrowing countenance,
        he was the first to give news of them to Charles.

53.   Ganelon gave him the news and, seeing the
        opening he desired to jump in and pour slander
        and ignominy on his absent enemy, he loosed his
        cruel tongue and unsparingly spoke out whatever
        came to mind, passing over in silence none of the
        wrongs that Rinaldo had done or could have done
        from the time of his birth.

54.   As dust, stirred up, whirls about and finds no
        resting place either in the sky or on earth; as water
        boiling over the fire rolls here and there and up
        and down in the pot; so Charles's thoughts swirl,
        and little can be resolved on this side or that. The
        plans he has already made do him no good; he
        must abandon everything and start all over again.

55.   If a father, who has always found joy and pleasure
        in being kind to his son, were to see him raise his
        knife against him, turned wicked and vicious
        without reason, he would not marvel at it more
        than Charles did, seeing Rinaldo transformed
        from a swan into a crow and turning his good
        lance without reason against France;

56.   Quel ch'averria a un nocchier che si trovasse
lontano in mar, e fremer l'onde intorno,
tornar di sopra, e andar le nubi basse
vedesse negre et oscurarsi il giorno;
che mentre a divietar s'apparecchiasse
di non aver da la fortuna scorno,
il governo perdesse, o simil cosa
alla salute sua più bisognosa;

57.   quel ch'averrebbe a una cittade astretta
da nimici crudel, privi di fede,
che d'alcun fresco oltraggio far vendetta
abbian giurato e non aver mercede;
che, mentre la battaglia ultima aspetta
e all'ultima difesa si provede,
vegga la munizione arsa e distrutta,
in ch'avea posto sua speranza tutta;

58.   quel ch'averria a ciascun che già credesse
d'aver condotto un suo desir a segno,
dove col tempo la fatica avesse,
l'aver, posto, gli amici, ogni suo ingegno;
e cosa nascer sùbito vedesse
pensata meno, e romperli il disegno:
quel duol, quell'ira, quel dispetto grave
a Carlo vien, come l'aviso n'have.

59.   Or torna a Carlo il conte di Pontiero,
e gli dà un altro aviso di Marsiglia,
ch'indi sciolta l'armata avea Ruggiero
per uscir fuor del stretto di Siviglia,
né ad alcun avea detto il suo pensiero;
e certo, poi che questa strada piglia,
gli è manifesto che, voltando intorno,
si troverà sorto in Guascogna un giorno.

56. What a helmsman would feel finding himself far
out at sea, with the waves tossing all around and
rolling over his boat, seeing the black clouds lower
and the day turning dark, who, while he readied
himself to avoid the tempest's fury, lost his rudder
or something similar most necessary for his safety;

57. What a city would feel, beset by cruel and faithless
enemies who have sworn to take vengeance for
some recent outrage and to have no mercy, that,
while it waits for the final battle and prepares itself
for a last defense, sees the munitions in which it
has put all its hope burned up and destroyed;

58. What anyone would feel who once believed that
he had brought to its fulfillment a desire to which
he had, over time, devoted his efforts, possessions,
friends, and all his ingenuity and who suddenly
were to see something unforeseen develop and
destroy his plan; that grief, that anger, that heavy
bitterness fell on Charles as soon as he heard the
news.

59. Now the Count of Ponthieu returns to Charles
and gives him another report from Marseilles that
Ruggiero had set sail from there with his fleet for
the straits of Seville[11] without telling anyone of his
plans; and, because he takes this route, it appears
that, coming around Spain, he will eventually put
ashore in Gascony, as well;

60.   E de la coniettura sua non erra:
      perché Marfisa ad un medesmo punto
      se n'era coi cavalli ita per terra,
      et a Rinaldo avea potere aggiunto.
      Or, se Carlo temea di questa guerra,
      ché Rinaldo lo fa restar consunto;
      quanto ha più da temer, se questi dui
      di tal valor, si son messi con lui?

61.   Gano con molta instanza lo conforta
      che di Rinaldo tolga la sorella,
      prima che di Provenza et Acquamorta
      seco gli faccia ogni città rubella,
      et al fratello apra quest'altra porta
      d'entrar in Francia sin ne le budella;
      ché ben deve pensar ch'ella il partito
      piglierà del fratello e del marito.

62.   E che mandasse sùbito a Ricardo,
      ch'avea l'armata in punto, anco gli disse,
      acciò che dal Fiamingo e dal Picardo
      ne l'Atlantico mar ratto venisse;
      et il rubello e truffator stendardo
      di Ruggier inimico perseguisse,
      che con tutte le navi s'avea, senza
      sua commission, levato di Provenza;

63.   e che sùbito a Orlando paladino
      con diligenza vada una staffetta
      ad avisarlo, come avea il cugino
      del perfido Aquitan preso la setta;
      e ch'egli dia la gente a Balduino,
      ripassi l'Alpi, e a Francia corra in fretta,
      e con lui meni tutta quella schiera
      che dianzi gli ha mandata di Baviera;

60. And this conjecture was confirmed by the fact that Marfisa was headed with her cavalry in the same direction by land and had joined her power with Rinaldo's. Now, if Charles had worried about this war because Rinaldo's defection left him shorthanded, how much more must he worry when two of such prowess as Marfisa and Ruggiero put in with him?

61. With great insistence, Ganelon urges Charles to arrest Rinaldo's sister before she causes all the cities of Provence and Aigues-Mortes to rebel with her and opens this other gateway for her brother's entry into the very entrails of France; for surely Charles must expect Bradamante to take the part of her brother and her husband.

62. Ganelon also told Charles to send a message immediately to Ricardo, who had his fleet in readiness, and tell him of the rebellion, so that he could come quickly from the Flemish and Picard seas to the Atlantic and pursue the rebellious and double-dealing standards of Ruggiero, who, without authorization, had made off with the whole fleet from Provence;

63. A diligent courier should go immediately to the paladin Orlando, to inform him that his cousin had taken the side of the treacherous Aquitaine and to order him to give his command to Baldovino, cross back over the Alps, and hurry quickly to France, bringing with him all the troops that Charles had previously sent him from Bavaria.

64.   e che tra via faccia cavalli e fanti,
      quanti più può, da tutte le contrade;
      non quelli sol che gli verranno inanti,
      ma che constringa a darne ogni cittade,
      altre mille, altre il doppio, altre non tanti,
      come più e men avran la facultade:
      e ch'egli dare il terzo gli volea
      di questi che in Boemia seco avea.

65.   Carlo pensava chi d'Orlando in vece,
      e chi degli altri dui poner dovea
      nella battaglia, che da diece a diece
      dianzi promessa a Cardorano avea.
      Come quel mulatiero, in somma, fece,
      ch'avea il coltel perduto e non volea
      che si stringesse il fodro vòto e secco,
      e 'n luogo del coltel rimesse un stecco:

66.   così, in luogo d'Orlando e di Ruggiero
      e di Rinaldo, fu da Carlo eletto
      Ottone, Avolio e il frate Berlingiero:
      ch'Avino infermo era già un mese in letto.
      Gli dà consiglio il conte di Pontiero
      che di Giudea si chiami Sansonetto,
      per valer meglio, quando a tempo giugna,
      che i tre figli di Namo in questa pugna.

67.   A danno lo dicea, non a profitto
      di Carlo, il traditor; perché all'offesa
      che di far in procinto ha il re d'Egitto,
      non sia in Ierusalem tanta difesa.
      A Sansonetto fu sùbito scritto,
      e dal corrier la via per Tracia presa,
      il qual, mutando bestie, sì le punse,
      ch'in pochi giorni a Palestina giunse.

64. Along the way he should gather as many knights and foot soldiers as he could from the countryside and not just those that come forward as volunteers; he should force every city to give him some men, some a thousand, others twice that number, others not so many, according to their ability; and Charles should give him a third of those he had with him in Bohemia.

65. Charles was considering who, instead of Orlando and the other two champions, he should put forward in the duel of ten against ten that he had promised Cardorano. As did the muleteer who, having lost his knife and not wanting to tie on his scabbard empty and bare, put in a stick in place of the blade,

66. So, in place of Orlando, Ruggiero, and Rinaldo, Charles chose Ottone, Avolio, and his brother Berlingiero, because Avino had already been sick in bed for a month. The Count of Ponthieu advises Charles to recall Sansonetto from Judea, for he would be worth more than all three of Namo's sons should he arrive in time for the battle.

67. The traitor meant this to harm Charles, not to help him; he wanted Jerusalem to have that much less defense against the attack which the King of Egypt was preparing to make. Sansonetto was sent for immediately, and a courier made his way through Thrace and, changing horses frequently, spurred them so hard that he arrived in Palestine in a few days.

68. Di tòr Marsiglia si proferse Gano,
    senza che spada stringa o abbassi lancia:
    vuol sol da Carlo una patente in mano
    da poter commandar per tutta Francia.
    Nulla propone il fraudolente in vano:
    se giova o nuoce, Carlo non bilancia;
    né véntila altrimenti alcun suo detto,
    ma sùbito lo vuol porre ad effetto.

69. Di quanto avea ordinato il Maganzese
    andò l'aviso all'Ungaro e al Boemme,
    ne le Marche, in Sansogna si distese,
    in Frisa, in Dazia, all'ultime maremme.
    Gano de' suoi parenti seco prese,
    seco tornati di Ierusalemme;
    e quindi se n'andò per tòr la figlia
    del duca Amon, con frode, di Marsiglia.

70. Di Baviera in Suevia, et indi, senza
    indugio, per Borgogna e Uvernia sprona;
    e molto declinando da Provenza,
    sparge il rumor d'andar verso Baiona:
    finge in un tratto di mutar sentenza,
    e con molti pedoni entra in Narbona,
    che per Francia in gran fretta e per la Magna
    raccolti e tratti avea seco in campagna.

71. Giunge in Narbona all'oscurar del giorno,
    e, giunto, fa serrar tutte le porte,
    e pon le guardie ai ponti e ai passi intorno,
    che novella di sé fuor non si porte.
    D'un corsar genoese (Oria od Adorno
    fosse, non so) quivi trovò a gran sorte
    quattro galee, con che predando gia
    il mar di Spagna e quel di Barberia.

68.   Ganelon offered to take Marseilles himself,
      without wielding a sword or lowering a lance; he
      only wants letters patent from Charles giving him
      the power to command all of France. The traitor
      proposes nothing that is not adopted; Charles does
      not weigh the benefits and drawbacks, nor does
      he debate any of Ganelon's counsels, but, rather,
      puts them into effect at once.

69.   News of everything that the Count of Mainz had
      plotted reached Hungary and Bohemia, stretched
      to the Marches, to Saxony, to Frisia, to Dacia, to
      the most distant shores. Ganelon took some of
      his kinsmen, who had returned with him from
      Jerusalem, and went to take the daughter of Duke
      Amone, by fraud, from Marseilles.

70.   He spurs from Bavaria to Swabia, from there,
      without delay, through Burgundy and the
      Auvergne, and, giving Provence a wide berth,
      spreads the rumor that he is going toward
      Bayonne; he pretends suddenly to change his
      mind and enters Narbonne with many foot
      soldiers he had hastily gathered together on his
      way through France and Germany and taken with
      him on campaign.

71.   He reached Narbonne at the darkening of day
      and, once inside the town, made all the gates fast
      and put guards at the bridges and passes round
      about so no news of his arrival might escape.
      Luckily for him, he found there four galleys
      belonging to a Genoese corsair (whether he was a
      Doria or an Adorno I don't know [12]), with which
      he had just been pillaging the seas of Spain and
      Barbary.

72.   Gano, dato a ciascun debiti premi,
      sopra i navigli i suoi pedoni parte;
      e, come biancheggiar vide gli estremi
      termini d'orïente, indi si parte,
      e va quanto più può con vele e remi:
      ma tien l'astuto all'arrivar quest'arte,
      che non si scuopre a vista di Marsiglia
      prima che 'l sol non scenda oltra Siviglia.

73.   La figliuola d'Amon, che non sa ancora
      che Rinaldo rubel sia de l'Impero,
      veduto il giglio che sì Francia onora,
      la croce bianca e l'uccel bianco e il nero,
      e poi Vertunno in su la prima prora,
      ch'avea l'insegna e il viso di Ruggiero,
      senza timor, senz'armi corse al lito,
      credendosi ire in braccio al suo marito;

74.   il qual sia, per alcun nuovo accidente,
      tornato a lei con parte de l'armata:
      non dal marito, ma dal fraudolente
      Gano si ritrovò ch'era abbracciata.
      Come chi còrre il fior volea, e il serpente
      truova che 'l punge; così disarmata,
      e senza poter farli altra difesa,
      dagli nimici suoi si trovò presa.

75.   Si trovò presa ella e la rocca insieme,
      ché non vi poté far difesa alcuna.
      Il popul, che ciò sente e peggio teme,
      chi qua chi là con l'armi si raguna;
      il rumor s'ode, come il mar che freme
      vòlto in furor da sùbita fortuna:
      ma poi Gano parlandogli, e di Carlo
      mostrando commission, fece acchetarlo.

72. Ganelon paid out the just price for each vessel;
then he divided his foot soldiers up among the
ships and, as he saw the far limits of the east begin
to brighten, departed and sailed as fast as he could
by canvas and oars for Marseilles. At his arrival, the
cunning Ganelon employed another stratagem
and waited to reveal himself to the view of
Marseilles until the sun went down beyond
Seville.

73. Amone's daughter, who still did not know that
Rinaldo was a rebel against the Empire, saw the
lily that France honors so, the white cross and the
white and black eagles,[13] and then Vertumnus on
the foremost prow, who had put on the arms and
countenance of Ruggiero; she ran fearless and
unarmed to the shore, believing she was running
into her husband's arms;

74. her husband, who because of some new
happenstance had returned to her with part of his
fleet: but she found herself embraced not by her
husband but by the fraudulent Ganelon. Like one
who wants to pick a flower, but finds a serpent
that stings, so Bradamante, unarmed and unable to
put up any defense, found herself taken by her
enemies.

75. She found herself taken together with her fortress,
for it could muster no defense. The populace,
hearing of this and fearing worse, assemble with
their arms, some here, some there; an uproar is
heard like a raging sea, rolled into a fury by an
unexpected storm; but then Ganelon calmed
them, speaking to them and showing Charles's
orders.

76. Disegna il traditor che di vita esca
     la sua inimica, innanzi ch'altri il viete;
     poi muta voglia, non che gli n'incresca
     né del sangue di lei non abbia sete;
     ma spera poter meglio con tal ésca
     Rinaldo e Ruggier trarre alla sua rete:
     e tolti alcuni seco, con speranza
     di me' guardarla, andò verso Maganza.

77. Dui scudier de la donna, ch'a tal guisa
     trar la vedean, montar sùbito in sella;
     e l'uno andò a Rinaldo et a Marfisa
     verso Guascogna a darne la novella;
     l'altro Orlando trovar prima s'avisa,
     che 'l campo non lontano avea da quella,
     da quella strada, per la qual captiva
     la sfortunata giovane veniva.

78. Orlando avendo in commissione avuto
     di dar altrui l'impresa de' Lombardi,
     et a' Franceschi accorrere in aiuto
     contra Rinaldo e gli fratei gagliardi,
     era già in ripa al Rodano venuto,
     e fermati a Valenza avea i stendardi;
     dove da Carlo esercito aspettava,
     altro n'avea et altro n'assoldava.

79. Venne il scudiero, e gli narrò la froda
     ch'alla donna avea fatto il Conte iniquo,
     e ch'in Maganza lungi da la proda
     del fiume la traea per calle obliquo;
     poi gli soggiunse: —Non patir che goda
     d'aver quest'onta il tuo avversario antiquo
     fatta al tuo sangue. Se ciò non ti preme,
     come potranno in te gli altri aver speme?—

76.   The traitor had planned to put his enemy to death
      before anyone prevented it; then he changed his
      mind, not because he felt sorry for her, or because
      he was not thirsty for her blood, but only because
      he hoped that with her as bait he would be better
      able to draw Rinaldo and Ruggiero into his net.
      So, taking some men with him (the better to keep
      guard over her), off he went toward Mainz.

77.   Two of the lady's squires who saw her taken in
      this fashion mounted their saddles at once, one
      going off toward Gascony to take the news to
      Rinaldo and Marfisa, the other deciding first to
      look for Orlando, whose camp was not far from
      the very same road on which the unlucky young
      woman went prisoner.

78.   Obliged by his orders to leave his campaign
      against the Lombards to another and to rush to the
      aid of the French against Rinaldo and the valiant
      siblings,[14] Orlando had already arrived at the banks
      of the Rhone and had halted his standards at
      Valence; he awaited there another army from
      Charles—in addition to the force he had on hand,
      and another he recruited of mercenaries.

79.   The squire came and told him about the fraud that
      the wicked Count had perpetrated on the lady
      and how he led her by an indirect route, far from
      the river's edge, toward Mainz; then he added:
      "Do not allow your old adversary to rejoice in
      dishonoring your blood this way. If this does not
      spur you to action, how will others be able to rest
      their hopes in you?"

80.   Di sdegno Orlando, ancor che giusto e pio,
      fu per scoppiar, perché volea celarlo,
      come di Gano il nuovo oltraggio udìo;
      e benché fa pensier di seguitarlo,
      pur se ne scusa e mostrasi restio,
      ché far non vuol sì grave ingiuria a Carlo,
      per commission del qual sa ch'avea Gano
      posto in Marsiglia e ne la donna mano.

81.   Così risponde, e tuttavia dirizza
      a far di ciò il contrario ogni disegno;
      ché l'onta sì de la cugina attizza,
      sì accresce il foco de l'antiquo sdegno,
      che non truova per l'ira e per la stizza
      loco che 'l tenga, e non può stare al segno:
      a pena aspettar può che notte sia,
      per pigliar dietro al traditor la via.

82.   Né Brigliador né Vaglientino prese,
      perché troppo ambi conosciuti furo;
      ma di pel bigio un gran corsier ascese,
      ch'avea il capo e le gambe e il crine oscuro:
      lassò il quartiero e l'altro usato arnese,
      e tutto si vestì d'un color puro:
      partì la notte, e non fu chi sentisse,
      se non Terigi sol, che si partisse.

83.   Gano per l'acque Sestie, indi pel monte
      alla man destra avea preso il camino;
      passò Druenza et Issara, ove il fonte
      a men di quattro miglia era vicino:
      ché nel paese entrar volea del conte
      Macario di Losana, suo cugino;
      e per terre di Svizzeri andar poi,
      e per Lorena, a' Maganzesi suoi.

80. Although he was just and pious, when he heard of
     Ganelon's latest outrage Orlando was on the point
     of bursting from trying to conceal his indignation;
     and even though he makes up his mind to pursue
     the Count, still he demurs and makes a show of
     reluctance because he does not want openly to do
     so grave an injury to Charles, at whose bidding he
     knows Ganelon laid hands on the lady and on
     Marseilles.

81. He answers one way and yet directs his every
     intention toward doing the opposite, for his
     cousin's dishonor so stirs him, so feeds the fire of
     his ancient wrath, that he cannot find room
     enough to hold in his anger and frustration and
     cannot stand his mark. He can hardly wait for
     night before taking the road after the traitor.

82. He took neither Brigliadoro nor Vaglientino,
     because both were too well known;[15] he mounted
     instead a big gray courser whose head, legs, and
     mane were black. He left behind his shield and
     other customary armor and clothed himself in
     pure white. He departed that night, and there was
     nobody except Terigi alone who knew that he
     had gone.

83. Ganelon had taken the road through Aix and
     from there had taken a right turn through the
     mountains; he crossed the Durance and Isere,
     whose source was less than four miles away, for
     he wanted to reach the territory of his cousin,
     Count Macario of Lausanne, and afterward to
     cut through Switzerland and Lorraine to his own
     lands at Mainz.

84.   Orlando venne accelerando il passo,
ch'ogni via sapea quivi o breve o lunga;
e come cacciator ch'attenda al passo
ch'a ferire il cingial nel spiedo giunga,
si mise fra dui monti dietro un sasso;
né molto Gano il suo venir prolunga,
che dinanzi e di dietro e d'ambi i lati
cinta la donna avea d'uomini armati.

85.   Lassò di molta turba andare inante
Orlando, prima che mutasse loco;
ma come vide giunger Bradamante,
parve bombarda a cui sia dato il foco:
con sì fiero e terribile sembiante
l'assalto cominciò, per durar poco:
la prima lancia a Gano il petto afferra,
e ferito aspramente il mette a terra.

86.   Passò lo scudo, la corazza e il petto;
e se l'asta allo scontro era più forte,
gli seria dietro apparso il ferro netto,
né data fòra mai più degna morte.
Pur giacer gli conviene a suo dispetto,
né quindi si può tòr, ch'altri nol porte:
Orlando il lassa in terra e più nol mira,
volta il cavallo e Durindana aggira.

87.   Le braccia ad altri, ad altri il capo taglia;
chi fin a' denti e chi più basso fende;
chi ne la gola e chi ne la inguinaglia,
chi forato nel petto in terra stende.
Non molto in lungo va quella battaglia,
ché tutta l'altra turba a fuggir prende:
gli caccia quasi Orlando meza lega,
indi ritorna e la cugina slega.

84.   Orlando, who knew every path in the region, short or long, came hurrying his steps and, like a hunter who waits at the pass for a boar to come running onto his spear, positioned himself behind a rock between two mountains. Ganelon, who had Bradamante surrounded in front, in back, and on both sides with armed men, was not long in coming.

85.   Orlando allowed many in the escort to go on ahead before he left his hiding place, but when he saw Bradamante arrive he was like a blast shot out of a cannon; with so fierce and terrible an aspect did he begin his assault, which lasted but a little while; his first lance struck Ganelon's breast and laid him bitterly wounded on the ground.

86.   It passed through his shield, cuirass, and breastplate and, if the shaft had been stronger at the impact, the point would have appeared cleanly through his back. No death would ever have been more deserved. As it is, Ganelon has no choice but to lie there, much to his chagrin, unable to escape unless someone is to carry him. Orlando leaves him on the ground and pays him no further heed, but turns his horse and whirls Durindana [16] about.

87.   He cuts the arms off some, the heads off others; some he cleaves to the teeth and others down farther; some he lays out on the ground stabbed in the throat, others in the groin, others through the chest. The battle goes on for only a little while because the rest of the troop takes flight. Orlando chases them half a mile away and then returns and unties his cousin.

88.   La quale, eccetto l'elmo, il scudo e il brando,
tutto il resto de l'armi ritenea:
ché Gano, per alzar sua gloria, quando
non più ch'una donzella presa avea,
pensò, avendola armata, ir dimostrando
che 'l medesimo onor se gli dovea
ch'ad Ercole e Teseo gli antiqui dènno
di quel ch'a Termodonte in Scizia fenno.

89.   Orlando, che non volse conosciuto
esser d'alcun, indi accusato a Carlo;
e per ciò con un scudo era venuto
d'un sol color, che fece in fretta farlo;
andò là dove Gano era caduto,
e prima l'elmo, senza salutarlo,
e dopo il scudo, la spada gli trasse,
e volse che la donna se n'armasse.

90.   Poi se n'andò fin che a Mattafellone,
il buon destrier di Gan, prese la briglia,
e ritornando fece ne l'arcione
salir d'Amon la liberata figlia;
né, per non dar di sé cognizïone,
levò mai la visiera da le ciglia:
poi, senza dir parola, il freno volse,
e di lor vista in gran fretta si tolse.

91.   Bradamante lo prega che 'l suo nome
le voglia dire, et ottener nol puote:
Orlando in fretta il destrier sprona, e come
corrier che vada a gara, lo percuote.
Va Bradamante a Gano, e per le chiome
gli leva il capo, e due e tre volte il scuote;
et alza il brando nudo ad ogni crollo,
con voglia di spiccar dal busto il collo.

88. Except for her helmet, her shield, and her sword,
     Bradamante had kept all her armor, for though he
     had taken no more than a damsel, Ganelon
     thought to heighten his glory by traveling with
     her armed and so showing how he was due the
     same honor that the ancients gave to Hercules
     and Theseus for their conquest of the Scythian
     Amazons by the banks of the Thermodon.

89. Orlando did not want to be recognized by anyone
     and afterward have his exploit revealed to Charles,
     and on that account he had come with a shield of
     just one color which he had had hurriedly made.
     He went to where Ganelon had fallen and
     without greeting him took away first his helmet
     and then his shield and sword and wished
     Bradamante to arm herself with them.

90. Then he went off and took hold of the bridle of
     Mattafellone, Ganelon's good steed, and returning
     made Amone's daughter, who was now free, get
     up in the saddle. In order not to give himself away,
     he never raised the visor from his brow. Without
     saying a word, he reined sharply about and hastily
     removed himself from their sight.

91. Bradamante begs him to tell her his name, but she
     cannot discover it. Orlando hurriedly spurs his
     horse and beats it like a jockey in a race.
     Bradamante went to Ganelon and lifted his head
     by the hair, shook it two or three times, and raised
     her naked sword at every shake, thinking of
     cutting his neck off his shoulders.

92.   Ma poi si avvide che, lasciandol vivo,
        potria Marsiglia aver per questo mezo,
        e gli faria bramar, d'ogn'agio privo,
        che di sé fosse già polvere e lezo.
        come ladro il legò, non che cattivo,
        e col capo scoperto al sole e al rezo,
        per lunga strada or dietro sel condusse,
        or cacciò innanzi a gran colpi di busse.

93.   Quella sera medesima veduto
        le venne quel scudier del quale io dissi
        ch'andò a Valenza a dimandare aiuto,
        né parve a lui che Orlando lo esaudissi;
        indi era dietro all'orme egli venuto
        di Gano, per veder ciò che seguissi
        de la sua donna, e per poter di quella
        ai fratelli portar poi la novella.

94.   A costui diede la capezza in mano,
        che pel collo, pei fianchi e per le braccia,
        sopra un debol roncin l'iniquo Gano
        traea legato a discoperta faccia.
        Curar la piaga gli fe' da un villano,
        che per bisogno in tal opre s'impaccia;
        il qual, stridendo Gano per l'ambascia,
        tutta l'empie di sal, e a pena fascia.

95.   Il Maganzese al collo un cerchio d'oro
        e prezïose annella aveva in dito,
        et alla spada un cinto di lavoro
        molto ben fatto e tutto d'or guarnito;
        e queste cose e l'altre che trovoro
        di Gano aver del ricco e del polito,
        la donna a Sinibaldo tutte diede,
        ch'era di maggior don degna sua fede.

92.   But then she realized that by letting him live she
       would be able to recover Marseilles, and she
       would make him wish, deprived of every comfort,
       that he were already dust and stench. She bound
       him like a thief, not just like a prisoner, and with
       his head bared to the sun and the cold she led him
       sometimes along the road behind her, sometimes
       chased him on ahead of her with great blows from
       her lance.

93.   That same evening she came across the squire I
       mentioned who had gone toward Valence to ask
       for help and who had not thought Orlando would
       grant it. He had followed Ganelon's tracks to see
       what had become of his lady and then to bring
       news of her to her brothers.

94.   Bradamante gave into his hands the end of the
       rope which drew the wicked Ganelon on a weak
       nag, bound by the neck, sides, and arms, his face
       exposed. She had his wounds cared for by a
       peasant who meddled with such work only in a
       pinch and who filled the wounds with salt and
       then wrapped them as best he could while
       Ganelon cried out from the pain.

95.   Ganelon had a chain of gold around his neck,
       precious rings on his fingers, and for his sword a
       belt that was of very fine workmanship and
       decorated all over with gold. These and all the
       other rich and exquisite things which they found
       in his possession the lady gave to Sinibaldo, whose
       loyalty was worthy of greater rewards.

96. A Sinibaldo, che così nomato
     era il scudier, con l'altre anco concesse
     la gemma in che Vertunno era incantato,
     ma non sapendo quanto ella gli desse;
     né sapendolo ancora a chi fu dato,
     con l'altre annella in dito se lo messe;
     stimòllo et ebbe in prezzo, ma minore
     di quel ch'avria, sapendo il suo valore.

97. Pel Delfinato, indi per Linguadoca
     ne va, dove trovar spera il fratello,
     ch'avea Guascogna, o ne restava poca,
     omai ridotta al suo voler ribello.
     Come la volpe che gallina od oca,
     o lupo che ne porti via l'agnello
     per macchie o luoghi ove in perpetuo adugge
     l'ombra le pallide erbe, ascoso fugge;

98. ella così da le città si scosta
     quanto più può, né dentro mura alloggia;
     ma dove trovi alcuna casa posta
     fuor de la gente, ivi si corca o appoggia:
     il giorno mangia e dorme e sta riposta,
     la notte al camin suo poi scende e poggia:
     le par mill'anni ogni ora che 'l ribaldo
     s'indugi a dar prigion al suo Rinaldo.

99. Come animal selvatico, ridotto
     pur dianzi in gabbia o in luogo chiuso e forte,
     corre di qua e di là, corre di sotto,
     corre di sopra, e non trova le porte;
     così Gano, vedendosi condotto
     da' suoi nimici a manifesta morte,
     cercava col pensier tutti gli modi
     che lo potesson trar fuor di quei nodi.

96.   Together with these other jewels, she gave
Sinibaldo (for so the squire was called) the gem in
which Vertumnus was held by enchantment; but
she did not realize how much she was giving him,
and neither did he. He put it with the other rings
on his fingers; he prized and treasured it, but less
than he would have had he known of its power.

97.   Bradamante proceeded through the Dauphiné and
from there through Languedoc, where she hoped
to find her brother, who by now had subjected all
or almost all Gascony to his rebellious will. As the
fox that carries off a hen or a goose, or the wolf
that carries off a lamb, flees covertly through
thickets and places where permanent darkness
overshadows the pale grass;

98.   so Bradamante keeps away from the cities as much
as she can and never sleeps within their walls, but
wherever she finds some dwelling in a place far
from people, there she lays herself down and rests.
During the day she eats and sleeps and stays out of
sight, and at night she descends to her route and
sets out once again. Every hour that she delays
consigning the scoundrel as a prisoner to her
Rinaldo seems a thousand years to her.

99.   As a wild animal, just recently forced into a cage
or strong enclosure, runs here and there, up and
down, and finds no way out; so Ganelon, seeing
himself led by his enemies to a certain death,
examined in his thoughts all the ways by which he
might free himself from those bonds.

100.   Pur la guardia gli lascia un dì tant'agio,
        che dà de l'esser suo notizia a un oste;
        e gli promette trarlo di disagio
        s'andar vuol a Baiona per le poste,
        et al Lupo figliuol di Bertolagio
        far che non sien le sue miserie ascoste:
        ch'in costui spera, tosto che lo intenda,
        ch'alli suoi casi alcun rimedio prenda.

101.   L'oste, più per speranza di guadagno
        che per esser di mente sì pietosa,
        salta a cavallo, e la sferza e 'l calcagno
        adopra, e notte o dì poco riposa:
        giunse, io non so s'io dica al Lupo o all'agno;
        so ch'io l'ho da dir agno in una cosa:
        ch'era di cor più timido che agnello,
        nel resto lupo insidïoso e fello.

102.   Tosto che 'l Lupo ha la novella udita,
        senza far il suo cor noto a persona,
        con cento cavallier de la più ardita
        gente ch'avesse, uscì fuor di Baiona;
        e verso dove avea la strada uscita
        che facea Bradamante, in fretta sprona;
        poi si nasconde in certe case guaste
        ch'era tra via, ma ch'a celarlo baste.

103.   L'oste quivi lasciando i Maganzesi,
        andò per trovar Gano e Bradamante,
        ché da l'insidie e dagli lacci tesi
        non pigliassero via troppo distante.
        Non molto andò che di lucenti arnesi
        guarnito un cavallier si vide inante,
        che cacciando il destrier più che di trotto,
        parea da gran bisogno esser condotto.

100.   Somehow his guard allows him enough ease one
        day that he makes an innkeeper aware of his
        position and promises to bring him out of poverty
        if he will go by post-horse to Bayonne and tell
        Lupo, Bertolagi's son, of his misery; for he hopes
        that Lupo will find some remedy for his troubles
        as soon as he hears of them.

101.   More from hope of profit than from a disposition
        to pity, the innkeeper jumps on his horse and plies
        his whip and heel, resting little by day or night. I
        don't know whether to say he reached Lupo the
        Wolf or Lupo the Lamb; I do know I have to call
        him a lamb in one respect, for his heart was more
        timorous than a lamb's, though the rest of him was
        an insidious and wicked wolf.

102.   As soon as this Lupo heard the news, without
        making his heart known to anyone, he left
        Bayonne with a hundred of the most courageous
        knights he had and spurred in haste to where the
        road Bradamante was taking came out; then he
        hid himself in some ruined houses that happened
        to be beside the way and that were big enough to
        conceal him.

103.   Leaving the men of Mainz there, the innkeeper
        went off to find Ganelon and Bradamante, lest
        they take a route too distant from the traps and
        snares set by Lupo. He did not go far before he
        saw in front of him a knight equipped with
        shining armor, who drove his horse at something
        more than a trot and appeared to be drawn on by
        some pressing need.

104.   Galoppandoli innanzi iva un valletto,
        due damigelle poi, poi veniva esso:
        le damigelle avean l'una l'elmetto,
        la lancia e 'l scudo all'altra era commesso.
        Prima che giunga ove lor possa il petto
        vedere o 'l viso, o più si faccia appresso,
        l'oste all'incontro la figlia d'Amone
        vede venir col traditor prigione.

105.   Poi vide il cavallier da le donzelle,
        tosto ch'a Bradamante fu vicino,
        ire a 'bracciarla, et accoglienze belle
        far l'una all'altra a capo umile e chino;
        e poi ch'una o due volte iterar quelle,
        volgersi e ritornar tutte a un camino:
        e chi pur dianzi in tal fretta venia,
        lasciar per Bradamante la sua via.

106.   Quest'era l'animosa sua Marfisa,
        la qual non si fermò, tosto ch'intese
        de la cognata presa, et in che guisa;
        e per ir in Maganza il camin prese,
        certa di liberarla, pur ch'uccisa
        già non l'avesse il Conte maganzese;
        e se morta era, far quivi tai danni,
        che desse al mondo da parlar mill'anni.

107.   L'oste giunse tra lor e salutolle
        cortesemente, e mostrò far l'usanza,
        ché la sera albergar seco invitolle,
        e finse che non lungi era la stanza;
        poi, mal accorto, a Gano accennar volle,
        e del vicino aiuto dar speranza:
        ma dal scudier che Gano avea legato
        fu il misero veduto et accusato.

104.   Galloping ahead of him went a valet, and then
        two damsels, and he came afterward; one of the
        damsels had his helmet; his lance and shield were
        entrusted to the other. Before the innkeeper can
        get to where he could see the breastplate or their
        faces, or draw any closer, he sees Amone's
        daughter coming from the other direction with
        the captive traitor.

105.   Then he sees the knight with the damsels go to
        embrace Bradamante as soon as he was near her,
        and each make the other fair greetings with heads
        bowed and modest; and after they have repeated
        their greetings, he sees them turn about and come
        back together on one road; and he sees the one
        who came before in such haste leave his path to
        join Bradamante.

106.   This was the high-spirited Marfisa, who never
        rested once she heard of her sister-in-law's capture
        and of the way in which it was done but took the
        road toward Mainz certain to free her if Ganelon
        had not already killed her, and if she were dead, to
        do such harm there as would give the world
        something to talk about for a thousand years.

107.   The innkeeper joined them and saluted them
        courteously and appeared to act normally, for he
        invited them to stay the night with him and
        feigned that his inn was not far off; then he
        foolishly tried to signal Ganelon to give him hope
        of help nearby; but the wretch was seen and
        denounced by the squire who kept Ganelon tied
        up.

108. Marfisa, ch'avea l'ira e la man presta,
      lo ciuffò ne la gola, e l'avria morto,
      se non facea la cosa manifesta
      ch'avea per Gano ordita, et il riporto;
      pur gli travolse in tal modo la testa,
      ch'andò poi, fin che visse, a capo torto.
      Le chiome in fretta armar, ch'eran scoperte,
      de le vicine insidie amendue certe.

109. Tolgon tra lor con ordine l'impresa,
      che Bradamante non s'abbia a partire,
      ma star del traditor alla difesa,
      ch'alcun nol scioglia né faccia fuggire;
      e che Marfisa attenda a fare offesa
      a' Maganzesi, ucciderli e ferire.
      Così ne van verso la casa rotta,
      dove i nimici ascosi erano in frotta.

110. L'altre donzelle e i dui scudier restaro,
      ch'eran senz'armi, non troppo lontano;
      Bradamante e Marfisa se n'andaro
      verso gli aguati, avendo in mezo Gano.
      Tosto che dritto il loco si trovaro,
      saltò Marfisa con la lancia in mano
      dentro alla porta, e messe un alto grido,
      dicendo: —Traditor, tutti vi uccido.—

111. Come chi vespe o galavroni o pecchie
      per follia va a turbar ne le lor cave,
      se gli sente per gli occhi e per l'orecchie
      armati di puntura aspera e grave;
      così fa il grido de le mura vecchie
      del rotto albergo uscir le genti prave
      con un strepito d'armi e, da ogni parte,
      tanto rumor ch'avria da temer Marte.

108. Marfisa, who was quick to anger and to raise her
      hand, seized the innkeeper by the throat and
      would have killed him had he not told her clearly
      everything Ganelon had plotted and how Lupo
      had responded; still, she twisted his head in such a
      way that he went about with it bent sideways as
      long as he lived. Alerted to the ambush nearby,
      both ladies hastened to arm their uncovered locks.

109. They divided the job between them
      systematically, so that Bradamante would not have
      to leave the traitor but would stay behind to guard
      him in case anyone should try to free his bonds or
      help him to escape. Marfisa was to attend to the
      attack on Lupo's men, to kill and wound them. So
      they proceeded toward the ruined house, where
      their enemies lay hidden in a group.

110. The other damsels and the two squires, who were
      unarmed, remained a little way off. Bradamante
      and Marfisa went out toward the ambush with
      Ganelon between them. The moment they found
      themselves right in front of the place, Marfisa leapt
      inside the door with her lance in hand and let out
      a great shout, crying: "Traitors, I will kill you all."

111. As one who in his folly goes and stirs up wasps or
      hornets or bees in their hives feels about his eyes
      and ears how they are armed with a deep and
      bitter sting; so Marfisa's shout makes the wicked
      men come out from the old walls of the ruined
      dwelling on every side, with a clatter of arms and
      such an uproar that Mars himself would have been
      afraid.

237

112.   Marfisa, che dovunque apparia il caso
più periglioso divenia più ardita,
con la lancia mandò quattro all'occaso,
che trovò stretti insieme in su l'uscita;
e col troncon, ch'in man l'era rimaso,
solo in tre colpi a tre tolse la vita.
Ma tornate ad udir un'altra volta
quel che fe' poi ch'ebbe la spada tolta.

112. Marfisa, who in the greatest danger became all the more fearless, used her lance to send to their sunset four that she found packed together near the door and with the trunk of the lance that remained in her hand she took the lives of three others in just three blows. But come back another time to hear what she did after she had taken out her sword.

Canto Quarto

1. Donne mie care, il torto che mi fate
    bene è il maggior che voi mai feste altrui:
    che di me vi dolete et accusate
    che nei miei versi io dica mal di vui,
    che sopra tutti gli altri v'ho lodate,
    come quel che son vostro e sempre fui:
    io v'ho offeso, ignorante, in un sol loco;
    vi lodo in tanti a studio, e mi val poco.

2. Questo non dico a tutte, ché ne sono
    di quelle ancor c'hanno il giudicio dritto,
    che s'appigliano al più che ci è di buono,
    e non a quel che per cianciare è scritto;
    dàn facilmente a un leve error perdono,
    né fan mortal un venïal delitto.
    Pur, s'una m'odia, ancor che m'amin cento,
    non mi par di restar però contento:

3. ché, com'io tutte riverisco et amo,
    e fo di voi, quanto si può far, stima,
    così né che pur una m'odii bramo,
    sia d'alta sorte o medïocre o d'ima.
    Voi pur mi date il torto, et io mel chiamo;
    concedo che v'ha offese la mia rima:
    ma per una ch'in biasmo vostro s'oda,
    son per farne udir mille in gloria e loda.

Canto 4

1. MY DEAR LADIES, the wrong you do me is surely
   greater than any you have ever done others, for
   you complain about me and accuse me of
   speaking ill of you in my verses—I, who have
   praised you above all others as one who is, and
   always was, your devoted servant. I have offended
   you inadvertently in just one passage; I praise you
   on purpose in so many others, yet it does me little
   good.[1]

2. I do not say this to all the ladies, for there are still
   some whose judgment is sound and who hold on
   to the greater part of what I write, which is good,
   rather than to the bits that are written in jest.
   These ladies pardon a small mistake easily and do
   not make a mortal sin of a venial one.
   Nevertheless, if but one lady hates me, I still don't
   feel I can rest contented even though a hundred
   others should love me.

3. For just as I love and revere all ladies and esteem
   you as much as can be, I do not want even one to
   hate me, whether she be of high, of middling, or
   even of the lowest rank. Still, you say I am in the
   wrong, and I acknowledge it. I admit that my
   poem may have offended you, but for every verse
   that is heard reproaching you, I am ready to write
   a thousand to be heard in your praise and to your
   glory.

4. Occasïon non mi verrà di dire
   in vostro onor, che preterir mai lassi;
   e mi sforzerò ancor farla venire,
   acciò il mondo empia e fin nel ciel trapassi;
   e così spero vincer le vostr'ire,
   se non sarete più dure che sassi:
   pur, se sarete anco ostinate poi,
   la colpa non più in me serà, ma in voi.

5. Io non lasciai per amor vostro troppo
   Gano allegrar di Bradamante presa,
   ché venir da Valenza di galoppo
   feci il signor d'Anglante in sua difesa;
   et or costui che credea sciorre il groppo
   di Gano, e far alle guerriere offesa,
   a vostro onor udite anco in che guisa,
   con tutti i suoi, trattar fo da Marfisa.

6. Marfisa parve al stringer de la spada
   una Furia che uscisse de lo inferno;
   gli usberghi e gli elmi, ovunque il colpo cada,
   più fragil son che le cannucce il verno;
   o che giù al petto o almen che a' denti vada,
   o che faccia del busto il capo esterno,
   o che sparga cervella, o che triti ossa,
   convien che uccida sempre ogni percossa.

7. Dui ne partì fra la cintura e l'anche:
   restar le gambe in sella e cadde il busto;
   da la cima del capo un divise anche
   fin su l'arcion, ch'andò in dui pezzi giusto;
   tre ferì su le spalle o destre o manche;
   e tre volte uscì il colpo acre e robusto
   sotto la poppa dal contrario lato:
   dieci passò da l'uno all'altro lato.

4. No opportunity will arise for me to speak in your honor that I shall ever allow to go by, and I shall even try to make such opportunities arise, so that your praises may fill the world and pass beyond up to the sky. In this way I hope to vanquish your wrath (if you are not harder than rocks); and if you are still obstinate, the guilt will be no longer mine but yours.

5. Out of love for you, I kept Ganelon from rejoicing too much in capturing Bradamante, for I made the lord of Anglant come at a gallop from Valence to her defense. And now you will hear how, in your honor, I have Marfisa deal with Lupo and all his men, who thought to loose Ganelon's bonds and do the two women warriors harm.

6. When she wielded her sword, Marfisa seemed a Fury out of Hell. Wherever her blows fall, hauberks and helmets are more fragile than reeds in winter; whether the blows cleave as far as the chest, or at least to the teeth, or separate the head from the shoulders, whether they scatter brains or crush bone, every one of them kills its man.

7. She cut two men apart between the belt and the haunches; their legs stayed in the saddle and their torsos fell to the ground. She clove one from the top of his head right down to the saddle bow and he fell in two perfect halves. She struck three men either on their left or right shoulder and three times her powerful cutting blow came out under the breast on the other side. She stabbed ten from one side right through to the other.

8.   Lungo saria voler tutti gli colpi
      de la spada crudel, dritti e riversi,
      quanti ne sveni, quanti snervi e spolpi,
      quanti ne tronchi e fenda porre in versi.
      Chi fia che Lupo di viltade incolpi,
      e gli altri in fuga appresso a lui conversi,
      poi che dal brando che gli uccide e strugge
      difender non si può se non chi fugge?

9.   Creduto avea la figlia di Beatrice
      d'esser venuta a far quivi battaglia,
      e si ritrova giunta spettatrice
      di quanto in armi la cognata vaglia:
      ché non è alcun del numero infelice
      ch'a lei s'accosti pur, non che l'assaglia:
      che fan pur troppo, senza altri assalire,
      se puon, volgendo il dosso, indi fuggire.

10.   D'ogni salute or disperato Gano,
      di corvi, d'avoltor ben si vede ésca;
      ché, poi che questo aiuto è stato vano,
      altro non sa veder che gli riesca.
      Lo trasser le cognate a Mont'Albano,
      che più che morte par che gli rincresca;
      e fin ch'altro di lui s'abbia a disporre,
      lo fan calar nel piè giù d'una torre.

11.   Ruggiero intanto al suo vïaggio intento,
      ch'ancor nulla sapea di questo caso,
      carcando or l'orza et or la poggia al vento,
      facea le prore andar volte all'occaso.
      Ogni lito di Francia più di cento
      miglia lontano a dietro era rimaso.
      Tutta la Spagna, che non sa a ch'effetto
      l'armata il suo mar solchi, è in gran sospetto.

8.   It would be tedious putting into verse all of her
      sword's cruel blows, forehand and backhand, how
      many slit veins, how many severed muscles or
      stripped flesh from bone, how many ripped open,
      how many hacked apart. Who would accuse Lupo
      and the others who fled with him of being
      cowards, when flight was the only defense against
      that murderous and destructive sword?

9.   Beatrice's daughter[2] thought she had come along
      to fight as well, but finds herself a witness to her
      sister-in-law's prowess; for there isn't one of that
      unhappy number who can even get near Marfisa,
      much less strike her a blow. It is all they can do if,
      without attacking anyone, they can turn their
      backs and flee from there.

10.   Bereft of every hope of deliverance, Ganelon now
      considered himself a certain meal for crows and
      vultures, for after this rescue had failed, he could
      think of no other with a chance of success. The
      sisters-in-law dragged him off to Montauban,
      which seemed to sorrow him more than death
      itself, and, until someone else should decide what
      to do with him, they dropped him down into the
      dungeons underneath a tower.

11.   Meanwhile, Ruggiero was busy about his voyage
      and, still knowing nothing of these events, set his
      sails first to the windward, then to the leeward
      before the breeze, and advanced his ships' prows
      toward the west. He left every shore of France a
      hundred miles or more behind him. All of Spain,
      not knowing why his fleet should plow its seas, is
      full of suspicion.

12. La città nominata da l'antico
    Barchino Annon, tumultüar si vede;
    Taracona e Valenza, e il lito aprico
    a cui l'Alano e il Gotto il nome diede;
    Cartagenia, Almeria, con ogni vico,
    de' bellicosi Vandali già sede;
    Malica, Saravigna, fin là dove
    la strada al mar diede il figliuol di Giove.

13. Avea Ruggier lasciato poche miglia
    Tariffa a dietro, e da la destra sponda
    vede le Gade, e più lontan Siviglia,
    e ne le poppe avea l'aura seconda;
    quando a un tratto di man, con maraviglia,
    un'isoletta uscir vide de l'onda:
    isola pare, et era una balena
    che fuor del mar scopria tutta la schena.

14. L'apparir del gran mostro, che ben diece
    passi del mar con tutto il dosso usciva,
    correr all'armi i naviganti fece,
    et a molti bramar d'essere a riva.
    Saette e sassi e foco acceso in pece
    da tutto il stuolo in gran rumor veniva
    di timpani e di trombe, e tanti gridi,
    che facea il ciel, non che sonare i lidi.

15. Poco lor giova ir l'acqua e l'aer vano
    di percosse e di strepiti ferendo:
    che non si fa per questo più lontano,
    né più si fa vicino il pesce orrendo;
    quanto un sasso gittar si può con mano,
    quel vien l'armata tuttavia seguendo:
    sempre le appar col smisurato fianco
    ora dal destro lato, ora dal manco.

12.   The city named after the ancient Hanno Barca[3] is
        up in arms, together with Tarragona and Valencia
        and the sunny shore which the Alan and the Goth
        named,[4] Cartagena, Almeria, every hamlet that
        was once the seat of warmongering Vandals,[5]
        Malaga and Salobreña, up to where the son of
        Jove left a path for the sea.[6]

13.   Ruggiero had left Tarifa a few miles behind,
        seeing Cadiz on the right-hand shore and Seville
        farther on. He had a following breeze astern
        when, a stone's throw away, he was amazed to see
        a small island rise up out of the waves. It looked
        like an island, but it was a whale raising its entire
        back out of the water and into view.

14.   The appearance of this enormous monster, the
        whole of whose back rose a good ten paces above
        the ocean, made the sailors run to their arms and
        many wish for a safe place on shore. The whole
        crew threw arrows and rocks and firebrands
        lighted with pitch, with a great sounding of drums
        and trumpets and cries that made the heavens, not
        to mention the coasts, resound.

15.   It does them little good to keep striking the water
        and the empty air with their blows and shouts, for
        they draw no farther away from the whale in this
        fashion, nor does the terrible fish get any closer.
        A stone's throw behind them, it comes along
        steadily following the fleet; it is always visible to
        them with its immeasurable flanks, now on the
        right side, now on the left.

16. Andar tre giorni et altre tante notti,
quanto il corso dal stretto al Tago dura,
che sempre di restar sommersi e rotti
dal vivo e mobil scoglio ebbon paura:
gli assalse il quarto dì, che già condotti
eran sopra Lisbona, un'altra cura:
ché scoperson l'armata di Ricardo
che contra lor venia dal mar Picardo.

17. Insieme si conobbero l'armate,
tosto che l'una ebbe de l'altra vista:
Ruggier si crede ch'ambe sian mandate
perché lor meno il Lusitan resista;
e non che, per zizanie seminate
da Gano, l'una l'altra abbia a far trista:
non sa il meschin che colui sia venuto
per ruinarlo, e non per darli aiuto.

18. Fa sugli arbori tutti e in ogni gabbia
e le bandiere stendere e i pennoni,
dare ai tamburi, e gonfiar guance e labbia
a trombe, a corni, a pifari, a bussoni:
come allegrezza et amicizia s'abbia
quivi a mostrar, fa tutti i segni buoni;
gittar fa in acqua i palischermi, e gente
a salutarlo manda umanamente.

19. Ma quel di Normandia, ch'assai diverso
dal buon Ruggier ha in ogni parte il core,
al suo vantaggio intento, non fa verso
lui segno alcun di gaudio né d'amore;
ma, con disir di romperlo e sommerso
quivi lasciar, ne vien senza rumore;
e scostandosi in mar, l'aura seconda
si tolle in poppa, ove Ruggier l'ha in sponda.

16. They went for three days and another three nights
    along the stretch from Gibraltar to the River
    Tagus, and they feared the whole time that they
    would be sunk and destroyed by this living,
    moving reef. On the fourth day they had already
    arrived just outside Lisbon when another care
    beset them, for they saw Ricardo's fleet coming
    toward them from the Sea of Picardy.

17. The two fleets recognized one another as soon as
    they had been sighted. Ruggiero thinks they have
    both been sent to defeat the King of Portugal,
    who will be less able to resist their combined
    forces, and not that one had come, through the
    dissension sown by Ganelon, to do the other
    harm. The poor man had no idea that Ricardo
    had come to destroy him and not to give him aid.

18. He orders banners and pennants to fly from all
    the masts and from every crow's nest; he has the
    sailors beat their drums and swell their cheeks and
    lips on trumpets, coronets, pipes, and horns; he
    puts up every welcoming sign, to demonstrate
    happiness and friendship. He has small boats put
    out on the water and sends men courteously to
    greet Ricardo.

19. But the Norman's heart is in a place entirely
    different from Ruggiero's, and he is intent on his
    advantage. He makes no sign to Ruggiero of joy
    or of love but, wanting to ram him and to leave
    him behind sunk, comes on without a sound and,
    moving away toward the sea, takes the following
    winds astern while Ruggiero receives them on the
    larboard side.

20. Poi che vide Ruggiero assenzo al mèle,
     armi a' saluti, odio all'amore opporse;
     e che, ma tardi, del voler crudele
     del capitan di Normandia s'accorse;
     né più poter montar sopra le vele
     di lui, né per fuggir di mezo tòrse,
     si volse e diede a' suoi duri conforti,
     ch'invendicati almen non fosser morti.

21. L'armata de' Normandi urta e fracassa
     ciò che tra via, cacciando Borea, intoppa;
     e prore e sponde al mare aperte lassa,
     da non le serrar poi chiovi né stoppa:
     ch'ogni sua nave al mezo, ove è più bassa,
     vince dei Provenzal la maggior poppa.
     Ruggier, col disvantaggio che ciascuna
     nave ha minor, ne sostien sei contr'una.

22. Il naviglio maggior d'ogni normando,
     che nel castel da poppa avea Ricardo,
     per l'alto un pezzo era venuto orzando:
     come su l'ali il pellegrin gagliardo,
     che mentre va per l'aria volteggiando,
     non leva mai da la riviera il sguardo;
     e vista alzar la preda ch'egli attende,
     come folgor dal ciel ratto giù scende.

23. Così Ricardo, poi che in mar si tenne
     alquanto largo, e vedut'ebbe il legno
     con che venia Ruggier, tutte l'antenne
     fece carcar fino all'estremo segno;
     e, sì come era sopra vento, venne
     ad investire, e riuscì il disegno:
     ché tutto a un tempo fur l'àncore gravi
     d'alto gittate ad attaccar le navi;

20.   By the time Ruggiero saw wormwood opposed to
        honey, weapons to greetings, hatred to love, and
        realized, too late, the cruel intent of the captain
        from Normandy, he was no longer able to
        outflank the other's sails or to get away through
        flight, so he turned and offered his men the hard
        comfort that they would at least not die
        unavenged.

21.   With Boreas[7] at their backs, the Norman fleet
        rams and destroys whatever it finds in its way and
        breaks open to the sea prows and gunwales which
        neither nails nor wax might close up afterward.
        For every one of their ships is taller at its
        midpoint, where it is lowest in the water, than the
        highest poop in the fleet from Provence. Along
        with the disadvantage of having smaller ships,
        Ruggiero is outnumbered six to one.

22.   The largest of all the Norman ships, which had
        Ricardo at its helm, came luffing a bit out to sea.
        As a vigorous falcon in flight, which never lifts its
        gaze from the ground while it glides through the
        air and, once it sees the prey for which it is
        waiting appear, descends quick as lightning down
        from the heavens;

23.   so, Ricardo, after keeping himself somewhat at a
        distance, when he spotted the vessel in which
        Ruggiero came on, loaded all his masts with sails,
        right up to the last jib and, as if he were riding the
        wind, came up to take him. The plan succeeded,
        for all at once heavy anchors were thrown from
        above as grappling hooks to pull the two ships
        together;

24.   e correndo alle gomone in aita
    più d'una mano, i legni gionti furo.
    Da pal di ferro intanto e da infinita
    copia de dardi era nissun sicuro:
    che da le gagge ne cadea, con trita
    calzina e solfo acceso, un nembo scuro:
    né quei di sotto a ritrovar si vanno
    con minor crudeltà, con minor danno.

25.   Quelli di Normandia, che di luogo alto
    e di numero avean molto vantaggio,
    nel legno di Ruggier féro il mal salto,
    dal furor tratti e dal lor gran coraggio;
    ma tosto si pentir del folle assalto:
    ché non patendo il buon Ruggier l'oltraggio,
    presto di lor, con bel menar de mani,
    fe' squarzi e tronchi e gran pezzi da cani;

26.   e via più a sé valer la spada fece,
    che 'l vantaggio del legno lor non valse,
    o perché contra quattro fosson diece:
    con tanta forza e tanto ardir gli assalse!
    Fe' di negra parer rossa la pece,
    e rosseggiar intorno l'acque salse:
    ché da prora e da poppa e da le sponde
    molti a gran colpi fe' saltar ne l'onde.

27.   Fattosi piazza, e visto sul naviglio
    che non era uom se non de' suoi rimaso,
    ad una scala corse a dar di piglio,
    per montar sopra quel di maggior vaso;
    ma veduto Ricardo il gran periglio
    in che incorrer potea, provide al caso:
    fu la provisïon per lui sicura,
    ma mostrò di pochi altri tener cura.

24.   With more than one hand running to help with
the cables, the two ships were joined. Meanwhile,
nobody was safe from the iron missiles and the
endless shower of darts which fell in a dark cloud
from the crow's nest along with pounded lime and
burning sulphur, nor do those below enter the
fray less cruelly or with lesser harm.

25.   The Normans, who had a great advantage in their
ship's superior height and in number, made the
deadly leap into Ruggiero's vessel, drawn on by
furor and their great courage; but they soon
repented of their foolish attack, for the good
Ruggiero refused to suffer this outrage and, with
his fair handiwork, promptly slashed and hacked
and carved them into dog's meat.

26.   His sword was far more useful to him than the
advantage the Normans had, with their taller ships
and ten men against four, was to them: with that
much strength and that much courage did he
attack them! He made the pitch seem red instead
of black, and the waters around the ship turned
crimson, for with his great blows he sent many
men leaping into the waves from the prow and the
poop and from both sides.

27.   He made himself an open space and, seeing there
was no man aboard the ship but those remaining
from his own crew, he ran for a ladder in order to
climb onto the larger vessel; but Ricardo saw the .
great peril into which he was running and looked
to the situation: his solution was good for himself
but showed he cared little for anyone else.

28. Mentre i compagni difendean il loco,
     andò alli schiffi e fe' gettarli all'acque:
     quattro o sei n'avisò; ma il numer poco
     fu verso agli altri a chi la cosa tacque.
     Poi fe' in più parti al legno porre il foco,
     ch'ivi non molto addormentato giacque;
     ma di Ruggier la nave accese ancora,
     e da le poppe andò sin alla prora.

29. Ricardo si salvò dentro ai batelli,
     e seco alcuni suoi ch'ebbe più cari;
     e sopra un legno si fe' por di quelli
     ch'in sua conserva avean solcati i mari:
     indi mandò tutti i minor vasselli
     a trar i suoi dei salsi flutti amari:
     che per fuggir l'ardente dio di Lenno
     in braccio a Teti et a Nettun si denno.

30. Ruggier non avea schiffo ove salvarse,
     ché, come ho detto, il suo mandato avea
     a salutar Ricardo et allegrarse
     di quel di che doler più si dovea;
     né all'altre navi sue, ch'erano sparse
     per tutto il mar, ricorso aver potea:
     sì che, tardando un poco, ha da morire
     nel foco quivi, o in mar se vuol fuggire.

31. Vede in prua, vede in poppa e ne le sponde
     crescer la fiamma, e per tutte le bande:
     ben certo è di morir, ma si confonde,
     se meglio sia nel foco o nel mar grande:
     pur si risolve di morir ne l'onde,
     acciò la morte in lungo un poco mande:
     così spicca un gran salto da la nave
     in mezo il mar, di tutte l'armi grave.

28. While his companions defended the place, he went to the skiffs and had them lowered into the water. He told four or six of his men of his plan, but they were few compared with the others to whom he kept the matter silent. Then he had fires set in various parts of his ship, which did not long lie dormant there: they spread and set Ruggiero's vessel ablaze as well, and the flames went right from stem to stern.

29. Ricardo saved himself in the dinghies and with him some of the men he held most dear. He had himself put onto one of the other ships that plowed the seas in his convoy and from there sent out smaller vessels to fish his men from the bitter salt waves; for in fleeing the burning God of Lemnos[8] they had given themselves up into the hands of Tethys and Neptune.[9]

30. Ruggiero had no skiff in which to save himself because, as I have said, he had sent his out to greet Ricardo and make merry over what he should instead have mourned. And he had no recourse to his other ships because they were scattered all over the sea. So, if he waits a little while longer, he will die there in the fire or, if he wishes to flee, in the ocean.

31. He sees the flames rise in the prow, and he sees them in the stern and on the sides, everywhere. He is quite sure of dying but in a quandary if it were better in the fire or in the great sea; finally he resolves to die in the waves, so that he may put off death a little longer. So, weighed down with all his armor, he takes a great leap off the ship into the middle of the sea.

32. Qual suol vedersi in lucida onda e fresca
 di tranquillo vivai correr la lasca
 al pan che getti il pescator, o all'ésca
 ch'in ramo alcun de le sue rive nasca;
 tal la balena, che per lunga tresca
 segue Ruggier perché di lui si pasca,
 visto il salto, v'accorre, e senza noia
 con un gran sorso d'acqua se lo ingoia.

33. Ruggier, che s'era abbandonato e al tutto
 messo per morto, dal timor confuso,
 non s'avvide al cader, come condutto
 fosse in quel luogo tenebroso e chiuso;
 ma perché gli parea fetido e brutto,
 esser spirto pensò di vita escluso,
 il qual fosse dal Giudice superno
 mandato in purgatorio o giù all'inferno.

34. Stava in gran tema del foco penace,
 di che avea ne la nuova Fé già inteso.
 Era come una grotta ampla e capace
 l'oscurissimo ventre ove era sceso:
 sente che sotto i piedi arena giace,
 che cede, ovunque egli la calchi, al peso:
 brancolando le man quanto può stende
 da l'un lato e da l'altro, e nulla prende.

35. Si pone a Dio, con umiltà di mente,
 de' suoi peccati a dimandar perdono,
 che non lo danni alla infelice gente
 di quei ch'al ciel mai per salir non sono.
 Mentre che in ginocchion divotamente
 sta così orando al basso curvo e prono,
 un picciol lumicin d'una lucerna
 vide apparir lontan per la caverna.

32. As in the fresh, clear water of a calm fish pond one
    sees carp run for the bread a fisherman throws or
    to food which falls from some branch along its
    banks; so the whale—which had followed
    Ruggiero on a long, watery dance in order at last
    to feed on him—seeing him jump, rushes there
    and with no trouble swallows him in a great gulp
    of water.[10]

33. Ruggiero, who had abandoned all hope and given
    himself up entirely for dead, was confused by fear
    and on falling did not realize how he had been
    brought into that dark, shadowy prison; but
    because it seemed fetid and ugly to him, he
    thought he was a spirit cut off from life who had
    been sent by the supreme Judge to Purgatory or
    down to Hell.[11]

34. He was terribly afraid of the penal fire which he
    had heard about before from his new Christian
    faith.[12] The pitch-dark stomach into which he had
    fallen was like a wide and spacious cavern. He
    feels sand lying beneath his feet, which gives way
    under his weight wherever he steps on it. Groping
    with his hands, he reaches out as far as he can to
    one side and the other, but touches nothing.

35. Humble in spirit, he begins to ask God's pardon
    for his sins, so that He might not damn him to
    join the unhappy people who are never to rise to
    Heaven. While thus he was praying devoutly on
    his knees, bowed and prostrate on the ground, he
    saw a tiny light from a lantern appear far off in the
    cavern.

36.　Esser Caron lo giudicò da lunge,
　　　che venisse a portarlo all'altra riva:
　　　s'avvide, poi che più vicin gli giunge,
　　　che senza barca a sciutto piè veniva.
　　　La barba alla cintura si congiunge,
　　　le spalle il bianco crin tutto copriva;
　　　ne la destra una rete avea, a costume
　　　di pescator; ne la sinistra un lume.

37.　Ruggier lo vedea appresso, et era in forse
　　　se fosse uom vivo, o pur fantasma et ombra.
　　　Tosto che del splendor l'altro s'accorse
　　　che feria l'armi e si spargea per l'ombra,
　　　si trasse a dietro e per fuggir si torse,
　　　come destrier che per camino adombra;
　　　ma poi che si mirar l'un l'altro meglio,
　　　Ruggier fu il primo a dimandar al veglio:

38.　—Dimmi, padre, s'io vivo o s'io son morto,
　　　s'io sono al mondo o pur sono all'inferno:
　　　questo so ben, ch'io fui dal mar absorto;
　　　ma se per ciò morissi, non discerno.
　　　Perché mi veggo armato, mi conforto
　　　ch'io non sia spirto dal mio corpo esterno;
　　　ma poi l'esser rinchiuso in questo fondo
　　　fa ch'io tema esser morto e fuor del mondo.

39.　—Figliuol,—rispose il vecchio—tu sei vivo,
　　　com'anch'io son; ma fòra meglio molto
　　　esser di vita l'uno e l'altro privo,
　　　che nel mostro marin viver sepolto.
　　　Tu sei d'Alcina, se non sai, captivo:
　　　ella t'ha il laccio teso, e al fin t'ha colto,
　　　come colse me ancora, con parecchi
　　　altri che ci vedrai, giovani e vecchi.

36. From afar, he judged it to be Charon coming to carry him to the other bank. He realized, after the figure came closer to him, that he was coming without a boat, with dry feet. His beard reached to his belt, white locks completely covered his shoulders, in his right hand he had a net, after the fashion of a fisherman, and in his left a light.

37. Ruggiero saw him close up and was in doubt whether he was a living man or only a ghost or a shade. As soon as the other was aware of the light that reflected off the armor and spread through the darkness, he drew back and turned to flee, like a horse that shies on the road; but after they could see one another better, Ruggiero was the first to ask the old man:

38. "Tell me, father, if I am alive or if I am dead, if I am in the world or if I am really in Hell: this I know well, that I was swallowed by the sea; but I cannot tell whether I died from it. Because I see myself armed, I am comforted that I may not be a spirit outside my body; but then, being closed up in this pit makes me fear that I am dead and beyond the world."

39. "Son," the old man answered, "you are alive, just as I am, but it would be far better for both of us if we were dead rather than buried alive in this sea monster. You are, if you don't know it, a captive of Alcina; she stretched the snare for you and has finally caught you just as she caught me and others you will see here, young and old.

40.   Vedendoti qui dentro, non accade
        di darti cognizion chi Alcina sia;
        che se tu non avessi sua amistade
        avuta prima, ciò non t'avverria.
        In India vedut'hai la quantitade
        de le conversïon che questa ria
        ha fatto in fere, in fonti, in sassi, in piante,
        dei cavallier di ch'ella è stata amante.

41.   Quei che, per nuovi successor, men cari
        le vengono, muta ella in varie forme;
        ma quei che se ne fuggon, che son rari,
        sì come esserne un tu credo di apporme,
        quando giunger li può negli ampli mari
        (però che mai non ne abbandona l'orme),
        gli caccia in ventre a quest'orribil pesce,
        donde mai vivo o morto alcun non esce.

42.   Le Fate hanno tra lor tutta partita
        e l'abitata e la deserta terra:
        l'una ne l'Indo può, l'altra nel Scita,
        questa può in Spagna e quella in Inghilterra;
        e ne l'altrui ciascuna è proibita
        di metter mano, et è punita ch'erra:
        ma comune fra lor tutto il mare hanno,
        e ponno a chi lor par quivi far danno.

43.   Tu vederai qua giù, scendendo al basso,
        degli infelici amanti i scuri avelli,
        de' quali è alcun sì antico, che nel sasso
        gli nomi non si puon legger di quelli.
        Qui crespo e curvo, qui debole e lasso
        m'ha fatto il tempo, e tutti bianchi i velli;
        che quando venni, a pena uscìan dal mento
        com'oro i peli ch'or vedi d'argento.

40. "Because I see you here I don't need to tell you who Alcina is, for if you had not once possessed her love, this would not have happened to you. You saw in India the many transformations—into beasts, fountains, rocks, and plants—this wicked woman has wrought on knights she once had taken as lovers.[13]

41. "Those that lose her favor because of newfound successors she changes into various forms; but as for those few who escape her, and I think I can assume you to be one of these, when she can overtake them on the high seas (for she never abandons their tracks), she drives them into the belly of this horrible fish, from which no one has ever departed dead or alive.

42. "The Fairies have divided up all the inhabited and uninhabited Earth among them; one governs in India, another in Scythia, this one Spain, and that one England. Each is prohibited from laying hands on the others' territory and will be punished if she errs, but they hold the sea in common among them all and they can do harm there to whomever they like.

43. "You will see below here, as we go down to the bottom, the dark tombs of her unfortunate lovers, some of which are so old that one cannot read their names on the stone. Here time has made me wrinkled and bent, exhausted and weak, and turned my hair all white. When I arrived, the silver whiskers you see now were golden and barely issued from my chin.

44.   Quanti anni sien non saprei dir, ch'io scesi
      in queste d'ogni tempo oscure grotte:
      che qui né gli anni annoverar né i mesi,
      né si può il dì conoscer da la notte.
      Duo vecchi ci trovai, dai quali intesi
      quel da che fur le mie speranze rotte:
      che più de la mia età ci avean consunto,
      et io gli giunsi a sepelire a punto.

45.   E mi narrar che, quando giovenetti
      ci vennero, alcun'altri avean trovati,
      che similmente d'Alcina diletti,
      di poi qui presi e posti erano stati:
      sì che, figliuol, non converrà ch'aspetti
      riveder mai più gli uomini beati,
      ma con noi che tre eramo, et ora teco
      siam quattro, starti in questo ventre cieco.

46.   Ci rimasi io già solo, e poscia dui,
      poi da venti dì in qua tre fatti eramo,
      et oggi quattro, essendo tu con nui:
      ch'in tanto mal grand'aventura chiamo
      che tu ci trovi compagnia, con cui
      pianger possi il tuo stato oscuro e gramo;
      e non abbi a provar l'affanno e 'l duolo
      che quel tempo io provai che ci fui solo.—

47.   Come ad udir sta il misero il processo
      de' falli suoi che l'han dannato a morte,
      così turbato e col capo demesso
      udia Ruggier la sua infelice sorte.
      —Rimedio altro non ci è—soggiunse appresso
      il vecchio—che di oprar l'animo forte.
      Meco verrai dove, secondo il loco,
      l'industria e il tempo n'ha adagiati un poco.

44. "I have no way of telling how many years it is
since I came down into this cave in whose
darkness all sense of time is lost. Here one cannot
count years or months, or tell the day from night.
I found two old men here from whom I learned
that which shattered my hopes: they had spent
more years in this place than I had yet lived, and I
arrived just in time to bury them.

45. "They told me that when they came here as
young men they found others, once similarly
beloved of Alcina, who had afterward been
captured and imprisoned here. So you must
expect, my son, never to see happy men again but
to live in this dark belly with us—we who have
been three and now with you are four.

46. "For a while I stayed here alone and then there
were two of us and there have been three for
twenty days now. Today, with you joining us, we
are made four, and I call it great good fortune that
in such evil circumstances you should find
company here with whom you can lament your
dark and miserable state and that you won't have
to experience the anguish and pain I felt in the
time I dwelt here all alone."

47. As a wretched man listens to the trial of the crimes
that have condemned him to death, so, distraught
and with head hung down, Ruggiero listened to
his unhappy fate. "There is no other remedy
here," the old man added next, "than to practice
fortitude. You will come with me to where,
according to the nature of this place, industry and
time have somewhat eased our lives.

48. Ma voglio proveder prima di cena,
     che qui sempre però non si digiuna.—
     Così dicendo, Ruggier indi mena,
     cedendo al lume l'ombra e l'aria bruna,
     dove l'acqua per bocca alla balena
     entra, e nel ventre tutta si raguna:
     quivi con la sua rete il vecchio scese,
     e di più forme pesci in copia prese.

49. Poi, con la rete in collo e il lume in mano,
     la via a Ruggier per strani groppi scorse:
     al salir et al scendere la mano
     ai stretti passi anco talor gli porse.
     Tratto ch'un miglio o più l'ebbe lontano,
     con gli altri dui compagni al fin trovorse
     in più capace luogo, ove all'esempio
     d'una moschea, fatto era un picciol tempio.

50. Chiaro vi si vedea come di giorno,
     per le spesse lucerne ch'eran poste
     in mezzo e per gli canti e d'ogn'intorno,
     fatte di nicchi di marine croste:
     a dar lor l'oglio traboccava il corno,
     ché non è quivi cosa che men coste,
     pei molti capidogli che divora
     e vivi ingoia il mostro ad ora ad ora.

51. Una stanza alla chiesa era vicina,
     di più famiglia che la lor capace,
     dove su bene asciutta alga marina
     nei canti alcun commodo letto giace.
     Tengono in mezo il fuoco la cucina:
     che fatto avea l'artefice sagace,
     che per lungo condutto di fuor esce
     il fumo, ai luoghi onde sospira il pesce.

48. "But first I want to provide us with some supper, for, whatever our plight here, we do not continually fast." So speaking, he leads Ruggiero away, the shadows and dark air yielding to his light, to a place where the water came into the whale's mouth and collected all together in its stomach. The old man went down there with his net and gathered in plenty of fish of different kinds.

49. Then, with the net over his shoulder and the lantern in his hand, he showed Ruggiero the way through unknown, tangled paths; sometimes he also gave him his hand climbing and descending through narrow passes. After he had led him for a mile or more, they finally found themselves with the other two companions in a more open space, where a little temple had been erected on the model of a mosque.

50. One saw there as clearly as if it were daylight because of the many lanterns made of the shells of crustaceans that were set up in the middle of the place, in the corners and all around. The oil horn supplying them overflowed, for there was nothing there that cost less because of the many sperm whales that the monster devoured and swallowed alive from one moment to the next.

51. Next to the church, there was a room big enough for larger company than theirs, where some comfortable bedding of well-dried seaweed could be found in the corners. They kept a fire in the middle of the kitchen which the wise craftsman had constructed so that the smoke would escape through a long conduit which drew it out to where the fish breathed.

52. Tosto che pon Ruggier là dentro il piede,
    vi riconosce Astolfo paladino,
    che mal contento in un dei letti siede,
    tra sé piangendo il suo fero destino.
    Lo corre ad abbracciar, come lo vede:
    gli leva Astolfo incontro il viso chino:
    e come lui Ruggier esser conosce,
    rinuova i pianti, e fa maggior l'angosce.

53. Poi che piangendo all'abbracciar più d'una
    e di due volte ritornati furo,
    l'un l'altro dimandò da qual fortuna
    fosson dannati in quel gran ventre oscuro.
    Ruggier narrò quel ch'io v'ho già de l'una
    e l'altra armata detto, il caso oscuro,
    e di Ricardo senza fin si dolse;
    Astolfo poi così la lingua sciolse:

54. —Dal mio peccato (che accusar non voglio
    la mia fortuna) questo mal mi avviene.
    Tu di Ricardo, io sol di me mi doglio:
    tu pati a torto, io con ragion le pene.
    Ma, per aprirti chiaramente il foglio
    sì che l'istoria mia si vegga bene,
    tu déi saper che non son molti mesi
    ch'andai di Francia a riveder mie' Inglesi.

55. Quivi, per chiari e replicati avisi
    essendo più che certo de la guerra
    che 'l re di Danismarca e i Dazii e i Frisi
    apparecchiato avean contra Inghilterra;
    ove il bisogno era maggior mi misi,
    per lor vietar il dismontar in terra,
    dentro un castel che fu per guardia sito
    di quella parte ov'è men forte il lito:

52.   As soon as Ruggiero set his foot inside, he
      recognized the paladin Astolfo, who was sitting
      unhappily on one of the beds, lamenting to
      himself over his hard destiny. As soon as he sees
      him, Ruggiero runs to embrace him; Astolfo
      raises his lowered face and, as he recognizes
      Ruggiero, renews his weeping and suffers even
      more.

53.   After they had exchanged tearful embraces more
      than once or twice, they asked one another by
      what fortune they had been damned to that great,
      dark belly. Ruggiero related what I have already
      told you about the two fleets, the confused
      situation, and complained endlessly about
      Ricardo. Astolfo then loosed his tongue as
      follows: [14]

54.   "This evil comes upon me because of my sins (for
      I do not want to accuse my fortune). You
      complain about Ricardo, I only about myself. You
      suffer these punishments wrongly, I with cause.
      But, to open the page at the beginning and see my
      story plainly, you must know that it is not many
      months since I left France to see my English
      people once again.

55.   "There I was assured by many clear reports that
      the King of Denmark, the Jutlanders, and the
      Frisians were preparing a war against England, and
      to deter their landing I placed myself where the
      need was greatest, in a castle that was positioned
      to guard that region where the shore was least
      fortified.

56. ché da quel canto il re mio padre Ottone
     temea che fosse l'isola assalita.
     Signor di quel castell'era un barone
     ch'avea la moglie di beltà infinita;
     la qual tosto ch'io vidi, ogni ragione,
     ogni onestà da me fece partita;
     e tutto il mio voler, tutto il mio core
     diedi in poter del scelerato amore.

57. E senza aver all'onor mio riguardo
     che quivi ero signor, egli vassallo
     (ché contra un debol, quanto è più gagliardo
     chi le forze usa, tanto è maggior fallo),
     poi che dei prieghi ire il rimedio tardo
     e vidi lei più dura che metallo,
     all'insidie aguzzar prima l'ingegno,
     et indi alla violenzia ebbi il disegno.

58. E perché, come i modi miei non molto
     erano onesti, così ancor né ascosi,
     fui dal marito in tal sospetto tolto,
     che in lei guardar passò tutti i gelosi.
     Per questo non pensar che 'l desir stolto
     in me s'allenti o che giamai riposi;
     et uso atti e parole in sua presenza
     da far romper a Giobbe la pacienza.

59. E perché aveva pur quivi rispetto
     d'usar le forze alla scoperta seco,
     dov'era tanto populo, in conspetto
     de' principi e baron che v'eran meco;
     pur pensai di sforzarlo, ma l'effetto
     coprire, e lui far in vederlo cieco;
     e mezzo a questo un cavalier trovai,
     il qual molt'era suo, ma mio più assai.

56. "My father, King Ottone, feared that the island might be attacked on that side. The lord of the castle was a baron who had a wife of infinite beauty. As soon as I saw her all reason, all honor left me, and I gave all my will, all my heart, into the power of a wicked love.

57. "Without regard for my honor, or for the fact that I was lord there while he was a vassal (for in using force against someone weaker, the more powerful a man is, the greater is his fault), when I saw that the remedy I sought came slowly despite my entreaties and that the lady was harder than metal, I decided to sharpen my wits, directing them first to deceit, and then to violence.

58. "And, as my manners were not very honorable and I did nothing to hide them, I was held in so much suspicion by the husband that he surpassed all jealous men in guarding his wife. Do not imagine that my mad desire relents or ever rests on that account; I do and say things in the man's presence that would break the patience of Job.

59. "And although I still had scruples about using force openly with him while there were so many people about and in the sight of the princes and barons who were there with me, I thought nonetheless how to overpower him by force, but to conceal the fact, and to make him blind to it as well. And to this end I found a knight who belonged very much to him, but very much more to me.

60. A' preghi miei, costui gli fe' vedere
com'era mal accorto e poco saggio
a tener dov'io fossi la mogliere,
che sol studiava in procacciargli oltraggio;
e saria più laudabile parere,
tosto che m'accadesse a far vïaggio
da un loco a un altro, com'era mia usanza,
di salvar quella in più sicura stanza.

61. Còrre il tempo potea la prima volta
che, per non ritornar la sera, andassi:
che spesso aveva in uso andar in volta
per riparar, per riveder i passi.
Gualtier (che così avea nome) l'ascolta,
né vuol ch'indarno il buon consiglio passi:
pensa mandarla in Scozia, ove di quella
il padre era signor di più castella.

62. Quindi segretamente alcune some
de le sue miglior cose in Scozia invia.
Io do la voce d'ir a Londra; e, come
mi par il tempo, un dì mi metto in via;
et ei con Cinzia sua (che così ha nome),
senza sospetto di trovar tra via
cosa ch'all'andar suo fosse molesta,
del castello esce, et entra in la foresta.

63. Con donne e con famigli disarmati
la via più dritta inverso Scozia prese:
non molto andò, che cadde negli aguati,
ne l'insidie che i miei li avean già tese.
Avev'io alcuni miei fedel mandati,
che co' visi coperti in strano arnese
gli furo adosso, e tolser la consorte,
e a lui di grazia fu campar da morte.

60. "At my beseeching, this man made the baron see
how ill-advised and foolish he was to keep his
wife where I was present, when my one ambition
was to procure his dishonor; and that it would be
wiser, the next time I made the rounds of our
defenses, as I was wont to do, to secure her in a
safer place.

61. "Because I often used to go about repairing and
inspecting the strategic passes, he could seize the
opportunity the first time I left without intending
to return the same evening. Walter (for this was
the baron's name) listens to the man and does not
allow the good advice to go unheeded. He
decides to send his wife to Scotland, where her
father was the lord of many castles.

62. "Whereupon he sends some shipments of his
wife's best things secretly to Scotland. I spread
word of a trip to London and, when I think it the
right moment, set out one day on my way. He
leaves the castle and goes into the forest with his
Cynthia (for this was the lady's name), without
expecting to meet any hindrance along the way.

63. "With the ladies and with his unarmed servants,
he took the most direct route toward Scotland.
He had not gone far before he fell into the
ambush, into the treachery, that my men had set
for him. I had sent some of my trusty men who
attacked him with masked faces and unknown
armor and took away his consort, while he was
lucky to escape with his life.

64.   Quella portano in fretta entro una torre,
fuor de la gente, in loco assai rimoto;
donde a me senza indugio un messo corre,
il qual mi fa tutto il successo noto.
Io già avea detto di volermi tòrre
de l'isola; e la causa di tal moto
era, ch'udiva esser Rinaldo a Carlo
fatto nemico, et io volea aiutarlo.

65.   Alli amici fo motto; e, come io voglia
passar quel giorno, inverso il mar mi movo;
poi mi nascondo, et armi muto e spoglia,
e piglio a' miei servigi un scudier novo;
e per le selve ove meno ir si soglia,
verso la torre ascosa via ritrovo;
e dove è più solinga e strana et erma,
incontro una donzella che mi ferma,

66.   e dice: "Astolfo, giovaràtti poco"
che mi chiamò per nome "andar di piatto;
che ben sarai trovato, e a tempo e a loco
ti punirà quello a chi ingiuria hai fatto."
Così dice; e ne va poi come foco
che si vede pel ciel discorrer ratto:
la vuo' seguir; ma sì corre, anzi vola,
che replicar non posso una parola.

67.   E se n'andò quel dì medesimo anco
a ritrovar Gualtiero afflitto e mesto,
che per dolor si battea il petto e 'l fianco,
e gli fe' tutto il caso manifesto:
non già ch'alcun me lo dicessi, e manco
che con gli occhi i'l vedessi, io dico questo;
ma, così, discorrendo con la mente,
veggo che non puote esser altramente.

64. "They take her in haste to a tower in a remote place far from populated areas; from there a messenger returns to me without delay to tell me the successful outcome of the whole affair. I had already spoken of wanting to leave the island, and my reason for this move was that I had heard Rinaldo had become Charles's enemy and that I wanted to give him aid.

65. "I bid my friends farewell and, as if I want to cross the channel that very day, make for the sea. Then I hide, change my armor and tunic, take a new squire in my service, and follow a secret road to the tower through woods where few men choose to travel. There, where it is most solitary, wild, and deserted, I come across a damsel who stops me,

66. "and says: 'Astolfo,' for she called me by name, 'it will do you little good to go in secret, for you will surely be discovered and sometime, somewhere, the man you have wronged will punish you.' So she says and then disappears like the lightning one sees speed so swiftly across the sky. I want to follow her, but she runs, or rather flies, so fast that I am unable to answer one word.

67. "And that same day she also went to find the miserable and dejected Walter, who was beating his breast and side in grief, and she laid bare the entire situation to him. I say this not because anyone actually told me she did, and less because I saw it with my own eyes, but, going over the case in my mind, I see it cannot have been otherwise.

68.   Conietturando, similmente, seppi
esser costei d'Alcina messaggera;
che dal dì ch'io mi sciolsi dai suoi ceppi,
sempre venuta insidïando m'era.
Come ho detto, costei Gualtier pei greppi
pianger trovò di sua fortuna fiera;
né chi offeso l'avea gli mostra solo,
ma il modo ancor di vendicar suo duolo.

69.   E lo pon, come suol porre alla posta
il mastro de la caccia i spiedi e i cani;
e tanto fa, ch'un mio corrier, ch'in posta
mandav'a Antona, gli fa andar in mani.
Io scrivea a un mio, ch'ivi tenea a mia posta
un legno per portarmi agli Aquitani,
il giorno ch'io volea che fosse a punto
in certa spiaggia per levarmi giunto.

70.   Né in Antona volea né in altro porto,
per non lasciar conoscermi, imbarcarmi:
del segno ancora io lo faceva accorto
col qual volea dal lito a lui mostrarmi,
acciò stando sul mar tuttavia sorto
mandasse il palischermo indi a levarmi;
et, all'incontro, il segno che dovessi
far egli a me in la lettera gli espressi.

71.   Ben fu Gualtier de la ventura lieto,
che sì gli apria la strada alla vendetta.
Fe' che tornar non poté il messo, e, cheto,
dov'era un suo fratel se n'andò in fretta,
e lo pregò che gli armasse in segreto
un legno di fedele gente eletta.
Avuto il legno, il buon Gualtiero corse
al capo di Lusarte, e quivi sorse.

68.   "Similarly conjecturing, I know that the damsel
      was a messenger from Alcina, who, from the day I
      loosed myself from her fetters, had constantly
      been plotting against me. As I said, she found
      Walter in the wilds lamenting his harsh fortune,
      and she told him not only who had injured him
      but also the way to avenge his grief.

69.   "And she positions him just as the master of the
      hunt positions the spearmen and the dogs at a
      pass. She so arranges matters that one of the
      couriers I was sending by post to Southampton
      falls into Walter's hands. I had written to one of
      my men who held a ship at my disposal there to
      take me to the Aquitaine, telling him the day that
      I wanted it on a certain beach ready for me to
      come and depart on it.

70.   "I didn't want to embark from Southampton or
      any other port because I didn't want to be
      recognized. I also told the man about a signal I
      would make to show myself on the beach so he
      could send a boat to pick me up from where he
      was standing at anchor; I also told him in the letter
      the signal that he would have to make to me in
      return.

71.   "Walter was delighted with his good fortune,
      which in this way cleared the path for his revenge.
      He made sure the messenger could not return and
      quietly hurried to a brother of his and begged him
      to arm a ship for him in secret with select and
      loyal men. The good Walter obtained his ship and
      hurried to Cape Lizard and anchored there.

72.   Vicino a questo mar sedea la rocca,
      dove aspettava in parte assai selvaggia,
      sì ch'apparir veggo lontan la cocca
      col segno da me dato in su la gaggia:
      io, d'altra parte, quel ch'a me far tocca
      gli mostro da la torre e da la spiaggia.
      Manda Gualtier lo schiffo, e me raccoglie,
      et un scudier c'ho meco, e la sua moglie.

73.   Né sé né alcun de' suoi ch'io conoscessi
      prima scopersi che sul legno fui;
      ove lasciando a pena ch'io dicessi:
      —Dio aiutami—, pigliar mi fece ai sui,
      che come vespe e galavroni spessi
      mi s'aventaro; e, comandando lui,
      in mar buttarmi, ove già questa fera,
      come Alcina ordinò, nascosa s'era.

74.   Così 'l peccato mio brutto e nefando,
      degno di questa e di più pena molta,
      m'ha chiuso qui, onde di come e quando
      io n'abbia a uscir, ogni speranza è tolta;
      quella protezïon tutta levando,
      che san Giovanni avea già di me tolta.—
      Poi ch'ebbe così detto, allentò il freno
      Astolfo al pianto, e bagnò il viso e 'l seno.

75.   Ruggier, che come lui non era immerso
      sì nel dolor, ma si sentia più sorto,
      gli studiava, inducendogli alcun verso
      de la Scrittura, di trovar conforto.
      —Non è—dicea—del Re de l'universo,
      l'intenzïon che 'l peccator sia morto,
      ma che dal mar d'iniquitadi a riva
      ritorni salvo, e si converti e viva.

72.   "In a very wild spot close by these waters sat the
        fortress where I was waiting and from which I saw
        the ship appear from afar with my signal given
        above the crow's nest. I, for my part, give the
        signal I was to show from the tower and from the
        beach. Walter sends his skiff and collects me, a
        squire I kept along with me, and his wife.

73.   "Neither Walter nor any of his men that I could
        recognize revealed themselves before I was in their
        boat. There, leaving me barely time to say 'God
        help me,' he had his men seize me; they threw
        themselves on me as thick as wasps and hornets. At
        his bidding, they threw me into the sea, where
        this beast, as Alcina had planned, was already
        hidden.

74.   "Thus my ugly and wicked sin, worthy of this
        punishment and of much worse, has shut me up
        here, without any hope of escape; and all the
        protection St. John once gave me has been taken
        away." [15] And after these words Astolfo gave free
        rein to his weeping and bathed his face and breast
        with tears.

75.   Ruggiero, who was not as immersed in his sorrow
        as was Astolfo but felt more calm, strove to find
        him some comfort by citing him some verses of
        Scripture. "It is not the intention of the King of
        the Universe," he said, "that the sinner should die,
        but that he should return safe from the sea of his
        iniquity to shore, and be converted and live. [16]

76. Cosa umana è a peccar; e pur si legge
     che sette volte il giorno il giusto cade;
     e sempre a chi si pente e si corregge
     ritorna a perdonar l'Alta bontade:
     anzi, d'un peccator che fuor del gregge
     abbi errato, e poi torni a miglior strade,
     maggior gloria è nel regno degli eletti,
     che di novantanove altri perfetti.—

77. Per far nascer conforto, cotal seme
     il buon Ruggier venìa spargendo quivi;
     poi ricordava ch'altra volta insieme
     d'Alcina in Orïente fur captivi;
     e come di là usciro, anco aver speme
     dovean d'uscir di questo carcer vivi.
     —S'allora io fui—dicea—degno d'aita,
     or ne son più, che son miglior di vita.—

78. E seguitò: —Se quando ne l'errore
     de la dannata legge ero perduto,
     e ne l'ozio sommerso e nel fetore
     tutto d'Alcina, come animal bruto,
     mi liberò il mio sommo almo Fattore;
     perché sperar non debbo ora il suo aiuto,
     che per la Fede essendo puro e netto
     di molte colpe, io so che m'ha più accetto?

79. Creder non voglio che 'l demonio rio,
     dal qual la forza di costei dipende,
     possa nuocere agli uomini che Dio
     per suoi conosce e che per suoi difende.
     Se vera fede avrai, se l'avrò anch'io,
     Dio la vedrà che i nostri cori intende:
     e vedendola vera, abbi speranza
     che non avrà il demonio in noi possanza.—

76. "It is a human thing to sin. One reads that even the just man falls seven times a day [17] and that the Goodness on High always renews his pardon to the man who repents and corrects himself. Moreover, for the sinner who may have wandered from the flock but who has then returned to a better way, there is more glory in the kingdom of the elect than for ninety-nine other perfect spirits." [18]

77. The good Ruggiero went sowing such seed as this in order to generate some comfort. Then he recalled that they had been prisoners of Alcina together on another occasion, in the East, and because they escaped from her there, they had reason to hope they could escape alive from this prison as well. "If I was worthy of help then," he said, "I am more worthy of it now, for I lead a better life."

78. And he continued: "If, when I was lost in the error of the damned creed and all immersed like a brute animal in the idleness and stench of Alcina, my most high and dear Maker freed me, then why should I not hope for His assistance now, now that I am purified and cleansed of my many sins by Faith, and I know that He finds me more acceptable?

79. "I will not believe that the wicked Devil on whom Alcina's power depends can harm men whom God recognizes and defends as His own. If you have true faith, and if I have it too, God, who understands our hearts, will see it; and when He sees it is genuine, you may have hope that the Devil will not have power over us."

80.   Astolfo, presa la parola, disse:
    —Questo ogni buon cristian de' tener certo.
    Non scese in terra Dio, né con noi visse,
    né in vita e in morte ha tanto mal sofferto,
    perché il nimico suo dipoi venisse
    a riportar di sua fatica il merto.
    Quel che sì ricco prezzo costò a lui,
    non lascerà sì facilmente altrui.

81.   Non manchi in noi contrizïone e fede,
    e di pregar con purità di mente;
    che Dio non può mancarci di mercede:
    Egli lo disse, e il dir suo mai non mente.
    Scritto ha nel suo Evangelio: "Ch'in me crede,
    uccide nel mio nome ogni serpente,
    il venen bee senza che mal gli faccia,
    sana gli infermi e gli demoni scaccia."

82.   E dice altrove: "Quando con perfetta
    fede ad un monte a commandar tu vada:
    'Di qui ti leva, e dentro il mar ti getta';
    che 'l monte piglierà nel mar la strada."
    Ma perché fede quasi morta è detta
    quella che sta senza fare opre a bada,
    procacciamo con buon'opre che sia
    più grata a Dio la tua fede e la mia.

83.   Proviam di trarre alla vera credenza
    quest'altri che son qui presi con nui;
    di che già fatto ho qualche esperïenza,
    ma poco un parer mio può contra dui.
    Forse saremo a mutar lor sentenza
    meglio insieme tu et io, ch'io sol non fui;
    e se potiam questi al demonio tòrre,
    non ha qua dentro poi dove si porre.

80. Astolfo began to speak and said: "Every good Christian ought to be sure of this one thing: God did not descend to earth and live with us and suffer so much evil in life and in death so that His enemy might come afterward to carry away the rewards of His labor. That which cost Him so rich a price He will not leave so easily for another.

81. "Let us not fail to be contrite and have faith and to pray with pure minds, for God cannot fail to show us His mercy. He said so Himself, and His words never lie. He has written in His Gospel, 'He that believes in me kills every serpent in my name, drinks poison without it doing him harm, heals the sick, and drives out devils.'[19]

82. "And He says elsewhere: 'When you go to the mountain with perfect faith and command, "Rise from here and throw yourself into the sea," the mountain will take its way to the sea.'[20] But because the faith that tarries without doing works is said to be almost dead,[21] let us strive to make your faith and mine more gracious unto God through good works.

83. "Let us try to lead these others that are imprisoned here with us to the true faith, which I have tried somewhat to do, but my one opinion can do little against their two. Perhaps we will be better able to change their minds together, you and I, than I was alone; and if we are able to save them from the Devil, he will then have no foothold in here.

84. E Dio, tutti vedendone fedeli
    pregar la sua clemenza che n'aiute,
    dal fonte di pietà scender dai cieli
    farà qua dentro un fiume di salute.—
    Così dicean; poi salmi, inni e vangeli,
    orazïon che a mente avean tenute,
    incominciar i cavallier devoti,
    e a porr'in opra i prieghi e i pianti e i voti.

85. Intanto gli altri dui con studio grande
    cercavan di far vezzi al novell'oste.
    Di vari pesci varie le vivande
    a rosto e lesso al foco erano poste.
    Poco inanzi, un naviglio da le bande
    di Vinegia, spezzato ne le coste,
    la balena s'avea cacciato sotto
    e tratto in ventre in molti pezzi rotto;

86. e le botte e le casse e gli fardelli
    tutti nel ventre ingordo erano entrati.
    Gli naviganti soli coi battelli
    ai legni di conserva eran campati:
    sì che v'è da dar foco, e nei piatelli
    da condir buoni cibi e delicati
    con zucchero e con spezie; et avean vini
    e còrsi e grechi, precïosi e fini.

87. Passavano pochi anni, ch'una o due
    volte non si rompesson legni quivi;
    donde i prigion per le bisogne sue
    cibi traean da mantenersi vivi.
    Poser la cena, come cotta fue;
    s'avessen pane o se ne fosson privi,
    non so dir certo: ben scrive Turpino
    che sotto il gorgozulle era un molino,

84. "And God, seeing all of us faithful and praying
that His mercy may help us, will make a river
of salvation flow down to this place from the
fountain of His pity in Heaven."[22] Thus they
spoke; then the devout knights began the psalms,
hymns, gospels, and prayers they could remember
and put their prayers and lamentations and vows
to work.

85. Meanwhile, the other two were striving with
great zeal to welcome their new guest. Various
meats from various fish had been put to roast and
boil on the fire. A little while earlier, the whale
had stove in the sides of a Venetian ship and
driven it under, gulping down bit by shattered bit
into its stomach.

86. All the casks and trunks and packing cases on
board came into the monster's voracious belly;
only the sailors escaped on lifeboats to their escort
ships. And so there was kindling for fire and sugar
and spices to season good, delicate foods on their
plates. And there were precious, fine wines, too,
from Corsica and Greece.

87. Few years passed without a ship or two being sunk
in this fashion. The prisoners took from them the
food they needed to keep themselves alive. They
served the dinner when it was cooked; I cannot
say for certain whether they had bread or were
without it; Turpin, I know, wrote that there was a
mill under the whale's tonsils,

88.   che con l'acque ch'entravan per la bocca
      del mostro, il grano macinava a scosse,
      il quale o in barcia o in caravella o in cocca
      rotta, là dentro ritrovato fosse.
      D'una fontana similmente tocca,
      ch'a ridirla le guance mi fa rosse:
      lo scrive pure, et il miracol copre
      dicendo ch'eran tutte magich'opre.

89.   Non l'afferm'io per certo né lo niego:
      se pane ebbono o no, lo seppon essi.
      Gli dui fedel, de' dui infedeli al prego,
      fen punto ai salmi, e a tavola son messi.
      Ma di Astolfo e Ruggier più non vi sego:
      diròvvi un'altra volta i lor successi.
      Finch'io ritorno a rivederli, ponno
      cenare ad agio, e dipoi fare un sonno.

90.   Intanto Carlo, alla battaglia intento
      che 'l re boemme aver dovea con lui,
      senza sospetto ignun che tradimento
      (quel che non era in sé) fosse in altrui,
      facea provar destrier, che cento e cento
      n'avea d'eletti alli bisogni sui;
      e gli migliori, a chi facea mestieri,
      largamente partia fra i suoi guerrieri.

91.   Non solo aver per sé buona armatura
      quanto più si potea forte e leggiera,
      ma trovarne ai compagni anco avea cura,
      che se mai lor ne fu bisogno, or n'era.
      Seco gli usava alla fatica dura
      due fïate ogni dì, mattino e sera;
      e seco in maneggiar arme e cavallo
      facea provarli, e non ferire in fallo.

88.   which, with the waters that entered through the
       monster's mouth, by fits and starts ground grain
       which had found its way there either in wrecked
       galleons or caravels or coracles. He also mentions
       a freshwater fountain which makes my cheeks
       blush to repeat it; still, he writes about it and
       defends the miracle saying that they were all works
       of magic.

89.   I certainly don't affirm this for certain, nor do I
       deny it; they know whether they had bread or
       not. At the request of the two infidels, the two
       faithful put an end to their psalms and sat down at
       the table. But I am going on no further about
       Astolfo and Ruggiero; I will tell you another time
       about what happened to them. Until I return to
       see them again, they can eat at their leisure and
       then take a nap.

90.   Meanwhile, Charles was intent on the battle that
       the Bohemian King was to have with him, and,
       suspecting no treason in anyone else (because
       there wasn't any in him), he had the horses tested,
       for he had hundreds and hundreds of choice ones
       to serve his needs. And he generously divided the
       best ones among those of his warriors who had
       most need of them.

91.   He was concerned not only to have the lightest
       and strongest armor possible for himself but to
       find such armor for his comrades, too, for if they
       had ever needed them, now was the time. He had
       them exercise with him at their hard calling twice
       every day, morning and evening, and he made
       them practice with him at handling their arms and
       horses and striking on target.

92.   Ma Cardoran, che non ha alcun disegno
di por lo stato a sorte d'una pugna,
viene aguzzando tuttavia l'ingegno,
sì come tronchi all'augel santo l'ugna.
Aspetta e spera d'Ungheria, e dal regno
de li Sassoni omai, ch'aiuto giugna:
la notte e il giorno intanto unqua non resta
di far più forte or quella cosa or questa.

93.   E ridur si fa dentro a poco a poco
e vettovaglia e munizione e gente,
ché per la tregua, in assediar quel loco
l'esercito era fatto negligente;
e parea quasi ritornata in gioco
la guerra ch'a principio era sì ardente;
e scemata di qui più d'una lancia,
contra Rinaldo era tornata in Francia.

94.   Sansogna e Slesia et Ungheria una bella
e grossa armata insieme posta avea:
la gente di Sansogna, e così quella
di Slesia, i pedestri ordini movea;
venir con questi, e la più parte in sella,
l'esercito de l'Ungar si vedea;
poi seguia un stuol di Traci e di Valachi,
Bulgari, Servïan, Russi e Polachi.

95.   Questi mandava il greco Costantino,
e per suo capitano un suo fratello;
sì come quel ch'a Carlo di Pipino
portava iniqua invidia et odio fello,
per esser fatto imperador latino
e usurparli il coronato augello.
Ben di lor mossa e di lor porse in via
avuto Carlo avea più d'una spia;

92. But Cardorano, who has no intention at all of submitting his state to the perils of a duel, is constantly sharpening his wits considering just how to cut off the talons of the holy imperial eagle. He waits and hopes for help to arrive from Hungary and, at any moment, from the Kingdom of the Saxons. Meanwhile he never stops fortifying now this defense, now that one, night and day.

93. Little by little he has supplies and munitions and men brought in, for the French army had grown careless in besieging the city because of the truce. The war, which in the beginning had been so fierce, now seemed almost to have turned into a game. More than one lance had been subtracted from Prague and sent back to fight against Rinaldo in France.

94. Saxony and Silesia and Hungary had put together a fine, big army. The men of Saxony and the men of Silesia, too, had mobilized their infantry, and the Hungarian army, most of it on horseback, was observed to be advancing with them. Then followed a troop of Thracians and Walachians, Bulgars, Serbs, Russians, and Poles.

95. Constantine the Greek sent these last, with a brother of his as their captain, because he bore vicious envy and deadly hatred toward Charles, the son of Pepin, for having become the Latin Emperor and for usurping the imperial eagle from him. Charles had certainly had more than one spy on their movements and on their setting out on the march.

96. ma, com'ho detto, Gano con diversi
mezi gli avea cacciato e fisso in mente
che si metteva insieme per doversi
mandar verso Ellesponto quella gente,
e tragittarsi in Asia contra i Persi
ch'avean presa Bittinia nuovamente;
e ch'era a petizion fatta et instanza
del greco imperator la ragunanza.

97. Né ch'ella fosse alli suoi danni volta
prima sentì, ch'era in Boemmia entrata;
sì che ben si pentì più d'una volta
che la sua più del terzo era scemata.
Già credendo aver vinto, quindi tolta
n'avea una parte et al nipote data.
Ma quel ch'oggi dir volsi è qui finito:
chi più ne brama udir, domani invito.

96.   But, as I have said, by diverse means Ganelon had
hammered home and fixed in his mind the idea
that their army was joining together in order to be
sent toward the Hellespont and to cross over into
Asia against the Persians, who had recently taken
Bithynia and that the alliance had been arranged at
the request and insistence of the Greek Emperor.

97.   Charles did not realize that this army was headed
in his direction and was intent on his undoing
until it had entered Bohemia; then indeed, and
more than once, he repented that his own army
had been reduced by more than a third. Believing
he had already conquered Prague, he had taken
away a good part of his forces and given them to
his nephew. But what I wanted to say today is
finished here; whoever wishes to hear more, I
invite you to do so tomorrow.

Canto Quinto

1.   Un capitan che d'inclito e di saggio
     e di magno e d'invitto il nome merta,
     non dico per ricchezze o per lignaggio,
     ma perché spesso abbia fortuna esperta,
     non si suol mai fidar sì nel vantaggio,
     che la vittoria si prometta certa:
     sta sempre in dubbio ch'aver debbia cosa
     da ripararsi il suo nimico ascosa.

2.   Sempre gli par veder qualche secreta
     fraude scoccar, ch'ogni suo onor confonda:
     ché pur là dove è più tranquilla e queta,
     più perigliosa è l'acqua e più profonda;
     perciò non mai prosperità sì lieta
     né tal baldanza a' suoi desir seconda,
     che lasciar voglia gli ordini e i ripari
     che faria avendo uomini e Dei contrari.

3.   Io 'l dirò pur, se bene audace parlo,
     che quivi errò quel sì lodato ingegno
     col qual paruto era più volte Carlo
     saggio e prudente e più d'ogn'altro degno:
     ma il vincer Cardorano, e vinto trarlo,
     glorïoso spettacolo, al suo regno,
     quivi gli avea così occupati i sensi,
     ch'altro non è che ascolti, vegga e pensi.

Canto 5

1. THE CAPTAIN WHO DESERVES to be called
    illustrious, wise, great, and invincible—not, I
    say, because of wealth or lineage but because of
    his proven experience against Fortune—will
    never trust so much in the superiority of his
    position that he promises himself certain victory;
    he is always in doubt whether his enemy possesses
    some secret means of defense.

2. He always seems to see some hidden stratagem
    about to spring and confound all the honor he has
    thus far won; for just where the water is most
    tranquil and calm, it is deepest and most
    dangerous; therefore, his victories can never be so
    happy nor his confidence ever so immoderate that
    he will abandon the precautions and defenses that
    he would make were he opposed by both men
    and gods.

3. Though I speak boldly, I will still say that here
    erred the much-praised discernment which many
    times had made Charles seem wise and prudent
    and more worthy than all other men; but the idea
    of defeating Cardorano and leading him
    conquered, a glorious spectacle, to his kingdom,
    had now so taken over Charles's senses that there
    was nothing else he would hear, or see, or think
    about.

4.   Né si scema sua colpa, anzi augumenta,
     quando di Gano il mal consiglio accusi.
     Per lui vuol dunque ch'altri vegga o senta,
     et ei star tuttavia con gli occhi chiusi?
     Dunque l'aloppia Gano e lo addormenta,
     e tutti gli altri ha dai segreti esclusi?
     Ben seria il dritto che tornasse il danno
     solamente su quei che l'error fanno.

5.   Ma, pel contrario, il populo innocente,
     il cui parer non è chi ascolti o chieggia,
     è le più volte quel che solamente
     patisce quanto il suo signor vaneggia.
     Carlo, che non ha tempo che di gente,
     né che d'altro ripar più si proveggia,
     quella con diligenzia, che si trova,
     tutta rivede e gli ordini rinova.

6.   E come che passar possa la Molta
     sul ponte che v'è già fatto a man destra,
     e sua gente ne li ordini raccolta
     ritrarre ai monti et alla strada alpestra;
     e ver' le terre Franche indi dar volta,
     o dove creda aver la via più destra:
     pur ogni condizion dura et estrema
     vuol patir, prima che mostrar che tema.

7.   Or quel muro ch'opposto avea alla terra
     tra un fiume e l'altro con sì lungo tratto,
     fa con crescer di fosse, e legne e terra,
     più forte assai che non avea già fatto;
     e con gente a bastanza i passi serra,
     acciò non, mentre attende ad altro fatto,
     questi di Praga, ritrovato il calle
     di venir fuor, l'assaltino alle spalle.

4.	And it does not lessen, but rather increases, his fault if he blames the bad counsel of Ganelon. Does he wish, then, that others should see and hear for him and that he should always remain with his eyes closed? That Ganelon should drug him and put him to sleep, while he excludes all others from his secrets? It would be truly just if the harm befell only those who make the mistake;

5.	but, on the contrary, it is the innocent people, whose opinion no one listens to or asks for, who are most often the only ones to suffer for the blunders of their lord. Charles, who has no time to provide himself with men or other means of defense, reviews with care all the men he does have, and he reorders the ranks.

6.	And although he could cross the Moldau on the bridge that was already built there on his right flank and withdraw his men, assembled in their ranks, to the mountains and the alpine road; and from there turn toward France or to wherever he might expect to find an easier passage; he nonetheless prefers to suffer every difficult and extreme condition before showing that he is afraid.

7.	Now he makes much stronger than he had before the wall that he had set up before the city between the two rivers, adding ditches and beams and earthworks; and he blocks its openings with enough men so that, while he attends to other business, the men of Prague might not discover a way of breaking out and attack him from behind.

8. L'un nimico avea dietro e l'altro a fronte,
    e vincer quello e questo animo avea.
    L'esercito de' Barbari su al monte
    passò l'Albi, vicino ove sorgea.
    Carlo tenea sopra l'altr'acqua il ponte,
    ch'uscìa verso la selva di Medea;
    e quello alla sua gente, che divise
    in tre battaglie, al destro fianco mise.

9. E così fece che 'l sinistro lato
    non men difeso era da l'altro fiume:
    si pose dietro l'argine e il steccato,
    da non poter salir senza aver piume.
    Il corno destro ad Olivier fu dato,
    del sangue di Borgogna inclito lume,
    che cento fanti avea per ogni fila,
    le file cento, con cavai seimila.

10. Ebbe il Danese in guardia l'altro corno,
    con numer par de fanti e de cavalli.
    L'imperator, di drappo azurro adorno
    tutto trapunto a fior de gigli gialli,
    reggea nel mezo; e i Paladini intorno,
    duchi, marchesi e principi vassalli,
    e sette mila avea di gente equestre,
    e duplicato numero pedestre.

11. All'incontro, il stuol barbaro, diviso
    in tre battaglie, era venuto inanti,
    men d'una lega appresso a questi assiso,
    e similmente avea i dui fiumi ai canti.
    Cento settanta mila era il preciso
    numer, ch'un sol non ne mancava a tanti;
    e in ogni banda con ugual porzioni
    partiti i cavalli erano e i pedoni.

8. He had one enemy behind him and another in front, and he boldly intended to defeat both. The army of the Barbarians crossed the Elbe up on the mountain, near where it had its source. Charles held the bridge over the other river, which flowed toward Medea's wood; and he put that on the right flank of his army, which he divided into three battalions.

9. And he arranged them so that his left side was no less well defended by the other river: in the rear was the barrier-wall and palisade, which could not be scaled without wings. The right flank of the army was given to Oliviero, the illustrious light of the blood of Burgundy, who had a hundred foot soldiers in every rank, a hundred ranks, and six thousand horsemen.

10. Uggiero the Dane had command over the other wing, with an equal number of foot soldiers and horsemen. The Emperor, dressed in an azure cloak all embroidered with yellow lilies, commands in the middle; about him he had the paladins, dukes, marquesses, and vassal princes, seven thousand of the equestrian rank, and twice that many foot soldiers.

11. On the other side, the Barbarian horde had come forward divided into three battalions; it was situated less than a mile from Charles's forces and likewise had the two rivers at its sides. Its exact number was one hundred and seventy thousand, not one less; and in every squadron horsemen and foot soldiers were divided in equal portions.

12.   Ogni squadra de' Barbari non manco
ivi quel giorno stata esser si crede,
che tutto insieme fosse il popul franco,
quanto ve n'era, chi a caval, chi a piede:
ma tal ardir e tal valor, tal anco
ordine avean questi altri, e tanta fede
nel suo signor, d'ingegno e di prudenza,
che ciascun valer quattro avea credenza.

13.   Ma poi sentir, che si trovar in fatto,
che pur troppo era un sol, non che a bastanza;
né di quella battaglia ebbono il patto
che lor promesso avea lor arroganza:
e potea Carlo rimaner disfatto
se Dio, che salva ch'in lui pon speranza,
non gli avesse al bisogno proveduto
d'un improviso e non sperato aiuto.

14.   E non poteron sì l'insidie astute,
l'arte e l'ingan del traditor crudele,
che non potesse più chi per salute
nostra morendo, volse bere il fele:
Gano le ordì, ma al fin l'Alta virtute
fece in danno di lui tesser le tele:
lo fe' da Bradamante e da Marfisa
metter prigione, e detto v'ho in che guisa.

15.   Quelle gli avean già ritrovato adosso
lettere e contrasegni e una patente,
per le quali apparea che Gano mosso
non s'era a tòr Marsiglia di sua mente,
ma che venuto il male era da l'osso:
Carlo n'era cagion principalmente;
e vider scritto quel ch'in mar appresso
per distrugger Ruggier s'era commesso.

12. Each Barbarian battalion there that day is believed
     to have been no less numerous than the whole
     French army put together, those on horseback and
     those on foot; but the French had so much
     courage, so much valor, so much discipline, and
     so much faith in their lord's intelligence and
     prudence that each believed himself to be worth
     four of the enemy.

13. Afterward, however, they learned from experience
     that just one of the enemy was not only enough,
     but too much; and the battle did not follow the
     plan their arrogance had promised them. Charles
     could have been left undone had not God, who
     saves whoever puts his hopes in Him, provided for
     his needs with unexpected and unhoped-for aid.

14. And the cruel traitor's astute deceptions, his art,
     and his treasons could not do so much that He
     could not do more: He who, dying for our
     salvation, wanted to drink gall. Ganelon arranged
     the threads, but in the end the Power on High
     wove the cloth to his harm; It had made him the
     prisoner of Marfisa and Bradamante, and I have
     told you in what way.

15. Those ladies had already found on him letters and
     countersigns and a patent from which it was
     apparent that Ganelon had not moved to take
     Marseilles on his own, but this sickness was bred
     in the bone: Charles was the principal cause
     behind it. The ladies also saw written there what
     had been arranged for the subsequent destruction
     of Ruggiero at sea.

297

16. E leggendo, Marfisa vi trovoro
    e Ruggier traditori esser nomati,
    perché, partiti da le guardie loro,
    in favor di Rinaldo erano andati;
    e per questo ribelli ai gigli d'oro
    eran per tutto il regno divulgati;
    e Carlo avea lor dietro messo taglia,
    sperando averli in man senza battaglia.

17. Marfisa, che sapea che alcun errore,
    né suo né del fratello, era precorso,
    pel qual dovesse Carlo imperatore
    contr'essi in sì grand'ira esser trascorso,
    di giusto sdegno in modo arse nel core,
    che, quanto ir si potea di maggior corso,
    correr pensò in Boemia e uccider Carlo,
    che non potrian suoi Paladin vietarlo.

18. E ne parlò con Bradamante, e appresso
    col Selvaggio Guidon, ch'ivi era allora:
    ché Mont'Alban gli avea il fratel commesso
    che vi dovesse far tanta dimora
    che Malagigi, come avea promesso,
    venisse; e l'aspettava d'ora in ora
    per dar a lui la guardia del castello,
    e poi tornar in campo al suo fratello.

19. Marfisa ne parlò, come vi dico,
    ai dui germani, e gli trovò disposti
    che s'abbia a trattar Carlo da nimico
    e far che l'odio lor caro gli costi;
    che si meni con lor Gano, il suo amico,
    e che s'un par di forche ambi sian posti;
    e che si scanni, tronchi, tagli e fenda
    qualunque d'essi la difesa prenda.

16. Reading on, they found Marfisa and Ruggiero
    named there as traitors because, having left their
    posts, they had gone to help Rinaldo; and for this,
    throughout all the realm, they were proclaimed
    traitors to the lilies of gold. Charles, moreover,
    had put a price on their heads, hoping to have
    them fall into his hands without a fight.

17. Knowing that no error, neither on her part nor
    her brother's, had occurred that could justify the
    great wrath which Emperor Charles turned
    against them, Marfisa burned with such righteous
    anger in her heart that she resolved to rush to
    Bohemia with as much speed as she could muster
    and to kill Charles; his paladins would not be able
    to stop her.

18. And she spoke of it with Bradamante and then
    with Guidon Selvaggio,[1] who was there at the
    time because Rinaldo had entrusted Montauban
    to him; he was to stay there until Malagigi came as
    he had promised to do; and Guidon was expecting
    him at any moment in order to give him the
    custody of the castle and then to return to his
    brother's army.

19. As I say, Marfisa spoke of it with the sister and
    brother, and she found them disposed to treat
    Charles as an enemy and to make their hatred cost
    him dearly; they would take his friend Ganelon
    along with them and hang both from one set of
    gallows, and whoever took up their defense
    should be put to the sword, ripped open, hacked
    apart, and cut in two.

20.   Guidon, ch'andar con lor facea pensiero
       né lasciar senza guardia Mont'Albano,
       espedì allora allora un messaggiero,
       ch'andò a far fretta al frate di Viviano;
       e gli parve che fosse quel scudiero
       che tratto avea quivi legato Gano;
       per narrar lui che la figlia d'Amone
       libera e sciolta, e Gano era prigione.

21.   Sinibaldo, il scudier, calò del monte,
       e verso Malagigi il camin tenne;
       e nol potendo aver in Agrismonte,
       più lontan per trovarlo ir gli convenne.
       Ma il dì seguente Alardo entrò nel ponte
       di Mont'Albano; e bene a tempo venne,
       ché, lui posto in suo loco, entrò in camino
       Guidon, senza aspettar più il suo cugino.

22.   Egli e le donne, tolto i loro arnesi,
       in Armaco e a Tolosa se ne vanno,
       due donzelle e tre paggi avendo presi,
       col conte di Pontier che legato hanno.
       Lasciànli andar, che forse più cortesi
       che non ne fan sembianti, al fin seranno:
       diciam del messo il qual da Mont'Albano
       vien per trovar il frate di Viviano.

23.   Non era in Agrismonte, ma in disparte,
       tra certe grotte inaccessibil quasi,
       dove imagini sacre, sacre carte,
       sacri altar, pietre sacre e sacri vasi,
       et altre cose appartinenti all'arte,
       de le quai si valea per vari casi,
       in un ostello avea ch'in cima un sasso
       non ammettea, se non con mani, il passo.

20. Guidon, who wanted to go with them but could
    not leave Montauban unguarded, immediately
    sent a messenger to make Viviano's brother[2]
    hurry; and he decided that the squire who had led
    Ganelon there in his shackles should be the one to
    tell Malagigi that Amone's daughter was free and
    unbound and Ganelon a prisoner.

21. The squire, Sinibaldo, swept down the mountain
    and made his way toward Malagigi; and being
    unable to track him down in Agrismonte, he had
    to go farther afield to find him. But the following
    day Alardo[3] arrived at the drawbridge to
    Montauban; and his coming was well timed, for
    Guidon stationed him in his place and started on
    his way without waiting any longer for his cousin.

22. Having taken up their arms, he and the ladies go
    off toward Armagnac and Toulouse, taking with
    them two damsels and three pages and the fettered
    Count of Ponthieu. Let them go, for perhaps in
    the end they will be more courteous than they
    appear to be: let us speak of the messenger who
    comes from Montauban to find Malagigi.

23. Malagigi was not in Agrismonte but some distance
    off, in certain almost inaccessible grottos, where
    he had holy images, holy writings, holy altars,
    holy stones, and holy vessels and other things
    pertaining to his art, which he drew upon for
    different occasions, in a dwelling that could not be
    reached except by climbing by hand to the top of
    a rocky cliff.

24.   Sinibaldo, che ben sapea il camino
       (ché vi venne talor con Malagigi,
       del qual da' tener'anni piccolino
       fin a' più forti stato era a' servigi),
       giunse all'ostello, e trovò l'indovino
       ch'avea sdegno coi spirti aerii e stigi,
       ché scongiurati avendoli due notti
       gli lor silenzi ancor non avea rotti.

25.   Malagigi volea saper s'Orlando
       nimico di Rinaldo era venuto,
       sì come in apparenza iva mostrando,
       o pur gli era per dar secreto aiuto:
       perciò due notti i spirti scongiurando,
       l'aria e l'inferno avea trovato muto;
       ora s'apparecchiava al ciel più scuro
       provar il terzo suo maggior scongiuro.

26.   La causa che tenean lor voci chete
       non sapeva egli, et era nigromante;
       e voi non nigromanti lo sapete,
       mercé che già ve l'ho narrato inante.
       Quando contra l'imperio ordì la rete
       Alcina, s'ammutiro in un instante,
       eccetto pochi, che serbati fòro
       da quelle Fate alli servigi loro.

27.   Malagigi, al venir di Sinibaldo,
       molto s'allegra udendo la novella
       che sia di man del traditor ribaldo
       in libertà la sua cugina bella,
       e ch'in la gran fortezza di Rinaldo
       si truovi chiuso in potestà di quella;
       e gli par quella notte un anno lunga,
       che veder Gano preso gli prolunga.

24. Sinibaldo, who knew the way well (for he had come there before with Malagigi, in whose service he had been from his tender years right up to his stronger ones), arrived at the lair and found the sorcerer angry with the aerial and Stygian spirits, for he had still not broken their silence after having conjured them for two nights running.

25. Malagigi wanted to know whether Orlando had really become Rinaldo's enemy, as he gave the appearance of being, or if he was about to give him secret help instead; conjuring the spirits for two nights to find out, he had discovered that the air and Hell had grown mute; now he was preparing, under the darkest night sky, to try a third, stronger, spell.

26. He did not know the reason why the spirits kept their voices quiet although he was a necromancer; and you, no necromancers, do know it, thanks to the fact that I have already told you the story. When Alcina had woven her plot against the Empire, they became silenced in an instant, except for the few whom the Fairies kept as their own servants.

27. At the arrival of Sinibaldo, Malagigi rejoices greatly to hear the news that his fair cousin has been freed from the knavish traitor's hands and that Ganelon now finds himself in her power, imprisoned inside Rinaldo's great fortress; and that night which delays him from going to see the captive Ganelon seems a year long to him.

28. Perciò s'affretta con la terza prova
     di vincer la durezza dei demoni;
     e con orrendo murmure rinova
     preghi, minacce e gran scongiurazioni,
     possenti a far che Belzebù si mova
     con le squadre infernali e legïoni.
     La terra e il cielo è pien di voci orrende;
     ma del confuso suon nulla s'intende.

29. Il mutabil Vertunno, ne l'anello
     che Sinibaldo avea sendo nascosto
     (sapete già come fu tolto al fello
     Gan di Maganza, e in altro dito posto:
     non che 'l scudier virtù sapesse in quello,
     ma perché il vedea bello e di gran costo),
     Vertunno, a cui il parlar non fu interdetto,
     là si trovò con gli altri spirti astretto.

30. E perché il silinguagnolo avea rotto,
     narrò di Gano l'opera volpina,
     ch'a prender varie forme l'avea indotto
     per por Rinaldo e i suoi tutti in ruina;
     e gli narrò l'istoria motto a motto,
     e da Gloricia cominciò e d'Alcina,
     fin che sul molo Bradamante ascesa
     per fraude fu con la sua terra presa.

31. Maravigliossi Malagigi, e lieto
     fu ch'un spirto a sé incognito gli avesse
     a caso fatto intendere un secreto
     che saper d'alcun altro non potesse.
     L'anel in ch'era chiuso il spirto inquieto,
     nel dito onde lo tolse, anco rimesse;
     e la mattina andò verso Rinaldo,
     pur con la compagnia di Sinibaldo.

28.   For this reason, he hurries with his third try at
       conquering the devils' obstinacy and with fearful
       mutterings renews his prayers, his threats and great
       spells, which have the power to move Beelzebub
       and his infernal troops and legions. The earth and
       sky are full of fearful voices; but nothing can be
       understood from the confused sound.

29.   The mutable Vertumnus, being hidden in the ring
       that Sinibaldo wore (you already know how it was
       taken from the wicked Ganelon of Mainz and put
       on another finger: not because the squire knew
       the power it possessed but because he thought it
       beautiful and very valuable), Vertumnus, for
       whom speech was not forbidden, found himself
       summoned there with the other spirits.

30.   And because he had a ready tongue, he told all
       about Ganelon's foxy deeds, how he had
       instructed Vertumnus to take various guises in
       order to lead Rinaldo and all his family to ruin:
       and he told him the story word for word, and he
       started with Gloricia and Alcina and went right up
       to when Bradamante went out on the jetty and
       was taken, along with her city, by his fraud.

31.   Malagigi was astonished and he was delighted that
       a spirit unknown to him should by chance have
       made him aware of a secret he could not have
       learned from any other. He put the ring in which
       the restless spirit was imprisoned back on the
       finger from which he had taken it and that
       morning went toward Rinaldo, still in the
       company of Sinibaldo.

32. Rinaldo dava il guasto alla campagna
     de li Turoni e la città premea;
     ché, costeggiando Arverni e quei di Spagna,
     col lito di Pittoni e di Bordea,
     se gli era il pian renduto e la montagna,
     né fatto colpo mai di lancia avea:
     ma già per l'avvenir così non fia,
     poi ch'Orlando al contrasto gli venia.

33. Orlando amò Rinaldo, e gli fu sempre
     a far piacer e non oltraggio pronto;
     ma questo amore è forza che distempre
     il veder far del re sì poco conto.
     Non sa trovar ragion per la qual tempre
     l'ira c'ha contra lui per questo conto:
     cagion non gli può alcuna entrar nel core,
     che scusi il suo cugin di tanto errore.

34. Or se ne vien il paladino innanti
     quanto più può verso Rinaldo in fretta;
     e seco ha cavallieri, arcieri e fanti,
     varie nazion, ma tutta gente eletta.
     Sa Rinaldo ch'ei vien; né fa sembianti
     quali far debbe chi 'l nimico aspetta:
     tanto sicur di quello si tenea
     ch'in nome suo detto 'l demon gli avea.

35. Da campo a Torse, ove era, non si mosse,
     né curò d'alloggiarsi in miglior sito.
     È ver che nel suo cuor maravigliosse
     che, dopo che Terigi era partito,
     avisato dal conte più non fosse,
     per tramar quanto era tra loro ordito:
     molto di ciò maravigliossi, e molto
     ch'avessi il baston d'or contra sé tolto;

32. Rinaldo was laying waste the countryside of the
    Tourangeaux and had their city hard pressed; for
    he had skirted the Auvergnois and the Spaniards,
    along with the coasts of Bordeaux and of Poitou,
    and the plains and the mountains had surrendered
    to him without his having struck a blow with his
    lance. It would not be the same from now on,
    however, for Orlando had come against him.

33. Orlando loved Rinaldo and was always ready to
    do his pleasure and not to injure him; but seeing
    him show such little respect for the King, Orlando
    had to dissolve that love. He can find no cause for
    restraining his anger against Rinaldo on this score;
    not a single reason can enter into his heart to
    excuse his cousin for so great a transgression.

34. Now the paladin marches forward as fast as he can
    to confront Rinaldo, bringing knights and archers
    and foot soldiers with him; they come from
    various nations, but all are select troops. Rinaldo
    knows that he is coming; but he does not behave
    like a man who is waiting for his enemy; he was
    so sure of what the demon, speaking in Orlando's
    name, had told him.

35. He did not stir from his camp at Tours, where he
    was, nor did he care to quarter his forces at a
    better site. It is true that he wondered in his heart
    that, after Terigi had departed, he had received no
    further notice from the Count about how they
    were to work out what had been plotted between
    them; he wondered a great deal at this and a great
    deal more that Orlando should have taken up the
    baton of gold [4] against him;

36.   e non gli avesse innanzi un dei mal nati
      del scelerato sangue di Maganza
      mandato a castigar de li peccati
      indegni di trovar mai perdonanza:
      ma tal contrari non puon far che guati
      fuor di quanto gli mostra la fidanza,
      né che per suo vantaggio se gli affronti,
      dove vietar gli possa guadi o ponti.

37.   Ben mostra far provisïon; ma solo
      fa per dissimulare e per coprire
      l'accordo ch'aver crede col figliuolo
      del buon Milon, da non poter fallire.
      Ma 'l Conte, che non sa di Gano il dolo,
      fa le sue genti gli ordini seguire;
      né questa né altra cosa pretermette,
      ch'a valoroso capitan si spette.

38.   Alla sua giunta, tutti i passi tolle,
      che non venga a Rinaldo vettovaglia;
      e di quanti ne prese, alcun non volle
      vivo serbar, ma impicca e i capi taglia.
      Quel donde più Rinaldo d'ira bolle,
      è che 'l cugin fa publicar la taglia,
      la qual su la persona il re de' Franchi
      bandita gli ha di cento mila franchi.

39.   Et ha fatto anco publicar per bando
      che 'l re vuol perdonar a tutti quelli
      che verran ne l'esercito d'Orlando
      e lasceran Rinaldo e gli fratelli.
      Rinaldo al fin si vien certificando
      ch'Orlando esser non vuol de li ribelli;
      e si conosce, in somma, esser tradito,
      ma quando non vi può prender partito.

36.   and also that Orlando had not already sent him
one of the base progeny of the wicked clan of
Mainz, for him to punish for sins that could never
deserve a pardon; but such contrary actions
cannot make him look beyond the picture that his
own trusting faith paints for him, or lead him to
confront Orlando in an advantageous position
where he could bar him from fords and bridges.

37.   He certainly appears to make provisions for his
defense, but only does so to cover up and hide the
agreement he believes that he has with good
Milone's son, which cannot fail. But the Count,
unaware of Ganelon's treachery, makes his men
follow orders and omits neither this nor any other
thing expected of a brave captain.

38.   At his arrival he takes all the passes, so that no
supplies may come to Rinaldo; and he will not
spare any of the prisoners he has taken but hangs
them instead and cuts off their heads. What makes
Rinaldo boil most with wrath is that his cousin
widely proclaims the reward of one hundred
thousand francs which the King of France has set
on Rinaldo's head.

39.   And Orlando has also had announced by
proclamation that the King wants to pardon all
those who will join Orlando's army and leave
Rinaldo and his brothers. At last Rinaldo comes
to understand that Orlando does not want to be
one of the rebels and realizes, in the end, that he
has been betrayed, but only when he can take no
recourse against it.

40.   Vede che se non vien al fatto d'arme,
ancor che nol può far con suo vantaggio,
di fame sarà vinto, se non d'arme,
ch'a lui nave ir non può né carïaggio;
e teme appresso, che la gente d'arme
un giorno non si levi a farli oltraggio:
ché non è cosa che più presto chiame
a ribellarsi un campo, che la fame.

41.   Mirava le sue genti, e gli parea
che di febre sentissero ribrezo:
sì la giunta d'Orlando ognun premea,
ch'avean creduto dover star di mezo.
Rinaldo, poiché forza lo traea,
fece tutto il suo campo uscir del rezo,
e cautamente, in quattro schiere armato,
al Conte il fe' veder fuor del steccato.

42.   Già prima i fanti e i cavallieri avea
con Unuldo partito e con Ivone;
quei di Medoco il duca conducea,
con quei di Villanova e di Rione,
da San Macario, l'Aspara e Bordea,
Selva Maggior, Caorsa e Talamone,
e gli altri che dal mar fino in Rodonna
tra Cantello s'albergano e Garonna.

43.   Usciti erano gli Auscii e gli Tarbelli
sotto i segni d'Unuldo alla campagna;
gli Cotüeni e gli Ruteni, e quelli
de le vallee che Dora e Niva bagna;
e gli altri che le ville e gli castelli
quasi vuoti lasciar de la montagna
che già natura alzò per muro e sbarra
al furore aquitano e di Navarra.

40. He sees that unless he comes to a test of arms,
     even though he cannot do so with his advantage,
     he will be defeated by hunger, if not by arms,
     because neither ship nor wagon can come to him;
     and he fears further that his troops may one day
     rise to do him harm, for there is nothing that
     invites a camp to revolt more quickly than
     hunger.

41. He was watching his men and they seemed to be
     shivering with fever, they were so terrified by the
     arrival of Orlando, who they had thought would
     remain neutral. Driven by necessity, Rinaldo
     made all his camp come out into the open and
     cautiously displayed it before the Count in four
     armed squadrons outside the stockade.

42. He had previously divided the foot soldiers and
     cavalry with Unuldo and Ivone; the Duke led
     those of Medoc, along with those of Villeneuve
     and Rion, of Saint-Macaire, Lesparre and
     Bordeaux, Grandselve, Cahors and Talmont and
     the others that dwell from the sea up to Rodome,
     between the Cantal massif and the Garonne.

43. The Auscii and Tarbelli had gone out into the
     field under the standards of Unuldo; with them
     the Convenae and Ruteni and those from the
     valleys that the Adour and the Nive wash;[5] and
     the others who had left almost empty the villages
     and castles of the mountains that nature once
     raised as a wall and barricade against the fury of
     Aquitaine and Navarre.[6]

44.   Rinaldo gli Vassari e gli Biturgi,
        Tabali, Petrocori avea in governo,
        e Pittoni e gli Movici e Cadurgi,
        con quei che scesi eran dal monte Arverno;
        e quei ch'avean tra dove, Loria, surgi,
        e dove è meta al tuo vïaggio eterno,
        le montagne lasciate e le maremme,
        con quei di Borgo, Blaia et Angolemme.

45.   Et oltre a questi, avea d'altro paese
        e fanti e cavallier di buona sorte;
        di quai parte avea prima, e parte prese
        dal suo signor, quando partì di corte;
        tutti all'onor di lui, tutti all'offese
        di suoi nimici pronti sino a morte.
        Dato avea in guardia questo stuol gagliardo
        a Ricciardetto et al fratel Guicciardo.

46.   Unuldo d'Aquitania era nel destro,
        Ivo sul fiume avea il sinistro corno;
        de la schiera di mezo fu il maestro
        Rinaldo, che quel dì molto era adorno
        d'un ricco drappo di color cilestro
        sparso di pecchie d'or dentro e d'intorno,
        che cacciate parean dal natio loco
        da l'ingrato villan con fumo e foco.

47.   E perché ad ogni incommodo occorresse
        (che non men ch'animoso, era discreto),
        contra quei de la terra il fratel messe,
        con buona gente, per far lor divieto
        che, mentre gli occhi e le man volte avesse
        a quei dinanzi, non venisser drieto,
        o venisser da' fianchi, e con gran scorno,
        oltre il danno, gli dessero il mal giorno.

44.   Rinaldo had under his command the Vasates and
        the Bituriges, Gabales, Petrocorii and the Pictones
        and the Lemovices and Cadurci, together with
        those who had come down from the peaks of
        Auvergne; and those that had left the mountains
        and the shores between where you spring, Loire,
        and where your eternal journey finds its goal, with
        those of Bourges, Blois, and Angoulême.

45.   And in addition to these, he had both foot soldiers
        and knights of good quality from other lands,
        some of whom he had had before, and some he
        had taken from his liege when he departed from
        the Court; all were ready to die for his honor and
        to avenge the wrongs his enemies had done him.
        Rinaldo had entrusted this valiant troop to his
        brothers Ricciardetto and Guicciardo.

46.   Unuldo of Aquitaine was on the right wing, Ivone
        on the left beside the river; Rinaldo was the
        master of the troops in the middle, dressed that
        day in a rich cloak of celestial hue, spotted around
        and about with bees of gold that seemed to have
        been chased from their nests by an ungrateful
        farmer with fire and smoke.[7]

47.   And that he might be prepared for any
        contingency (for he was no less discreet than he
        was valorous), Rinaldo sent his brother with some
        good men against those inside Tours, to prevent
        them from adding insult to injury and attacking
        him from behind or on his flanks while he had his
        eyes and hands turned toward those before him.

313

48. Da l'altra parte il capitan d'Anglante
quelli medesimi ordini gli oppone:
fa lungo il fiume andar Teone innante,
figliuolo e capitan di Tassillone;
da l'altro corno, al conte di Barbante,
alla schiera di mezo egli s'oppone.
Bianca e vermiglia avea la sopravesta,
ma di ricamo d'or tutta contesta.

49. Ne l'un quartiero e l'altro la figura
d'un rilevato scoglio avea ritratta,
che sembra dal mar cinto, e che non cura
che sempre il vento e l'onda lo combatta.
L'uno di qua, l'altro di là procura
pigliar vantaggio, e le sue squadre adatta
con tal rumor e strepito di trombe
che par che triemi il mar e 'l ciel ribombe.

50. Già l'uno e l'altro avea, con efficace
et ornato sermon, chiaro e prudente,
cercato d'animar e fare audace
quanto potuto avea più la sua gente.
Era d'ambi gli eserciti capace
il campo, sino al mar largo e patente;
ché non s'era indugiato a questo giorno
a levar boschi e far spianate intorno.

51. Gli corridori e l'arme più leggiere,
e quei che i colpi lor credono al vento,
or lungi, or presso, intorno alle bandiere
scorrono il pian con lungo avvolgimento;
mentre gli uomini d'arme e le gran schiere
vengon de' fanti a passo uguale e lento,
sì che né picca a picca o piede a piede,
se non quanto vuol l'ordine, precede.

48.   On the other side, the captain of Anglant makes
the same arrangements against Rinaldo: he has
Teone, Tassillone's son and captain, go up ahead
along the river; he gives command of the other
wing to the Count of Brabant, and he himself
stands opposite the middle squadron. He wore a
tunic of white and red, but all woven with golden
embroidery.

49.   The design of the garment was divided in four
quarters, in two of which was depicted the figure
of a protruding reef, which seems to be girded by
the sea and not to care that the wind and the sea
are always beating against it. Here Orlando, there
Rinaldo strives to seize the advantage and
reorganizes his battalions with so much noise and
clamor of trumpets that it seems that the sea
trembles and the heavens resound.

50.   With a persuasive and decorous, clear and prudent
speech, each one had already tried to encourage
and embolden his men as much as he could. The
field was ample for both the armies, wide and
open right up to the sea; for they had not waited
until now to clear the woods and level the ground
all around.

51.   The skirmishers and more lightly armed troops
and those archers who entrust their blows to the
wind scour the plain, now from afar, now close
up, swirling widely around and about the
battalions, while the men-at-arms and the great
troops of foot soldiers come on at a slow and
steady pace, so that pike does not precede pike
nor foot precede foot one step farther than the
formation requires.

52.   L'un capitano e l'altro a chiuder mira
dentro 'l nimico, e poi venirli a fianco.
Teon, per questo, il corno estende e gira,
e Ivo il simil fa dal lato manco.
Andar da l'altra parte non s'aspira,
ché l'acqua vi facea sicuro e franco
a Rinaldo il sinistro, al Conte serra
il destro corno il gran fiume de l'Erra.

53.   L'un campo e l'altro venìa stretto e chiuso,
con suo vantaggio, stretto ad affrontarsi:
tutte le lance con le punte in suso
poteano a due gran selve assimigliarsi,
le quai venisser, fuor d'ogn'uman uso,
forse per magica arte, ad incontrarsi.
Cotali in Delo esser doveano, quando
andava per l'Egeo l'isola errando.

54.   All'accostarsi, al ritener del passo,
all'abbassar de l'aste ad una guisa,
sembra cader l'orrida Ircina al basso,
che tutta a un tempo sia dal piè succisa:
un fragor s'ode, un strepito, un fracasso,
qual forse Italia udì quando divisa
fu dal monte Apennin quella gran costa
che su Tifeo per soma eterna è imposta.

55.   Al giunger degli eserciti si spande
tutto 'l campo di sangue e 'l ciel di gridi:
a un volger d'occhi in mezo e da le bande
ogni cosa fu piena d'omicidi:
in gran confusïon tornò quel grande
ordine, e non è più chi regga o guidi,
o ch'oda o vegga; ché conturba e involve,
assorda e accieca il strepito e la polve.

52.   Each captain looks to close on his enemy and then
      to come at him on his flank. For this reason Teone
      extends his wing and turns toward the center, and
      Ivone does the same on his left. They do not even
      think about outflanking one another on the other
      side because the great river Loire leaves Rinaldo's
      left secure and protected and encloses the Count's
      right wing.

53.   Each army draws together in close and tight
      formation, exploiting its advantage, ready for
      battle; all the lances with their points on high
      could have been likened to two great forests
      which had come to meet one another, beyond all
      human experience, perhaps through some magical
      art. Such must the forests have appeared on Delos
      when the island went wandering through the
      Aegean.[8]

54.   As they neared one another and halted, lowering
      their lances in one motion, it seems as if the
      horrid Black Forest were falling to the ground, cut
      down at its foot all at the same instant: a din is
      heard, a clamor, a crash, similar, perhaps, to what
      Italy heard when the island mass of Ischia was torn
      away from the Apennines and laid as an eternal
      burden upon Typhoeus.[9]

55.   At the meeting of the armies the entire field spills
      over with blood and the heavens with cries: in one
      sweep of the eyes, from the flanks to the center,
      everything was full of killing; that great military
      order turned to great confusion, and there is no
      one who commands or rules any longer, or hears
      or sees; the clamor and the dust rise and envelop,
      deafen and blind.

56.   A ciascuno a bastanza, a ciascun troppo
      era d'aver di se medesmo cura.
      La fanteria fu per disciorre il groppo,
      perduto 'l lume in quella nebbia oscura:
      ma quelli da cavallo al fiero intoppo
      già non ebbon la fronte così dura;
      le prime squadre sùbito e l'estreme
      di qua e di là restar confuse insieme.

57.   Le compagnie d'alcuni, che promesso
      s'avean di star vicine, unite e strette,
      e l'un l'altro in aiuto essersi appresso
      né si lasciar se non da morte astrette,
      in modo si disciolser che rimesso
      non fu più 'l stuol fin che la pugna stette;
      e di cento o di più ch'erano stati,
      al dipartir non furo i dui trovati.

58.   Ché da una parte Orlando e da l'altra era
      Rinaldo entrato, e prima con la lancia
      forando petti e più d'una gorgiera,
      più d'un capo, d'un fianco e d'una pancia;
      poi, l'un con Durindana, e con la fera
      Fusberta l'altro, i dui lumi di Francia,
      a' colpi, qual fece in Val Flegra Marte,
      poneano in rotta e l'una e l'altra parte.

59.   Come nei paschi tra Primaro e Filo,
      voltando in giù verso Volana e Goro,
      nei mesi che nel Po cangiato ha il Nilo
      il bianco uccel ch'a' serpi dà martoro,
      veggiàn, quando lo punge il fiero asilo,
      cavallo andare in volta, asino e toro,
      così veduto avreste quivi intorno
      le schiere andar senza pigliar soggiorno.

56. It was enough, it was too much, for each man to look out for himself. The infantry were ready to break their ranks, unable to see in the cloudy darkness: but neither did those on horseback put up a very determined front at that fierce clash. In both armies, the first squadrons and the last were quickly mixed up together.

57. The companies of some who had promised to stand by one another united and in close formation, to be ready to help each other and not to separate unless compelled by death, dissolved in such a way that the troop was not reformed as long as the battle lasted; and of the hundred men or more that they had been before, no two were found at their departure.

58. For Orlando had entered the battle from one side and Rinaldo from the other, first with their lances piercing breasts and more than one throat, more than one head, side, and belly; then, the one with Durindana and the other with savage Fusberta, these two lights of France routed both sides, this one and that, with blows such as Mars struck in the Valley of Phlegra.[10]

59. As in the pastures between Primaro and Filo, rolling down toward Volano and Goro,[11] in the months when the white bird that deals death to snakes has exchanged the Nile for the Po[12], one may see a horse, an ass, or a bull run in circles when the angry horsefly stings it, so here you would have seen the troops run about without pause for rest.

60.   A Rinaldo parea che, distornando
      da quella pugna il cavallier di Brava,
      gli suoi sarebbon vincitori, quando
      sol Durindana è che gli afflige e grava;
      di lui parea il medesimo ad Orlando:
      che se da le sue genti il dilungava,
      facilmente alli Franchi e alli Germani
      cederiano i Pittoni e gli Aquitani.

61.   Perciò l'un l'altro, con gran studio e fretta
      e con simil desir, par che procacci
      di ritrovarsi, e da la turba stretta
      tirarse in parte ove non sia ch'impacci.
      Per vietarli il camin nessun gli aspetta,
      non è chi lor s'opponga o che s'affacci;
      ma in quella parte ove gli veggon volti,
      tutti le spalle dàn, nissuno i volti.

62.   Come da verde margine di fossa
      dove trovato avean lieta pastura,
      le rane soglion far sùbita mossa
      e ne l'acqua saltar fangosa e scura
      se da vestigio uman l'erba percossa
      o strepito vicin lor fa paura;
      così le squadre la campagna aperta
      a Durindana cedono e a Fusberta.

63.   Gli duo cugin, di lance proveduti
      (che d'olmo l'un, l'altro l'avea di cerri),
      s'andaro incontro, e i lor primi saluti
      furo abbassarsi alle visiere i ferri.
      Gli dui destrier, che senton con ch'acuti
      sproni alli fianchi il suo ciascun afferri,
      si vanno a ritrovar con quella fretta
      che uccel di ramo o vien dal ciel saetta.

60. It seemed to Rinaldo that, if the Knight of Brava[13] were diverted from that battle, his men would be victorious, for it is only Durindana that wounds and injures them; the same idea occurred to Orlando about him, that if he could lead Rinaldo away from his men, the Pictones and Aquitani would easily yield to the Franks and Germans.

61. For this reason, each seems with great eagerness and haste and with similar desire to bring about a single combat with the other and to draw themselves away from the serried ranks to a place where no one would get in the way. Nobody lingers to block their way, there is no one who would oppose or confront them; but they all turn their backs—none turn their faces—and run in the opposite direction from where they see the two of them headed.

62. As, from the green edge of a ditch where they have found happy feeding, frogs will make a sudden movement and leap into the dark and muddy water if a human footstep striking the grass, or a nearby noise, makes them afraid; so the troops yield the open field to Durindana and Fusberta.

63. Equipped with their lances (one made of elm, the other of oak), the two cousins rode against each other, and their first greetings were to lower the iron points and direct them at one another's visor. The two horses, who feel how sharp are the spurs with which their riders strike their flanks, rush to meet one another with the speed of a bird flying from a branch, or an arrow from the sky.

64. Negli elmi si feriro a mezo 'l campo
     sotto la vista, al confinar dei scudi:
     suonar come campagne, e gittar vampo,
     come talor sotto 'l martel gl'incudi.
     Ad amendui le fatagion fur scampo,
     che non potero entrarvi i ferri crudi:
     l'elmo d'Almonte e l'elmo di Mambrino
     difese l'uno e l'altro Paladino.

65. Il cerro e l'olmo andò, come se stato
     fosser di canne, in tronchi e in schegge rotto:
     messe le groppe Brigliador sul prato,
     ma, come un caprio snel, sorse di botto.
     L'uno e l'altro col freno abbandonato,
     dove piacea al cavallo, era condotto,
     coi piedi sciolti e con aperte braccia,
     roverscio a dietro, e parea morto in faccia.

66. Poi che per la campagna ebbono corso
     di più di quattro miglia il spazio in volta,
     pur rivenne la mente al suo discorso,
     e la memoria sparsa fu raccolta:
     tornò alla staffa il piè, la mano al morso,
     e rassettati in sella dieder volta;
     e con le spade ignude aspra tempesta
     portaro al petto, agli omeri e alla testa.

67. Tutto in un tempo, d'un parlar mordente
     Rinaldo a ferir venne, e di Fusberta,
     al cavallier d'Anglante, e insiememente
     gli dice—Traditor—a voce aperta;
     e la testa che l'elmo rilucente
     tenea difesa, gli fe' più che certa
     ch'a far colpo di spada di gran pondo
     si ritrovava altro che Orlando al mondo.

64.   In the middle of the field they struck each other
       on their helmets beneath the visor, at the edge of
       their shields; the blows resounded like bells and
       throw off sparks like the anvil sometimes does
       under the hammer. Enchantments were the
       salvation of both; the cruel iron could not
       penetrate the helmets of Almonte and Mambrino
       that protected the one and the other paladin.[14]

65.   The oak and the elm were broken into bits and
       splinters as if they had been made of cane:
       Brigliadoro fell backward on his croup upon the
       meadow, but like a nimble goat rose up at once.
       With his reins abandoned each knight was taken
       wherever his horse pleased, his feet loose and his
       arms splayed, bent over backward and to all
       appearances dead.

66.   After they had run in opposite directions through
       the field for the space of more than four miles,
       somehow their minds recovered their trains of
       thought and their scattered memories came back
       together; their feet returned to the stirrups, their
       hands to the reins, and, reseated in the saddle, they
       turned about; and with their naked swords they
       brought a bitter storm down upon each other's
       chests, shoulders, and heads.

67.   At one and the same moment, Rinaldo struck the
       knight of Anglant with biting words and with
       Fusberta and cries out "Traitor" to him in an
       audible voice; and his ringing head, which the
       shining helmet kept protected, made Orlando
       more than certain that there was someone other
       than himself to be found in the world who could
       strike blows of great weight.

68. Per l'aspro colpo il senator romano
    si piegò fin del suo destrier sul collo;
    ma tosto col parlare e con la mano
    ricompensò l'oltraggio e vendicollo:
    gli fe' risposta che mentia, e villano
    e disleal e traditor nomollo;
    e la lingua e la mano a un tempo sciolse,
    e quella il core e questa l'elmo colse.

69. Multiplicavan le minacce e l'ire,
    le parole d'oltraggio e le percosse;
    né l'un l'altro potea tanto mentire
    che detto traditor più non gli fosse.
    Poi che tre volte o quattro così dire
    si sentì Orlando dal cugin, fermosse;
    e pianamente domandollo come
    gli dava, e per che causa, cotal nome.

70. Con parole confuse gli rispose
    Rinaldo, che di còlera ardea tutto;
    Carlo, Orlando e Terigi insieme pose
    in un fastel, da non ne trar construtto:
    come si suol rispondere di cose
    donde quel che dimanda è meglio instrutto.
    —Pian, pian, fa ch'io t'intenda,—dicea Orlando
    —cugino; e cessi intanto l'ira e 'l brando.—

71. In questo tempo i cavallieri e i fanti
    per tutto il campo fanno aspra battaglia,
    né si vede anco in mezo, né dai canti
    qual parte abbia vantaggio e che più vaglia.
    Le trombe, i gridi, i strepiti son tanti,
    che male i duo cugin alzar, che vaglia,
    la voce ponno, e far sentir di fuore
    perché l'un l'altro chiami traditore.

68.   The Roman Senator[15] fell all the way forward on
      his horse's neck because of this bitter blow; but
      soon with words and with his hands he repaid and
      avenged the injury; he answered Rinaldo that he
      lied, and called him a villain and disloyal and a
      traitor; and he loosed his tongue and his hand at
      the same time, and the first struck Rinaldo's heart,
      the last his helmet.

69.   Their threats and their furies multiplied, together
      with their insults and their blows; nor could one
      so give the lie to the other that he was no longer
      called a traitor. After Orlando heard his cousin call
      him this three or four times, he stopped; and
      calmly demanded of him how and for what reason
      he called him such a name.

70.   Rinaldo answered him with confused words, for
      he was burning all over with rage; he lumped
      Charles, Orlando, and Terigi all together in an
      incomprehensible bundle: like one responding
      about things of which the person asking is better
      informed. "Slowly, slowly, cousin, speak so I can
      understand you," said Orlando, "and in the
      meantime hold off your anger and your sword."

71.   At this moment their knights and infantry are
      warring bitterly throughout the entire field, nor
      can one see, either in the center or on the flanks,
      which side has the advantage or is prevailing. So
      great is the din of trumpets, shouts, and arms that
      the two cousins are not able to raise their voices
      effectively above it and to make audible why the
      one should call the other traitor.

72. Per questo fur d'accordo di ritrarsi
e diferir la pugna al nuovo sole;
poi, la mattina, insieme ritrovarsi
nel verde pian con le persone sole;
e qual fosse di lor certificarsi
il traditor, con fatti e con parole.
Fatto l'accordo, dier subito volta,
e per tutto sonar féro a raccolta.

73. Al dipartir vi fur pochi vantaggi;
pur, s'alcun ve ne fu, Rinaldo l'ebbe:
che, oltre che prigioni e carrïaggi
vi guadagnasse, a grand'util gli accrebbe,
ché alloggiò dove aver da li villaggi
copia di vettovaglie si potrebbe.
L'altra mattina, com'era ordinato,
si trovò solo alla campagna armato.

[Qui mancano molte stanze]

74. Scendono a basso a Basilea et al Reno,
e van lungo le rive insino a Spira,
lodando il ricco e di cittadi pieno
e 'l bel paese ove il gran fiume gira.
Entrano quindi alla Germania in seno,
e son già a Norimbergo, onde la mira
lontan si può veder de la montagna
che la Boemia serra da la Magna.

75. .   .   .   .
.   .   .   .
.   .   .   .
.   .   .   .
Venner, continüando il lor vïaggio,
su 'n monte onde vedean giù ne la valle
la pugna che Sassoni, Ungari e Traci
facean crudel contra i Francesi audaci:

72.   For this reason they agreed to withdraw and put
        off the battle to the next day; then, in the
        morning, to meet alone on the green field and to
        certify with deeds and words which of them was
        the traitor. Having agreed, they quickly turned
        about and made the retreat sound on all sides.

73.   Neither side had much of an advantage at the
        disengagement; still, if either did, it was Rinaldo,
        for in addition to the prisoners and wagons he
        won there, he received the further great benefit of
        being able to move his army's camp to where it
        would be able to have a supply of provisions from
        the villages. The next morning, as had been
        arranged, he found himself armed and alone on
        the battlefield.

        [There is a gap in the narrative at this point. The
        canto resumes with a description of the journey of
        Bradamante, Marfisa, and Guidon in search of
        Charles and of their arrival above Prague.]

74.   They descend to Basel and to the Rhine and go
        along its banks up to Speyer, praising the lovely
        countryside where the great river winds, rich and
        full of cities. From there they enter into the heart
        of Germany and are already at Nuremberg,
        whence one can see in the distance the mountains
        that wall off Bohemia from the Main.

75.   Continuing their journey,[16] they came to a
        mountain from which they saw down in the valley
        the cruel onslaught the Saxons, Hungarians, and
        Thracians were making against the daring French.

76.   e gli aveano a tal termine condotti,
      per esser tre, come io dicea, contr'uno;
      e sì gli avean ne l'antiguardia rotti,
      che senza volger volto fuggia ognuno:
      né per fermargli i capitani dotti
      de la milizia avean riparo alcuno;
      anzi, i primi che 'n fuga erano volti,
      i secondi e i terzi ordini avean sciolti.

77.   L'ardite donne, con Guidone, e 'nsieme
      gli altri venuti seco a questa via,
      sul monte si fermar che da l'estreme
      rive d'intorno tutto il pian scopria:
      dove sì Carlo e li suoi Franchi preme
      la gente di Sansogna e d'Ungheria,
      e l'altre varie nazïoni miste,
      barbare e greche, ch'a pena resiste.

78.   Con gran cavalleria russa e polacca,
      l'esercito di Slesia e di Sansogna
      guida Gordamo; e sì fiero s'attacca
      con la gente di Fiandra e di Borgogna,
      e sì l'ha rotta, tempestata e fiacca
      al primo incontro, che fuggir bisogna;
      né può Olivier fermargli, ch'è lor guida,
      e prega invano e 'nvan minaccia e grida.

79.   Or, mentre questo et or quell'altro prende
      ne le spalle, nel collo e ne le braccia,
      volge per forza l'un, l'altro riprende,
      che 'l nemico veder non voglia in faccia;
      Gordamo di traverso a lui si stende,
      e s'un corsier ch'a tutta briglia caccia
      sì con l'urto il percuote e sì l'afferra
      con la gross'asta, che lo stende in terra.

76. They had brought the French to such a pass that it was three against one, as I said earlier; and they had so broken through Charles's vanguard that all the Frenchmen fled without looking back: and their captains, for all their learning in the art of the war, did not have any remedy that would stop them; on the contrary, the first ranks that had turned in flight had dispersed the second and third as well.

77. The fearless ladies, with Guidon and the others who had come with them on this trip, stopped on the mountain that overlooked the whole field up to its outermost river banks: there the men of Saxony and Hungary, and the other, various mixed nations, Barbarian and Greek, so pressed Charles and his Frenchmen that he could scarcely hold out against them.

78. With a large Russian and Polish cavalry, Gordamo leads the army of Silesia and Saxony; and he attacks the men of Flanders and Burgundy so fiercely and has so dispersed, stormed, and broken them at the first encounter that they have to flee; nor can Oliviero, who is their leader, stop them, and in vain he implores them and in vain threatens and exhorts them.

79. He seizes now one man and now another by the shoulders, by the neck, and by the arms and turns one back by force, berates another who will not look the enemy in the face; meanwhile, Gordamo charges toward Oliviero from the side and, on a horse to which he gives full rein, strikes him with such force and so catches him with his massive lance that he lays him on the ground.

80.   Non lunge da Olivier era un Gherardo
       et un Anselmo: il primo è di sua schiatta,
       ché di don Buoso nacque, ma bastardo
       (però avea il nome del vecchio da Fratta);
       il secondo fiamingo, il cui stendardo
       seguia una schiera in sue contrade fatta:
       restar questi dui soli alle difese,
       fuggendo gli altri, del gentil marchese.

81.   Gherardo col caval d'Olivier venne,
       e si volea accostar perché montassi;
       et Anselmo, menando una bipenne,
       gli andava innanzi e disgombrava i passi:
       quando Gordamo alzò la spada, e fenne
       con un gran colpo i lor disegni cassi:
       ché da la fronte agli occhi a quello Anselmo
       divise il capo, e non li valse l'elmo.

82.   Tutto ad un tempo, o con poco intervallo,
       con la spada a due man menò Baraffa,
       venuto quivi con Gordamo, et hallo
       accompagnato il dì sempre alla staffa;
       e le gambe troncò dietro al cavallo
       de l'altro sì, che parve una giraffa:
       ch'alto dinanzi e basso a dietro resta.
       Sopra Gherardo ognun picchia e tempesta;

83.   e tanto gli ne dàn che l'hanno morto
       prima ch'aiutar possa il suo parente.
       Dolse a Olivier vederli far quel torto,
       ma vendicar non lo potea altrimente;
       perché, da terra a gran pena risorto,
       avea da contrastar con troppa gente;
       pur, quanto lungo il braccio era e la spada,
       dovunque andasse si facea far strada.

80. Not far from Oliviero were one Gherardo and
     Anselmo: the first one of Oliviero's stock, being
     the son of Lord Buoso but a bastard (even though
     he had the name of the old Knight of Fratta); the
     second a Fleming, whose standard was followed
     by a troop drawn up in his country. The others
     taking flight, these two alone stayed to defend the
     gentle marquess.

81. Gherardo came up on Oliviero's horse and tried
     to draw close enough for him to mount it; and
     Anselmo, carrying a double-edged axe, went in
     front of him and cleared the way; then Gordamo
     raised his sword and shattered all their plans with
     one great blow; for he split that Anselmo's head
     from the forehead to the eyes, and his helmet did
     him no good at all.

82. All at the same moment, or with little interval,
     Baraffa struck with his two-handed sword; he
     came there as Gordamo's squire and had
     accompanied him all day at his stirrup; and he cut
     off the back legs of the other's horse so that it
     looked like a giraffe: for it stood tall in front and
     short behind. Everyone strikes and showers blows
     upon Gherardo;

83. and they give him so many blows that they have
     killed him before he can help his kinsman. It
     sorrowed Oliviero to see them do that wrong,
     but he could not do anything to avenge it; for
     having risen from the ground with great effort,
     he had to contend with too many of the enemy;
     still, wherever he went, he carved out a path as
     wide as his arm and sword.

84.   E se non fosser stati sì lontani
     da lui suoi cavallieri in fuga volti,
     che fuggian come il cervo inanzi a' cani
     o la perdice alli sparvieri sciolti;
     tra lor per forza de piedi e di mani
     saria tornato, e gli avria ancor rivolti:
     ma che speme può aver perché contenda,
     che forza è ch'egli muoia o che s'arrenda?

85.   Ecco Gordamo, senza alcun rispetto
     ch'egli a cavallo e ch'Olivier sia a piede,
     arresta un'altra lancia, e 'n mezzo il petto
     a tutta briglia il Paladino fiede;
     e lo riversa sì, che de l'elmetto
     una percossa grande al terren diede.
     Tosto ch'in terra fu, sentì levarsi
     l'elmo dal capo, e non potere aitarsi:

86.   ché li son più di venti adosso a un tratto,
     su le gambe, sul petto e su le braccia;
     e più di mille un cerchio gli hanno fatto:
     altri il percuote et altri lo minaccia;
     chi la spada di mano, chi gli ha tratto
     dal collo il scudo, e chi l'altre arme slaccia.
     Al duca di Sansogna al fin si rende,
     che lo manda prigione alle sue tende.

87.   Se non tenea Olivier, quando avea ancora
     l'arme e la spada, la sua gente in schiera,
     come fermarla e come volgerl'ora
     potrà, che disarmato e prigion era?
     Fuggesi l'antiguardia, et apre e fora
     l'altra battaglia, e l'urta in tal maniera
     che, confondendo ogn'ordine, ogni metro,
     seco la volge e seco porta indietro.

84. And if his cavalry had not turned and fled so far
behind him, running like a stag before hounds or
a partridge before loosed hawks, he would have
made his way, fighting on foot, back to them and
would have turned them around to battle once
again: but what hope can he have to fight for,
when he must either die or surrender?

85. But now Gordamo, without any scruple that he is
on horseback and Oliviero on foot, couches
another lance and strikes the paladin at full tilt in
the middle of his breast; and he bowls him over
with such force that he hit the ground hard with
his helmet. As soon as he was on the ground he
felt the helmet lifted from his head, and he was
helpless.

86. For all at once there are more than twenty men at
his legs, at his chest, and at his arms; and more
than a thousand made a circle around him: some
strike, others threaten him; one has dragged the
sword from his hand, another the shield from his
neck, another unlaces his other armor. Finally he
yields to the Duke of Saxony, who sends him a
prisoner to his tents.

87. If Oliviero did not hold his men in their ranks
when he still had his arms and sword, how will he
be able to stop and turn them about now, when
he has been disarmed and made a prisoner? The
vanguard flees backward and opens and cuts a
passage through the rest of the following army,
colliding with it in such a way that, mixing up
every rank and formation, it puts the army to
flight as well and carries it along behind.

88.   E perché Praga è lor dopo le spalle,
        i fiumi a canto e gli Alemanni a fronte,
        non sanno ove trovar sicuro calle
        se non a destra, ov'era fatto il ponte;
        e però a quella via sgombran la valle
        con li pedoni i cavallieri a monte;
        ma non riesce, perché già re Carlo
        preso avea il passo e non volea lor darlo.

89.   Carlo, che vede scompigliata e sciolta
        venir sua gente in fuga manifesta,
        la via del ponte gli ha sùbito tolta,
        perché ritorni, o ch'ivi faccia testa;
        né vi può far però ripar, ché molta
        l'arme abbandona e di fuggir non resta;
        e qualche un, per la tema che l'affretta,
        lascia la ripa e nel fiume si getta.

90.   Altri s'affoga, altri nuotando passa,
        altri il corso de l'acqua in giro mena;
        chi salta in una barca e 'l caval lassa,
        chi lo fa nuotar dietro alla carena;
        o dove un legno appare, ivi s'ammassa
        la folta sì, che, di soverchio piena,
        o non si può levar se non si scarca,
        o nel fondo tra via cade la barca.

91.   Non era minor calca in su l'entrata
        del ponte, che da Carlo era difesa;
        e sì cresce la gente spaventata,
        a cui più d'ogni biasmo il morir pesa,
        che 'l re non pur, con tutta quella armata
        che seco avea, ne perde la contesa,
        ma, con molt'altri uomini e bestie a monte,
        nel fiume è rovesciato giù del ponte.

88.   And because Prague is behind their shoulders, the
      rivers at their sides, and the Germans in front of
      them, they do not know where to find a safe path
      except on the right, where the bridge had been
      built; and therefore, with horsemen piling on top
      of foot soldiers, they clear out of the valley by this
      route; but they do not succeed, because King
      Charles had already taken the crossing and did not
      wish to give it up to them.

89.   Charles, who sees his confused and disbanded
      men coming in open flight, quickly took away
      their path across the bridge so that he might turn
      them around or make a stand there; but he is
      unable to stem the tide, because so many men are
      abandoning their arms and continue to run; some,
      because of the fear that panics them, leave the
      bank and throw themselves into the river.

90.   One drowns, another crosses swimming, another
      the water's current drags in circles; one leaps into a
      boat and leaves his horse, one makes his horse
      swim behind the skiff; and where a boat appears,
      the army crowds in so thickly that, full to
      overflowing, the vessel either cannot leave unless it
      empties or it sinks to the bottom along its way.

91.   The crowd was no less packed at the entrance to
      the bridge, which Charles was defending; and the
      terrified men, for whom death weighs more than
      any shame, grow to such a number that the King,
      with all the forces he had with him, not only loses
      the struggle but, piled together with many other
      men and beasts, is himself thrown over into the
      river beneath the bridge.

92.   Carlo ne l'acqua giù dal ponte cade,
        e non è chi si fermi a darli aiuto;
        che sì a ciascun per sé da fare accade,
        che poco conto d'altri ivi è tenuto:
        quivi la cortesia, la caritade,
        amor, rispetto, beneficio avuto,
        o s'altro si può dire, è tutto messo
        da parte, e sol ciascun pensa a se stesso.

93.   Se si trovava sotto altro destriero
        Carlo, che quel che si trovò quel giorno,
        restar potea ne l'acqua di leggiero,
        né mai più in Francia bella far ritorno.
        Bianco era il buon caval, fuor ch'alcun nero
        pelo, che parean mosche, avea d'intorno
        il collo e i fianchi fin presso alla coda:
        da questo al fin fu ricondotto a proda.

92.   Charles falls into the water below the bridge, and
there is no one who stops to give him help, for
each man has so much to do to take care of
himself that there is little concern for others there:
there courtesy, charity, love, respect, gratitude for
favors received in the past, or anything else one
can say is put aside, and each one thinks only
about himself.

93.   If Charles had found himself on any horse other
than the one on which he rode that day, he could
easily have remained in the water and never
returned to fair France again. His good horse was
white, except for some spots of black which
looked like flies and which he had about his neck
and flanks right up to the tail: by this horse
Charles was finally brought back to shore.

Notes to the Translation

Canto 1

1. This stanza appears in the manuscript of the *Cinque Canti* that was discovered in the nineteenth century but not in the printed editions of the poem that were published in the sixteenth century. Except for its final couplet, the stanza corresponds to *Furioso* 46.68 (40.45) in the editions of 1516 and 1521, which describe the discontent of Ganelon's clan of Mainz at the wedding festivities of Ruggiero and Bradamante. Two members of the clan, Pinabello and Bertolagi, have been killed during the *Furioso*, the first by Bradamante (22.97), who wreaks vengeance on Pinabello for having attempted to kill her at the end of Canto 2, the second by her brother Ricciardetto and her cousin Aldigiero, with the assistance of Ruggiero and Marfisa (26.13).

2. This stanza appears only in the 1545 edition of the *Cinque Canti* (Venice: Aldo Manuzio), preceded by an explanatory sentence to the effect that the beginning of the first canto is missing. The 1548 edition of the *Cinque Canti* (Venice: Giolito) begins with stanza 1.

3. For Demogorgon, see the Introduction. In ancient Rome the Lustrum was a purificatory sacrifice made every five years after the census. It became a term for any passage of five years.

4. That is, from the west (the Hebrus is in Spain), east, north, and south.

5. In the apocryphal Acts of Peter, Simon Magus, for whom the sale of ecclesiastical offices was named, challenged Peter to a show of miracles before Nero and had himself carried aloft by devils. The prayers of the saint resulted in his falling to his death.

6. Morgana, or Morgan le Fay, the wicked sister of Arthur in Arthurian legend, is in the *Furioso* the sister of the Fairy Alcina and the half-sister of Logistilla in the *Furioso* 6.38; Logistilla allegorically represents Reason, and her two half-sisters represent the two lower parts of the Platonic soul. In the *Orlando Innamorato* II.8−9 and 13, where Morgana is the personification of Fortune, Orlando captures her and frees a number of damsels and knights, including Morgana's beloved favorite Gigliante, from her prison beneath a lake. See the Introduction.

7. See the *Orlando Innamorato* II.4.16−19, 40−45; II.13.22f.

8. Orlando made Morgana swear by Demogorgon not to do him any further harm (*Orlando Innamorato* II.13.29); see the Introduction.

9. The story of the love between Ruggiero and Alcina and of Ruggiero's subsequent escape from Alcina's enchanted island through the intervention of the good witch Melissa is recounted in the *Furioso* 7−8 and 10.

10. The eagle is the emblem of the Holy Roman Empire, ruled by Charles.

11. Ruggiero, who despite his Christian parentage was raised as a pagan, is baptized in the *Furioso* 41.59.

12. Orlando was the son of Berta, Charles's sister, and Milone of Clairmont, the brother of Amone; some versions say that Orlando was fathered by Charles himself. Ganelon married the widowed Berta and so became the hero's stepfather.

13. Orlando destroys Fallerina's garden in the *Orlando Innamorato* II.4−5.

14. Astolfo rescues an amnesiac Orlando and other knights from Dragontina in the *Orlando Innamorato* I.9.

15. All Fairies that played roles in earlier romances. For Silvanella, see the *Orlando Innamorato* II.17.56−60; for the White and Brown fairies, see the *Innamorato*

III.2.40–60 and the *Furioso* 15.57–92. The allusion to Borso is mysterious, though it may refer to Borso d'Este (1413–1471), Duke of Ferrara, later evoked at 2.120.

16. The hero Brandimarte is killed in battle and dies in the *Furioso* 42.14.

17. A marketplace during the Feast of the Assumption in Venice.

18. That is, where the sun and, figuratively, all things decline. "Occidere" in Latin means "to set, to fall down, to perish."

19. Ganelon's discontent comes in the aftermath of the war that occupies the plot of the *Orlando Furioso*, the conflict that Charles has fought and won against the North African King Agramante and Marsilio, the King of Spain.

20. The episode of Alcina's visit to Envy and of Envy's ensuing visit to Ganelon is modeled on the passage in Ovid's *Metamorphoses* (2.760f.) in which Minerva seeks out Envy to send her to poison the heart of Aglauros.

21. Tenarus was a promontory on the Peloponnesus where Hercules was said to have dragged the chained Cerberus. Avernus, in Campania, was the site of Aeneas's descent to the Underworld.

22. Pepin the Short usurped the throne from Childeric III, the last of the Merovingian kings.

23. Aurora is the goddess of dawn. The dreams of early morning were traditionally thought to be the truest and most prophetic.

24. Ariosto has here added to Ovid's description of Envy breathing her poison into Aglauros a reminiscence of the Virgilian fury Allecto, who thrusts her serpent into the breast of Amata in the *Aeneid* (7.346f.) and foments the war, at once foreign and civil, in the last six books of Virgil's epic.

25. These are the guests at the wedding of Bradamante

and Ruggiero: they were too many to be housed in the city of Paris and were hosted in tents and pavilions outside its walls. See the *Furioso* 46.74–75 and the Introduction.

26. Bradamante, the woman warrior and sister of Rinaldo.

27. Ariosto's argument appears to be pointed and personal here. In 1519 he and his family were denied the inheritance of his cousin, the deceased Rinaldo di Francesco Ariosti, which reverted as vacant fief to the property of Duke Alfonso d'Este. Ariosto bitterly describes this event in the same letter to Mario Equicola in which he writes of having made "some little addition" to the *Orlando Furioso* (see the Introduction, note 25), perhaps the *Cinque Canti* themselves.

28. Aachen was the capital of the historical Charlemagne.

29. Ariosto refers not only to the Germanic invasions of the Roman Empire but also to the repeated French and Spanish invasions of his contemporary Italy beginning in 1494.

30. Croesus was the last King of ancient Lydia, whose wealth became proverbial. Leon Battista Alberti (1404–1472) and Donato Bramante (1444–1514) were great Renaissance architects; the Roman Marcus Vitruvius Pollio, who lived in the time of Augustus Caesar, wrote the celebrated treatise, *De architectura*.

31. The giants hurl these three islands against the Gods in Claudian's *Gigantomachia* (85–86, 114–128). Lemnos was a home of the architect and fire god Vulcan.

32. One of the rivers of Hell.

33. The ship of St. Peter was a symbol of the Church.

34. Ganelon is correct but unfair: Ruggiero waits until the very end of the *Furioso* to leave the side of his liege-lord Agramante, the son of Troiano and the pagan commander-in-chief, in order to convert to Christianity and marry Bradamante: he refuses to do so on many earlier occasions in the poem, even after he

learns that his own father had been put to death by Troiano. His troops totally defeated, Agramante is killed by Orlando.

35. Pinabello and Bertolagi; see stanza *a* and note 1 above. It is Bradamante who actually kills Pinabello, although this fact is not generally known in the *Furioso* or here.

36. For the myth of the shape-changing Vertumnus, a Roman god of orchards and fruit who presided over the changing seasons, see Ovid, *Metamorphoses* 14.642f. Ariosto has made this classical deity into a demon.

37. The cousin of Rinaldo and Orlando, Malagigi is a magician and necromancer in the Carolingian romances. He will appear in Canto 5, stanza 24.

38. The Cimmerians live in Scythia and southern Russia. The wind is blowing from the west.

Canto 2

1. Ariosto echoes the parable of the good shepherd in John 10:11–16.

2. The tyrant of Pherae in ancient Thessaly was named Alexander. The three tyrants mentioned here are grouped together in Cicero's *De Officiis* 2.7.25–26, a passage that Ariosto invokes here. Like Ariosto's Suspicion, Dionysius was afraid of having a barber shave his beard: he resorted to singeing his whiskers with a coal.

3. Rhadamanthus, king of Crete and the mythical son of Jove, was held to be one of the infernal judges; see *Aeneid* 6.566–667.

4. The Garfagnana is a mountainous region north of Lucca that was part of the Este domains; Ariosto was governor there between 1522 and 1525. The Via Flaminia and the Via Appia were the great Roman roads that connected Rome to northern and southern Italy.

5. Lethe, the River of Oblivion. See stanza 23 below.

6. The fleur-de-lis, the heraldic symbol of the French monarchy.

7. These regions of Italy belonged to the States of the Church in Ariosto's time. The poet may be recalling the recent career of Cesare Borgia, who attempted, between 1499 and 1503, to carve out a personal domain in this area. See Machiavelli's famous discussion of Cesare's career in Chapter 7 of *The Prince*.

8. That is, the French or Franks, who descended from the Sicambri, one of the ancient Germanic tribes, themselves, in turn, supposedly descended from Trojan refugees; see Canto 1.45.

9. Namo, Duke of Bavaria, was one of the older friends and counselors of Charles. Charles had deprived King Gordamo, Lord of Saxony, of his territory.

10. Belgium and Holland.

11. Compare stanzas 36 and 37 with Lucan, *Pharsalia* 2.20–36.

12. An apparent topical allusion to the mission of Bernardo Bibbiena, Cardinal of Santa Maria in Portico, to France in 1518–1519. For this and the next stanza, see the Introduction.

13. The sword and crozier are traditional symbols of temporal and ecclesiastical power; they refer here respectively to Desiderius and Pope Leo.

14. The winged horse Pegasus opened Hippocrene, the spring on Mount Helicon sacred to the Muses, with a kick of its hoof. Medea fled King Creon of Corinth in a flying chariot after she had killed Creon's daughter, the new wife of Jason, as well as her own sons by Jason.

15. These two stories of Roman republican virtue and of honor owed to an enemy are recounted in Frontinus, 4.2 and Livy, 5.27, and coupled by Valerius Maximus, 6.5.1. They are also coupled—and contrasted—by Machiavelli in the *Discourses* 3.20.

16. The episode of the cutting down of the forest is modeled on Lucan, *Pharsalia* 3.399f. In turn, this passage, along with Lucan's original, would inspire the extended treatment of the enchanted woods in Tasso's *Gerusalemme liberata* 13 and 18.

17. Ovid recounts, in *Metamorphoses* 7.402–424, that Medea fled Corinth for Athens, where she married King Aegeus, and almost succeeded in having him poison Theseus before her plot was discovered.

18. The children of Helios included Medea, Pasiphae, Circe, and Phaedra; cursed by Venus, they all suffered from obsessive and violent loves.

19. That is, for a thousand years.

20. Compare the condition of the fairy Manto in the *Furioso* 43.98.

21. The Oriflamme, the sacred banner of St. Denis, was a banderole of red silk on a lance carried as a war standard by the early French kings.

22. Dukes Borso and Ercole I d'Este ruled Ferrara from 1450–1471 and 1471–1505, respectively.

CANTO 3

1. Alcina.

2. Miltiades led the Greeks to victory over the Persians under Darius at Marathon (490 B.C.); Themistocles commanded the Greek fleet that defeated the Persian armada of Xerxes at Salamis (480 B.C.).

3. Orlando.

4. Aquilante and Grifone; see stanza 47 below.

5. A city in Gascony near Pau.

6. The standard and the horn were the customary emblems of a courier.

7. Ruggiero is to sail to and through Gibraltar—the pillars of Hercules—and on to Lisbon, which, by a false

etymology, was fabled to have been founded by Ulysses.

8. Bradamante.

9. Ruggiero.

10. Rinaldo's sword.

11. Gibraltar.

12. The Doria and Adorno were two of the leading families of Genoa in Ariosto's time. Dionisotti (1960) suggests that the offhand and unflattering treatment of them here is another indication that the *Cinque Canti* were written before 1522, when the Adorno returned from exile to power in the city and before 1528, when Andrea Doria joined the forces of Charles V. In a stanza added to the 1532 *Furioso* (15.30), Ariosto praises Doria not as a corsair but, rather, as the scourge of pirates who has made the seas safe for the emperor.

13. Bradamante is taken in by a series of reassuringly familiar heraldic emblems: the fleur-de-lis of France, the white cross of Charles, the white eagle of Ruggiero, and the black eagle of the Holy Roman Empire.

14. Ruggiero and Marfisa.

15. Brigliadoro is the name of Orlando's horse in the *Furioso*; Vaglientino (Vegliantino) is the name of his horse in Pulci's *Morgante*.

16. Orlando's sword (Durendal in *The Song of Roland*).

Canto 4

1. Ariosto offends and alternately defends ladies in many places in the *Orlando Furioso*, which draws on the tradition of the *querelle des femmes*. The "one passage" he refers to here is probably the novella of Giocondo and Astolfo in Canto 28, for which the narrator apologizes in advance at the opening of the canto (28.1–3). For similar apologetic addresses to the ladies of his audience, see the openings of Cantos 20, 22, 29, and 30.

2. Bradamante.

3. Barcelona.

4. Catalonia; a fanciful etymology derives the name from "Goth-Alania."

5. Andalusia.

6. The pillars of Hercules; that is, Gibraltar.

7. The north wind.

8. Vulcan, the ancient god of fire. See stanza 1.79 above.

9. Ancient deities and personifications of the sea; Tethys is the wife of Ocean.

10. The episode inside Alcina's whale is inspired and partly modeled on a similar adventure in Lucian's mock *True History* 1.30f. The same work features a voyage to the moon (1.10–27), which, with Lucian's other satire, the *Icaromenippus*, is the model for the voyage that Ariosto's Astolfo makes to the moon in the company of St. John the Evangelist in the *Furioso* 34.67f. The presence of Astolfo in Alcina's whale links Ariosto's two imitations of Lucian's fantasy.

11. Jonah, swallowed by the great fish, cries out as if in the underworld (Jonah 2:3).

12. Ruggiero is converted in the *Furioso* 41.59.

13. When in the *Orlando Furioso* Ruggiero arrives at Alcina's island in the East Indies, he first encounters Astolfo, his predecessor in Alcina's love, who has been transformed into a myrtle tree. Astolfo was carried to Alcina's island on the back of her whale; now Ruggiero will discover him in the belly of the beast. See the *Furioso* 6.26f and *Orlando Innamorato* II. 13.58–14.8.

14. Astolfo's present narration parallels the long story he recounts, transformed into a myrtle tree on Alcina's island, to Ruggiero in the *Furioso* 6.32f.

15. With St. John's permission, Astolfo recovers his own lost wits as well as those of Orlando during his visit to the moon in the *Furioso* 34.86; the narrator an-

nounces, however, that although Astolfo thereafter lived wisely for a long time, he would commit an error that would cause him to lose his wits once again, a prophecy that is confirmed in this episode.

16. Ezekiel 33:11. The metaphor that Ruggiero uses is a particularly apt one, because he was converted when he was on the verge of drowning at sea in the *Furioso* (41.47f.).

17. Proverbs 24:16.

18. Luke 15:7.

19. Mark 16:18.

20. Matthew 17:20.

21. James 2:26.

22. Isaiah 66:12.

Canto 5

1. Guidon Selvaggio is the half-brother of Rinaldo and Bradamante, the bastard son of Amone. See the *Furioso* 20.6.

2. Malagigi.

3. Another brother of Rinaldo and Bradamante.

4. The insignia of the commander.

5. Both in this stanza and the next, Ariosto uses the Latin names of the ancient Gaulish tribes (Auscii, Tarbelli, etc.) that were said to inhabit the Aquitaine in classical times by Pliny in his *Natural History* 4.108–109.

6. The Pyrenees.

7. Rinaldo's emblem, depicting him as the victim of ingratitude, appeared at the end of the 1516 edition of the *Orlando Furioso*, along with the motto, "Pro bono malum." See the Introduction.

8. Delos, the birthplace of Apollo and Diana, floated about the Mediterranean until it was secured to one spot by the grateful Apollo. See the *Aeneid* 3.73f.

9. Zeus struck the rebellious giant, Typhoeus, with light-ning and then overwhelmed him with the mountain that is now Ischia. See the *Aeneid* 9.716; *Furioso* 16.23; 26.52; 33.24.

10. The Phlegraean fields were the site of the battle be-tween the Gods and the rebellious giants.

11. Ariosto describes an area near the estuary of the Po around Comacchio in the Este Duchy.

12. The bird is the stork, and the season is summer.

13. Orlando.

14. Orlando and Rinaldo each wear enchanted armor that makes them invulnerable. Their helmets are intro-duced in the *Furioso* 1.28 as the spoils of encounters with the Saracen knights Almonte and Mambrino.

15. Orlando.

16. The first four verses of stanza 75 are missing.

349

Designer: Wolfgang Lederer
Compositor: G & S Typesetters, Inc.
Text: 10/12 Bembo
Display: Bembo
Printer and Binder: BookCrafters